国家出版基金项目
NATIONAL PUBLICATION FOUNDATION

一代宗师 梅兰芳

The Master Mei Lanfang

【上】

名誉主编／梅葆玖
主　编／王文章
副主编／秦华生

文化艺术出版社
Culture and Art Publishing House

图书在版编目（C I P）数据

一代宗师梅兰芳 / 王文章主编 . -- 北京：文化艺术出版社，
2014.10
（京剧艺术大师梅兰芳研究丛书）
ISBN 978-7-5039-5876-2
Ⅰ.①一… Ⅱ.①王… Ⅲ.①梅兰芳（1894~1961）—传记—画
册 Ⅳ.①K825.78-64

中国版本图书馆CIP数据核字(2014)第229955号

一代宗师梅兰芳

（京剧艺术大师梅兰芳研究丛书）

名誉主编　梅葆玖
主　　编　王文章
副 主 编　秦华生
编　　辑　孙利华　邢春蕾
翻　　译　毛小雨
责任编辑　金　燕
装帧设计　顾　紫
出版发行　文化艺术出版社
地　　址　北京市东城区东四八条52号　（100700）
网　　址　www.whyscbs.com
电子邮箱　whysbooks@263.net
电　　话　（010）84057666（总编室）　84057667（办公室）
　　　　　84057691—84057699（发行部）
传　　真　（010）84057660（总编室）　84057670（办公室）
　　　　　84057690（发行部）
经　　销　全国新华书店
印　　刷　北京荣宝燕泰印务有限公司
版　　次　2015 年 8月第 1 版
印　　次　2015 年 8 月第 1 次印刷
开　　本　635×965 毫米　1/8
印　　张　82
字　　数　50千字　图片1100余幅
书　　号　ISBN 978-7-5039-5876-2
定　　价　780.00 元（上下）

总序

王文章

今年是梅兰芳艺术大师诞辰120周年。为了总结他的艺术成就，回顾他卓越的艺术创造，学习和继承他的艺术遗产和高尚精神，中国艺术研究院在院图书馆和梅兰芳纪念馆珍藏的丰富文献资料的基础上，编辑出版《京剧艺术大师梅兰芳研究丛书》，其中包括：

1.《梅兰芳演出剧本选集》

2.《梅兰芳演出戏单集》

3.《梅兰芳演出曲谱集》

4.《梅兰芳往来书信集》

5.《一代宗师梅兰芳》

6.《齐如山谈梅兰芳》、《父亲梅兰芳》、《忆艺术大师梅兰芳》、《梅兰芳若干史实考论》、《品梅记》、《梅兰芳京剧艺术研究》

上述书籍之外，《梅兰芳访美京剧图谱》也将同时增订再版。以上书籍中有许多资料是第一次公开面世，如“演出戏单”和“往来书信”等。还有第一次翻译出版的1919年梅兰芳首次访日演出后由日本汇文堂出版的日文版《品梅记》，还有法籍华人傅秋敏博士根据其1998年在法国出版的法文版专著《梅兰芳戏剧艺术研究》和博士论文翻译撰写的《梅兰芳京剧艺术研究》等。这套系列丛书的出版，会从梅兰芳表演艺术本体及社会人文历史的变迁中，从艺术史的角度整体性地反映出梅兰芳与京剧及社会演变的关系。这些文献资料的出版，相信会为研究一代京剧艺术大师梅兰芳开拓更加宽阔的社会人文视野。

梅兰芳作为一代创立完整表演艺术体系的京剧艺术大师，首先是他在艺术上深入继承传统，并勇于改革创新，发展、提高了京剧旦脚乃至京剧艺术的整体水平，形成了具有标志性、代表性的京剧梅派艺术。他出身梨园世家，从小经过严格的戏曲艺术基础训练，11岁登台演出，20岁左右即形成轰动性的舞台艺术影响，但这时也是他进行艺术革新尝试、创演时装新戏的开始。正是他继承传统又发展传统，锐意革新，在不断超越前人和超越自己的过程中，把京剧旦脚艺术开创到前所未有的艺术高峰。

梅兰芳作为一代具有广泛性群众影响的京剧艺术大师，不仅是因为他具有精湛的表演艺术，更因为他品德高尚，德艺双馨。他把为观众演好戏放在心中至高无上的地位；他扶危济困，提携同仁，待人诚恳，仁爱宽善。正是他对广大观众的无私奉献，才赢得观众的竭诚拥戴。

梅兰芳作为享誉世界的京剧艺术大师，还因为他以建立在对京剧艺术深入理解基础上的文化自信，抱着极大的热情，筚路蓝缕，在世界艺术舞台上努力传播京剧艺术。梅兰芳于1919年、1924年、1956年三次去日本，1930年去美国，1935年和1952年两次去苏联访问演出，其精湛的表演无不引起巨大轰动。这些演出，特别是1930年的访美演出，梅兰芳和他的剧团做了艰苦、细致的筹备，个中艰辛，外人难以体会。梅兰芳以自己的表演，真正让世界了解了中国戏曲的独特魅力，打破了当时欧美戏剧界把写实主义戏剧视作唯一正统舞台艺术的格局，增强了中国人对以京剧为代表的中国戏曲艺术的自信力和自豪感，加强了中西文化艺术的交流。

梅兰芳作为中国人爱戴并引以自豪的京剧艺术大师，还因为他在民族危亡之际，将个人安危置之度外，蓄须明志，不为敌伪演出，以大义凛然的爱国情怀，彪炳青史，为人景仰。梅兰芳先生正是以这样的气节，表现了一位艺术家对祖国和人民的真挚情怀。

梅兰芳大师为我们留下了珍贵的艺术遗产和精神遗产，在今天我们按照习近平总书记提出的立足中华优秀传统文化，培育和弘扬社会主义核心价值观而努力之时，梅兰芳大师的艺术遗产和精神遗产尤其值得我们珍视。梅兰芳曾是中国艺术研究院前身之一的中国戏曲研究院的首任院长，使我们作为今天中国艺术研究院的一员，更对梅兰芳大师怀有一种特殊的感情。在他诞辰120周年之际，我们整理编辑出版《京剧艺术大师梅兰芳研究丛书》，正是表达对他留下的这份丰富戏曲遗产的珍视，以及对他艺术实践和思想精神的研究、继承和弘扬。

2014年10月13日

Foreword

Wang Wenzhang

This year is the 120 anniversary of the birth of the great master Mei Lanfang. In order to summarize his artistic achievements, review his outstanding artistic creation, learn and inherit his artistic heritage and noble spirit, the scholars of the National Art Academy of China compile and publish Research Series on Mei Lanfang,the Great Master of Beijing Opera basing on the rich collections of the Academy Library and Mei Lanfang Memorial Museum as follows:

1. *The Anthology of Scripts Performed by Mei Lanfang*
2. *The Collection of Playbills of Mei Lanfang's Performance*
3. *The Collection of Music Scores of Mei Lanfang's Performance*
4. *The Collection of the Contacting Letters by Mei Lanfang*
5. *The Great Master Mei Lanfang*
6. *Qi Rushan's Talks about Mei Lanfang, My Father Mei Lanfang, A Recall of the Great Master Mei Lanfang, A Textual Research of Historical Facts about Mei Lanfang, Appreciation of Mei's Art, A Study of Mei Lanfang's Art of Beijing Opera*

Besides the books mentioned above, A Collection of Illustrative Plates of Beijing Opera Performed During Mei Lanfang's Visit to the United States will also be revised and reprinted. Many materials in the above books are first released to the public, such as "performance playbill" and "contacting letters" and so on. The Chinese version of Appreciation of Mei's Art translated from Japanese version, which was published by IBNUNDO in the year of 1919 in which Mei Lanfang performed in Japan, and A Study of Mei Lanfang's Art of Beijing Opera translated by French Chinese Dr. Fu Qiumin from French version published in 1998, and his monograph A Study of Mei Lanfang's Art of Beijing Opera based on his doctoral thesis. Both of them are put out first in Chinese. The series will reflect the relationship between Mei Lanfang and Beijing Opera and the evolution of society from the perspective of art history and showcase the change of Mei Lanfang's performing arts with the development of social and human history. I believe that the publication of series will develop more broad humane vision of society for the research of the great Beijing Opera master Mei Lanfang.

As a great master of Beijing Opera who created a complete performing system, Mei Lanfang inherited the tradition in the arts deeply and had the courage to reform, innovate, develop, and improve the overall level of dan role and Beijing Opera so that he formed an iconic and representative performing school of Mei. He was born in Liyuan (Pear Garden, means performing circle) family and had a strict training of Chinese drama from childhood. He made debut at age of 11 and formed a stage art sensational effect about 20 years old. At that time, he started his art innovation attempt to perform new plays with fashions. He not only inherited the tradition but also developed and innovated it. He constantly transcended predecessors and surpassed himself in the process of the Beijing opera art and dan roles to reach an unprecedented peak of art.

As a great master of Beijing Opera with a broad mass effect, Mei Lanfang not only had a superb performance art, but also was excellent in both performing skills and moral integrity. He put the supreme position in the heart to play a good show for the audience. He would like to help colleagues, treat people with sincerity, kindness and goodness. Since he devoted without selfishness to a large audience, and won the audience's wholehearted support.

As a great master of Beijing Opera with a world-renowned fame, Mei Lanfang spread the art of Beijing Opera in the world stage with the in-depth understanding of the art of Beijing Opera on the basis of cultural self-confidence. He was a pioneer in the field with a great enthusiasm. Mei Lanfang visited Japan three times in 1919, 1924 and 1956, and toured to the United States in 1930. In 1935 and 1952, he visited the Soviet Union twice. His exquisite performing all caused great sensation. For these performances, especially the 1930 US tour, Mei Lanfang and his troupe made painstaking and meticulous preparation. It is hard for outsiders to understand. Mei Lanfang really let the world understand the unique charm of Chinese opera with his performance, and broke the stereotype to treat realistic drama as the only legitimate stage art pattern by the European and American theatre circle at that time. He enhanced the self-confidence and sense of pride of the Chinese people who treat Beijing opera as the Chinese traditional drama, and promoted the Chinese and Western cultural exchange.

Mei Lanfang, the great master of Beijing Opera who is beloved and taken pride in by the Chinese people, was disregard of his personal safety on the occasion of national peril and grew a moustache not to perform for the enemy and puppet government. His patriotism without fear of death will be forever splendid in history and admired. Mr. Mei Lanfang was in such integrity, showing an artist sincere feelings for the motherland and the people.

The great master Mei Lanfang left us a precious artistic heritage and spiritual heritage. While today we follow the proposal of the General Secretary Xi Jinping to foster and promote the socialist core values with efforts based on the Chinese traditional culture, the great master Mei Lanfang's artistic heritage and spiritual heritage is especially worthy of our cherishing. Mei Lanfang was the first dean of the Chinese Opera Research Institute which is the predecessor of the National Art Academy of China, so that we, as a member of the Academy, have a special feeling to the great master. In his 120th anniversary of birth, we have finished the editing and publishing Research Series on Mei Lanfang, the Great Master of Beijing Opera. It expresses that we cherish this rich heritage treasures, as well as inheriting and carrying forward his artistic practice and the spirit of thought.

October 13th, 2014

梅蘭芳

生平简介
Biography

梅兰芳先生（1894—1961）是我国戏曲艺术大师，杰出的京剧表演艺术家。他一生热爱祖国、热爱人民，把全部精力献给了京剧艺术事业。在半个多世纪的舞台实践中，他继承传统、勇于革新、一丝不苟、精益求精，将我国戏曲艺术的精华集于一身，创造了众多优美而令人难忘的艺术形象，积累了大量优秀剧目，发展并提高了京剧旦脚的演唱和表演艺术，形成了具有独特风格、大家风范的艺术流派——梅派。

梅兰芳创造了多种性格鲜明的舞台艺术形象，展现了中国妇女各种美好的品德与个性，有的端庄淑静，有的英武豪放，有的娇憨活泼，有的聪慧机敏，等等。他善于运用歌唱、念白、身段、舞蹈等技巧，把人物的心理状态刻画入微，融化在美的形象之中。因此，他在国内外一致被誉为伟大的演员和美的化身。

梅兰芳是我国向海外传播京剧艺术的先驱者，他曾于1919 年、1924 年和 1956 年三次访问日本，1930 年访问美国，1935 年和1952 年两次访问苏联，演出获得盛誉。美国的南加利福尼亚大学和波摩那学院分别授予他荣誉文学博士学位。他在国外的演出不仅增加了各国人民对中国文化艺术的了解，使我国京剧艺术赢得国际声誉，也给予外国戏剧以积极影响。同时结识了众多国际知名戏剧家、作家、画家、歌唱家、舞蹈家、电影艺术家等，与他们建立了诚挚的友谊。以梅兰芳为代表的中国戏曲表演艺术被认为是当今世界三大表演体系之一。

1949 年，梅兰芳应邀参加了第一届全国文学艺术工作者代表大会和第一届中国人民政治协商会议。中华人民共和国成立后，梅兰芳先后当选为全国人民代表大会代表，中国政协常委，中国文学艺术界联合会副主席和中国戏剧家协会副主席。先后担任中国戏曲研究院院长，中国京剧院院长，中国戏曲学院院长。1959 年加入中国共产党。梅兰芳为祖国的文化艺术建设作出了多方面的贡献。

Mei Lanfang (1894-1961), was an outstanding Beijing Opera artist. He was a grandmaster of the traditional Chinese drama. Mei Lanfang was a patriot and deeply loved his people. Mei Lanfang dedicated his whole life to the art of Beijing Opera. During his stage career for over half a century, he combined the best Beijing Opera traditions from the past and adapted them to a new stage to enrich the performance. He had constantly sought to improve his artistic skills and created many unforgettable artistic imagery by putting together the best local and national operas. His performance had excellent acting, singing and dancing. He turned the Beijing Opera into a colorful and comprehensive art at the highest stage. As a result, he formed his original style which developed into "Mei Lanfang School"—a school with unique and graceful characteristic. Mei created a new path for his Beijing Opera contemporaries. He is one of the greatest artist in the history of the traditional Chinese drama with the embodiment of beauty.

Mei Lanfang was a pioneer for introducing Beijing Opera to the world. He was instrumental in promoting cultural exchanges among China and other countries. He had successful tours to Japan in 1919, 1924 and 1956, the United States in 1930, and the Soviet Union in 1935 and 1952. During the tours, he earned international fame and recognition. Furthermore, he popularized the traditional Chinese drama among foreign audiences. He also helped foreigners better understand Chinese art and culture. Through his performances and world tours, Beijing Opera obtained world fame and recognition in the foreign stage. The performing art of the Chinese theatre represented by Mei Lanfang is recognized as one of the world's three main contemporary styles of performing art.

After the founding of the People's Republic of China in 1949, Mei Lanfang was elected as a deputy to the National People's Congress and a member of the Standing Committee of the National Committee of the People's Political Consultative Conference. He was also elected as the Vice-chairman of the All-China Federation of Literary and Art Circles and of the Dramatists' Union. He became President of the Institute of Chinese Opera Research and of the College of Chinese Opera, as well as Director of the National Beijing Opera Theatre. Mei Lanfang participated in numerous social works and activities. He joined the Communist Party of China in 1959 and made significant contributions to the socialist construction of his motherland in his late years. Mei Lanfang is a symbol of China's performing art and the pride of his people and nation.

目录

壹·崭露头角

梨园世家……010
投师学艺……015
京城搭班……020
沪港成名……032

贰·承前启后

改革创新……054
时装新戏……074
梅舞芳歌……132
名旦之首……166

叁·文化大使

民间外交……182
出访日本……202
美国之行……224
访苏旅欧……292

肆·德艺双馨

抗战剧目……344
蓄须明志……354
剃须登台……366
赈灾济贫……394

伍·老骥伏枥

社会活动……412
各地演出……432
率团访日……492
电影生涯……514

陆·家庭交友

良师益友……536
梅氏夫人……551
梅氏子女及孙辈……558

柒·梅韵流芳

大师辞世……584
梅门桃李……590
纪念活动……616
梅馆故居……620
泰州市梅兰芳纪念馆……624

附录

CONTENTS

1. Cut a Striking Figure

Born in a Theatrical Family 010

Learning Stage Art from Good Teachers 015

Joined Troupes and Gave Performances 020

The First Time to Shanghai and Hong Kong 032

2. Innovations in Performing Art

Reformation and Innovation 054

New Plays in Modern Dresses 074

Mei Lanfang's Singing and Dancing 132

The Leading of Four Famous Dans 166

3. Visiting Abroad Win Appraise from Overseas

Meeting Foreign Guests 182

Visiting Japan Twice 202

Successful U.S. Tour 224

Visiting the Soviet Union 292

4. Excellence in Both Performing Skills and Moral Integrity

Patriotic Plays 344

Grew Moustache to Keep Himself Away From the Stage 354

Came Back on Stage Again 366

Raised Relief Funds to Aid the Victims of Natural Calamities and the Poor 394

5. Vitality and Splendour

Social Activities 412

Performances All Around the Country 432

Visiting Japan with China Beijing Opera Delegation 492

On Screen 514

6. Mei Lanfang's Family and His Domestic Life

Good Teachers and Helpful Friends 536

Mei Lanfang's Wife 551

Mei's later Generations 558

7. The Influences of Mei Everlasting

The Death of the Great Master 584

Mei's Disciples 590

Commemorative Activities 616

Mei Lanfang Memorial Museum 620

TaiZhou Mei Lanfang Memorial Museum 624

Appendix

壹

崭露头角
Cut a Striking Figure

梅兰芳，名澜，字畹华。原籍江苏泰州，1894年10月22日（农历九月二十四日）生于北京的一个戏曲世家。8岁开始学戏，师事吴菱仙，学京剧正工青衣戏。11岁首次登台，后搭喜连成科班借台练戏，向秦稚芬和胡二庚学习花旦戏，向茹莱卿学习武功。继而搭鸣盛和班、双庆班、玉成班在京演出，先后与当时名角合演，声誉鹊起。20岁时，首次赴沪演出，声名大噪。

Mei Lanfang was born in Beijing on October 22nd, 1894 in an actor's family. He started to learn Beijing Opera stage art at the age of eight and made his public debut at the age of eleven.

The teachers who had taught Mei were Wu Lingxian, Qin Zhifen,Hu Ergeng and Ru Laiqing.

Mei's fame as a prominent actor began in 1913, when he was invited to Shanghai to give performances for the first time at the age of twenty.

《穆柯寨》

梅兰芳饰穆桂英

Mei Lanfang as Mu Guiying in *Mu's Village Fortress*

《虹霓关》

梅兰芳饰东方氏

Mei Lanfang as Lady Dongfang in *Rainbow Pass*

《御碑亭》

梅兰芳饰孟月华

Mei Lanfang as Meng Yuehua in *The Pavilion of Imperial Monument*

《四郎探母》

梅兰芳饰铁镜公主

Mei Lanfang as Princess Tiejing in *Silang Visits His Mother*

梨园世家
Born in a Theatrical Family

1894年10月22日，梅兰芳出生在北京前门外李铁拐斜街的一个梨园世家中。梅兰芳的祖父梅巧玲（1842—1882）为清代同治、光绪年间著名的京剧、昆曲演员，"同光十三绝"之一。父亲梅竹芬（1874—1897）亦为清末京、昆旦脚演员，英年早逝。母亲杨长玉（1876—1908）是梨园名宿杨隆寿之女。伯父梅雨田（1865—1912）为京剧著名琴师，长期为谭鑫培操琴。梅兰芳7岁时入私塾读书，受家庭环境熏陶，8岁即开始拜师学艺。

Mei Lanfang was born in Beijing on October 22nd in a famous theatrical family. His grandfather Mei Qiaoling, was a famous Dan (female role) actor and the leader of the"Four Happiness Troupe" Sixi Company in the later half of the 19th century. Mei's father was also a Dan actor in the end of the Qing dynasty. Mei's uncle Mei Yutain was a very famous musician and an excellent fiddle player. Mei's grandfather on his mother's side Yang Longshou was also a famous actor as well as an excellent teacher of Beijing opera actors. Mei first attended a private primary school at 7 years old. One year later, he began his learning in theatre.

梅兰芳出生地住宅大门，北京前门外李铁拐斜街
The house in which Mei Lanfang was born(Li Tieguai Xiejie Street, Beijing)

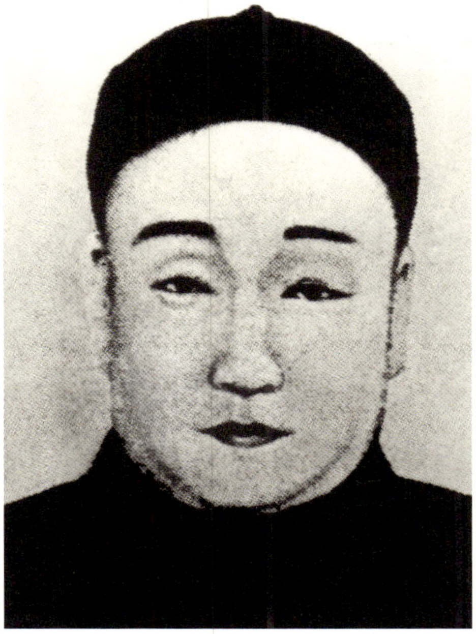

梅巧玲 Mei Qiaolin (1842—1882)

梅兰芳的祖父，原名芳，正名芳普，字筱波，一字雪芬，号慧仙，别号蕉园居士，自号梅道人，乳名阿昭，寓所名"景和堂"，又称景和堂主人，绰号胖巧玲。他是清朝同治、道光时期技艺非凡、声名赫赫的京剧表演艺术家，是徽班进京后由演唱徽调、昆腔衍变为京剧的十三位奠基人之一。因其在京剧旦脚表演艺术方面的突出成就，被清末画家沈蓉圃绘入《同光十三绝》画谱而流芳千古。梅巧玲天资聪慧，学戏刻苦，扮相雍容端丽，表演细腻逼真，念白文雅脱俗，京昆不挡，以花旦著称，兼工青衣和昆旦，破除了花旦只重念做，青衣专重唱功的界限，实为花衫行创造之滥觞。

Mei Lanfang's grandfather Mei Qiaoling was a famous Dan actor in the late Qing Dynasty, and he was the first generation of Dan actors in China. He was also one of "Thirteen peerless actors during the reign of Emperors Tongzhi and Guangxu". He had administrated "Sixi Troupe". He was always praised by colleagues, because he was generous, philanthropicminde and had both ability and political integrity.

上图 | 梅兰芳祖父梅巧玲
Grandfather Mei Qiaoling

下左 | 梅巧玲饰萧太后
Mei Qiaoling as the role of Dowager Xiao

下右 | 梅兰芳祖母陈太夫人（1841—1924）
（名小生陈金爵之女）
Grandmother Madame Chen Mei(1841-1924)
(Daughter of Actor Cheng Jinjue)

梅兰芳与祖母合影
Mei Lanfang and his Grandmother

梅竹芬 Mei Zhufen（1874—1897）

梅兰芳的父亲，别名梅肖芬，字凌云，小字二锁。梅巧玲的次子。他先学的是老生，又改小生，最后改唱青衣、花旦。他的昆曲、皮黄都是向梅巧玲学的，凡是梅巧玲唱过的戏，他都会唱，而且唱得极似。他的长相酷似父亲，因而又名“梅肖芬”。梅巧玲去世后，他上台唱《雁门关》、《富贵全》等戏的时候，好似梅巧玲再生。梅竹芬为人忠厚老实、性情温和，当时搭京城颇有名气的迟家“福寿班”，班里只要有人闹脾气告假不唱，班主总是请他代唱，加上外串堂会戏与戏园营业戏的频繁演出，使他的身体受到极大损伤，26岁时因患时疫医治无效，几天后就过早地离开了人世。当时梅兰芳年仅4岁。

Father Mei Zhufen (1874-1897) was a Dan actor, who died early. He was called "Mei Xiaofen", because he was like his father very much, especially in the opera *De Zhengfang*, *Yanmen Pass* and *Riches and Honor*.

左图｜梅兰芳的父亲梅竹芬
Father Mei Zhufen
右图｜梅兰芳的母亲杨长玉（1876—1908）
Mother Yang Changyu (1876-1908)

梅雨田 Mei Yutian（1865—1912）

梅兰芳的伯父。京剧琴师，是著名的皮黄音乐演奏家，胡琴、笛子、鼓等，样样精通。长期为谭鑫培伴奏，对谭派艺术起到烘云托月的作用，深得谭氏器重，有“胡琴圣手”之称。他与孙佐臣为胡琴演奏上的两大流派，影响深远，后世胡琴更多承袭梅雨田派。梅派伴奏风格平正大方，规矩严谨，格局高而韵味醇。

Uncle Mei Yutian (1865-1912) was a famous opera musician, who was elected to the court of Qing, and played Jinghu for Tan Xinpei for a long time. When Mei Lanfang performed his first play *Yu Tangchun* (a love story) at Wenming Teahouse in 1911, his uncle played music for him.

左图｜梅兰芳的伯父梅雨田
Uncle Mei Yutian

右图｜梅兰芳的伯母胡氏（演员胡喜禄侄女）
Aunt Madame Hu Mei (Niece of actor Hu Xilu)

投师学艺

Learning Stage Art from Good Teachers

9岁那年，我到姐丈朱小芬家里学戏……吴菱仙是我们开蒙的老师。

I started learning the art of Chinese opera at age 9 from my brother-in-law Zhu Xiaofen... Wu Lingxian is my first teacher.

—— 梅兰芳 *by Mei Lanfang*

梅兰芳投师吴菱仙后，第一出戏学的是《战蒲关》，嗣后又学了《祭江》、《二进宫》、《三娘教子》、《桑园会》、《彩楼配》、《三击掌》和《宇宙锋》等正工青衣戏。14岁时向秦稚芬和胡二庚学花旦戏。16岁时由梅雨田亲授《武家坡》和《玉堂春》等戏。20岁时拜陈德霖、乔蕙兰、李寿山和陈嘉樑为师，学了许多昆曲剧目，又从路三宝学习《贵妃醉酒》等戏。梅兰芳自幼刻苦练功，勤奋好学，转益多师，广征博采，戏路极广，为日后成为一代大师奠定了坚实的基础。

Wu Lingxian taught Mei Lanfang *Fight in Puguan Pass*, *Sacrifice at Riverside*, *Enter the Court Twice*, *The Third Mistress Teaches Her Son* and so forth. When he was fourteen, he learned from Qin Zhifen, Hu Ergeng. Later, he learned *Wu's Slope*, *Su San* from his uncle Mei Yutian. When he was twenty, he found Chen Delin to be his master and learned many plays of Kunqu Opera, Trough the learning of so many plays, he got a very good background of Beijing Opera performing art which brought successes in his life and carricd him to be the great master of Beijing Opera.

梅兰芳与老师吴菱仙

Mei Lanfang and his teacher Wu Lingxian

梅兰芳（中）与老师吴菱仙（右）和小伙伴朱幼芬（左）

Mei Lanfang (central) with Wu Lingxian(right) and Zhu Youfen(left)

吴菱仙 Wu Lingxian

本名吴永明，祖籍浙江省嘉兴市永安堂吴人。吴菱仙曾经在梅巧玲的四喜班里担任青衣演员。1902年，吴菱仙受梅雨田的委托，成为8岁梅兰芳的开蒙老师，开始教梅兰芳学戏。当时吴菱仙已有50多岁。因与梅兰芳的祖父梅巧玲共事多年，交往甚厚。教戏时特别认真，从教学第一出开蒙戏《战蒲关》开始，吴菱仙共教梅兰芳正工青衣戏30多出。

Wu Lingxian is the disciple of Shi Xiaofu who is one of the famous "Thirteen peerless actors during the Reign of Emperors Tongzhi and Guangxu". He was over 50 then, compared with Zhu Xiaoxia, he was more patient. Since then, Mei Lanfang started his Beijing Opera career. He was the teacher who introduced Mei Lanfang to Beijing Opera field of study.

1919年，梅兰芳（右一）与陈德霖（前）、王瑶卿（右二）、王蕙芳（左二）、姚玉芙（左一）在汉口合影
Mei Lanfang (right 1) with Chen Delin (sitting), Wang Yaoqing (right 2), Wang Huifang (left 2) and Yao Yufu (left 1) (1919)

陈德霖 Chen Delin（1862—1930）

名鋆璋，字麓畊，号漱云。陈德霖是清代光绪以来青衣演员的代表人物，其主要特色在于继承老派青衣演唱的传统，偏于阳刚一路，而在唱法上较前人略有变化，是近代青衣的重要流派，世称“陈派”。陈德霖热心教育事业，一生收徒甚众，桃李满天下。王瑶卿、梅兰芳、王蕙芳、王琴侬、姚玉芙、姜妙香并称“六大弟子”。

Chen Delin was good at both Beijing Opera and Kunqu, both military and civilian. Chen Delin's voice was clear and smooth, full of strength. He paid more attention to the play content; he combined figure character with inner world perfectly. He made many creations on singing; he improved Qingyi to a higher level. He had the honorable reputation Father of Qingyi. Mei is his favourite apprentice. He taught Mei Lanfang many plays.

谭鑫培与王瑶卿饰演《南天门》
Tan Xinpei and Wang Yaoqing in *The South Heaven Gate*

王瑶卿 Wang Yaoqing（1881—1954）

原名瑞臻，字稚庭，号菊痴，晚号瑶青。京剧表演艺术家、教育家，在梨园界被尊奉为“通天教主”。王瑶卿46岁时因嗓子变坏而离开舞台，致力于戏曲教育事业，在戏曲教育方面堪称一代宗师。他在继承前人表演艺术的基础上，将青衣、花旦、武旦融为一体，创造了“花衫”行当，在唱腔、表演、服装、化妆等方面都做了大胆的改革。他的京白清晰柔和，独具特色，把口语化的台词念得有感情、有韵味，抑扬顿挫，悦耳动听。他的唱功明丽刚健，遒劲爽脆，恰如其分地表现了人物思想感情的变化。“四大名旦”梅兰芳、程砚秋、尚小云、荀慧生均受其真传。

Wang Yaoqing is the student of Qingyi ancestor Mei Qiaoling and Yu Ziyun, and he is the teacher of Mei Lanfang and Cheng Yanqiu. He made great creative contributions to Beijing Opera's Dan acting. On the primary stage, in Dan category, Qingyi and Huadan were strictly divided. Qingyi actor only needs to sing well, no expressions or actions. Huadan only needs to express vividly and acts smoothly, no strict demand on singing. This was changed by Mei's grandfather Mei Qiaoling, and Hu Xilu, Yu Ziyun. Wang Yaoqing made a breakthrough on foundation of the changes. He broke the limitations and made "Huashan" role, which combines singing with acting.

梅兰芳的师承关系

①吴菱仙（青衣戏）
Wu Lingxian(qingyi role)
②陈德霖（青衣戏）
Chen Delin (qingyi role)
③王瑶卿（花衫戏）
Wang Yaoqing (huashan role)
④梅雨田（青衣戏）
Mei Yutian (qingyi role)
⑤茹莱卿（武工）
Ru Laiqing (martial role)
⑥乔惠兰（昆曲）
Qiao Huilan (Kunqu Opera)
⑦李寿山（昆曲）
Li Shoushan (Kunqu Opera)
⑧秦稚芬（花旦戏）
Qin Zhifen(huadan role)
⑨路三宝（刀马旦）
Lu Sanbao (daomadan role)
⑩钱金福（武工）
Qian Jinfu (martial role)
⑪陈嘉梁（昆曲）
Chen Jialiang (Kunqu Opera)
⑫丁兰荪（昆曲）
Ding Lansun (Kunqu Opera)

京城搭班
Joined Troupes and Gave Performances

我虽然不是科班出身，但提到我幼年时的舞台生活是离不开“喜连成”的。
Even though I wasn't from traditional Peking Opera's professional training at school(Keban), my adolescence life never left the performing troupes "Xi Lian Cheng".

——梅兰芳　*by Mei Lanfang*

1904年，梅兰芳11岁时首次登台，在“斌庆班”参加昆曲《长生殿·鹊桥密誓》的演出，饰剧中织女。14岁起在“喜连成”科班搭班演出。17岁搭“鸣盛和班”，18岁搭“双庆班”，20岁搭“玉成班”演出。梅兰芳在北京持续不断的演出，尤其是19岁时和伶界大王谭鑫培合演《桑园寄子》以及同其他名脚的合作演出，确立了他作为优秀旦脚演员在北京剧坛上的地位。

Mei gave his first stage show at eleven to play a supporting role in a Kunqu opera *Longevity Palace in 1904 at the age of 11*. The character he played was a spinning girl. And then, he joined *Xi Lianchen* Troupe at 14,*Ming Shenghe* Troupe at 17, *Shuangqing* Troupe at 19, *Yu Cheng* Troupe at 20. He performed frequently in Beijing, through the cooperations with the great masters such as Tan Xinpei and others, Mei gradually won his reputation as a good actor of Dan role in Beijing.

梅兰芳与王蕙芳
Mei Lanfang and Wang Huifang

上图｜梅兰芳与学艺伙伴朱幼芬

Mei Lanfang and his opera schoolmate Zhu Youfen

下左｜梅兰芳（中）在王瑶卿家与王少卿、王幼卿（1913）

Mei Lanfang (central), Wang Shaoqing and Wang Youqing at Wang Yaoqing's house(1913)

下右｜梅兰芳与学艺伙伴姚玉芙

Mei Lanfang and his opera schoolmate Yao Yufu

梅兰芳与幼年学艺时的小伙伴
前排左起：刘砚芳、姚玉芙、梅兰芳、王春林
二排左起：曹小凤、孙砚庭、姜妙卿、迟玉林
三排左起：罗小宝、姚佩兰、姜妙香、朱幼芬
Mei Lanfang and his opera schoolmates
Front,from left to right: Liu Yanfang, Yao Yufu, Mei Lanfang, and Wang Chunlin
2nd row, from left to right: Cao Xiaofeng, Sun Yanting, Jiang Miaoqing and Chi Yulin
3nd row, from left to right: Luo Xiaobao, Yao Peilan, Jiang Miaoxiang, and Zhu Youfen

“喜连成”搭班 Joining Xiliancheng Troupe

梅兰芳14岁时正式搭叶春善先生创办的“喜连成”科班（后改名“富连成”），与老生雷喜福、花脸侯喜瑞以及同学周信芳、贯大元等同台演出，受到了观众的欢迎。梅兰芳在“喜连成”里除了演出营业戏和行会戏之外，在其他时间还要继续向吴菱仙学戏。在搭“喜连成”的一段时间里，梅兰芳一年平均要演出300余场，紧张的生活，繁重的演出，艰苦的学习，使梅兰芳进入了舞台生涯最紧张的阶段。

After four years' performing experience, Mei lanfang got the opportunity to join the professional class "Xiliancheng Troupe" (later changed to "Fuliancheng Troupe") to perform. From 14 to 17, when he was in "Xiliancheng Troupe", he gained strong essential techniques.

《女起解》，梅兰芳饰苏三，萧长华饰崇公道
Mei Lanfang as Su San and Xiao Changhua as Chong Gongdao in *Sending Criminal Su san Under Escort*

在18岁以前，我专唱这一类青衣戏。
Before the age of 18, I Specially Performed Qingyi plays.

——梅兰芳　*by Mei Lanfang*

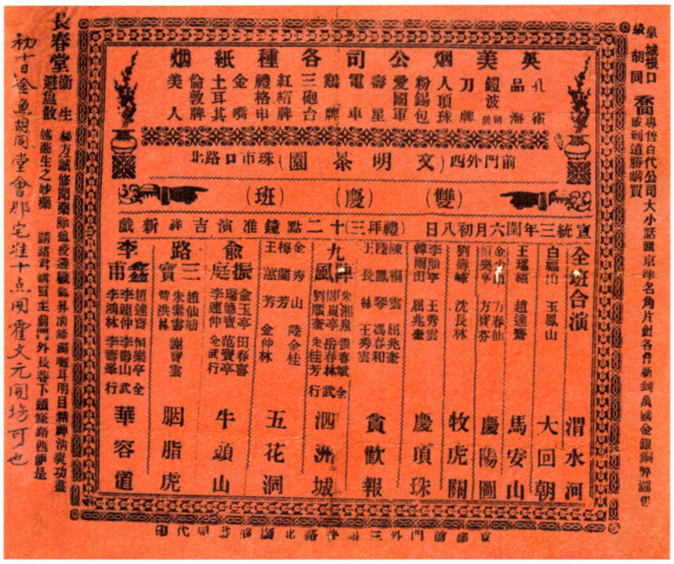

英美烟公司各種紙烟

文明茶園　前門外西珠市口路北

雙慶班

宣統三年閏六月初八日（禮拜三）十二點鐘准演吉祥新戲

渭水河　大回朝　馬安山　慶陽圖　牧虎關　慶頂珠　貪歡報　泗洲城　五花洞　牛頭山　胭脂虎　華容道

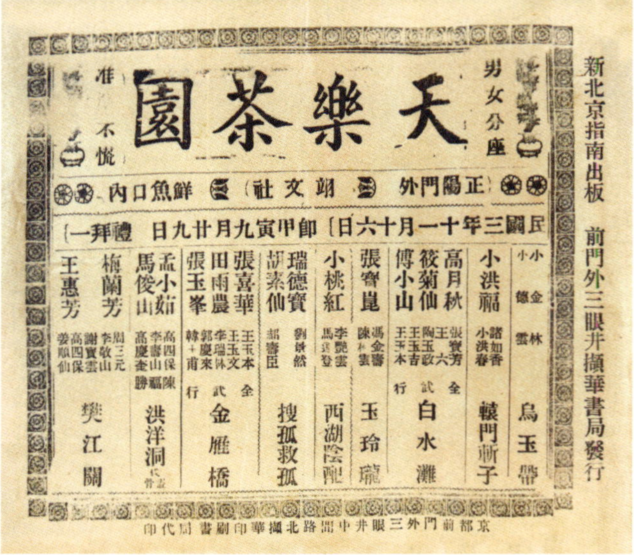

天樂茶園

男女分座　准不悞

正陽門外（鮮魚口內）

民國三年十一月十六日（即甲寅九月廿九日禮拜一）

烏玉帶　轅門斬子　白水灘　玉玲瓏　西湖陰配　搜孤救孤　金雁橋　洪洋洞　樊江關

梅蘭芳　王惠芳

新北京指南出板　前門外三眼井擷華書局發行

京都前門外三眼井中間路北擷華印刷書局代印

上左｜《五花洞》，梅兰芳饰潘金莲，王少卿饰武大郎
Mei Lanfang as Pan Jinlian and Wang Shaoqing as Wu Dalang in *Five Flowers Cave*

上右｜《樊江关》，梅兰芳饰薛金莲
Mei Lanfang as Xue Jinlian in *Fanjiang Pass*

下左｜梅兰芳演出《五花洞》戏单
A program of *Five Flowers Cave*

下右｜梅兰芳演出《樊江关》戏单
A program of *Fanjiang Pass*

《虹霓关》（头本），梅兰芳饰东方氏
Mei Lanfang as Lady Dongfang in *Rainbow Pass*(1st Part)

《虹霓关》（二本），梅兰芳饰丫环

Mei Lanfang as the Maid in *Rainbow Pass*(2nd Part)

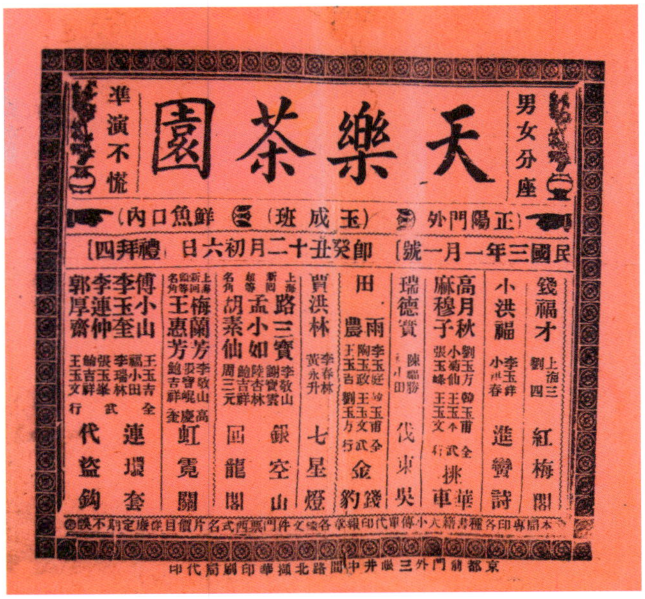

男女分座 天樂茶園 準演不慌

正陽門外（玉成班）鮮魚口內

民國三年一月一號　即癸丑十二月初六日　禮拜四

錢福才　上海三　劉四　紅梅閣

小洪福　李玉昇　小洪春　進蠻詩

高月秋　麻穆子　劉玉方　小菊仙　張玉峰　韓玉甫　王玉本　王玉文　全武行　挑華車

瑞德寶　陳鴻勝　王小田　伐東吳

田雨農　李玉庭　陶玉政　王玉吉　孫玉甫　王玉文　劉玉方　全武行　金錢豹

賈洪林　李春林　黃永升　七星燈

上海新到超等名角　路三寶　孟小如　胡素仙　李敬山　謝寶雲　陸杏林　鮑吉祥　周三元　銀空山　回龍閣

上海新到頭等名角　梅蘭芳　王惠芳　李敬山　姜妙香　鮑吉祥　高慶奎　虹霓關

傅小山　李玉奎　李連仲　郭厚齋　王玉吉　福小田　李瑞林　張玉峯　鮑吉祥　王玉文　全武行　連環套　代盜鈎

本局專印各種書籍大小傳單代印報章各樣文件門票西式名片價目從廉定期不誤

京都前門外三眼井中間路北擷華印刷局代印

上左｜《虹霓关》（头本），梅兰芳饰东方氏，路三宝饰王伯党

Mei Lanfang as Lady Dongfang and Lu Sanbao as Wang Bodang in *Rainbow Pass*(1st Part)

上右｜《虹霓关》（头本），梅兰芳反串王伯党，王惠芳饰东方氏

Mei Lanfang as Wang Bodang and Wang Huifang as Lady Dongfang in *Rainbow Pass*(1st Part)

下图｜梅兰芳演出《虹霓关》戏单（1914）

A program of Mei's acting in *Rainbow Pass*(1914)

左页 |《彩楼配》，梅兰芳饰王宝钏

Mei Lanfang as Wang Baochuan in *Betrothal at the Colour Tower*

上左 |《战蒲关》，梅兰芳饰徐艳贞

Mei Lanfang as Xu Yanzhen in *The Battle of Pu Pass*

上中 |《御碑亭》，梅兰芳饰孟月华

Mei Lanfang as Meng Yuehua in *The Pavilion of Imperial Monument*

上右 |《桑园会》，梅兰芳饰罗敷

Mei Lanfang as Luo Fu in the Meeting at *the Mulberry Garden*

上左 |《三娘教子》，梅兰芳饰王春娥
Mei Lanfang as Wang Chun E in *Mother Educated Her Stepson*
上中 |《梅龙镇》，梅兰芳饰李凤姐
Mei Lanfang as Li Fengjie in *The Meilong Town*
上右 |《金针刺红蟒》，梅兰芳饰红蟒
Mei Lanfang as Lady Red Python in *The Red Python and the Golden Pin*

《汾河湾》，梅兰芳饰柳迎春，王凤卿饰薛仁贵

Mei Lanfang as Liu Yingchun and Wang Fengqing as Xue Rengui in The *Fen River Bend*

沪港成名

The First Time to Shanghai and Hong Kong

辛亥革命后，……我初步感觉到，这种专重唱工的青衣戏，不能满足观众的要求，所以就在青衣之外，兼学了二本《虹霓关》、《樊江关》、《汾河湾》、《穆柯寨》这些偏重身段表情和武工的戏，使戏路宽广丰富一些。

After 1911 revolution...... I realized that I wasn't able to satisfy the audience with only Qingyi operas. As a result, I learned other operas Rainbow Pass, Fan Jiang Pass, By The Fen River Bend, Mu's Villige Fortress.These operas emphasized body emotions and kongfu. It made opera broader and more enriching.

—— 梅兰芳　*by Mei Lanfang*

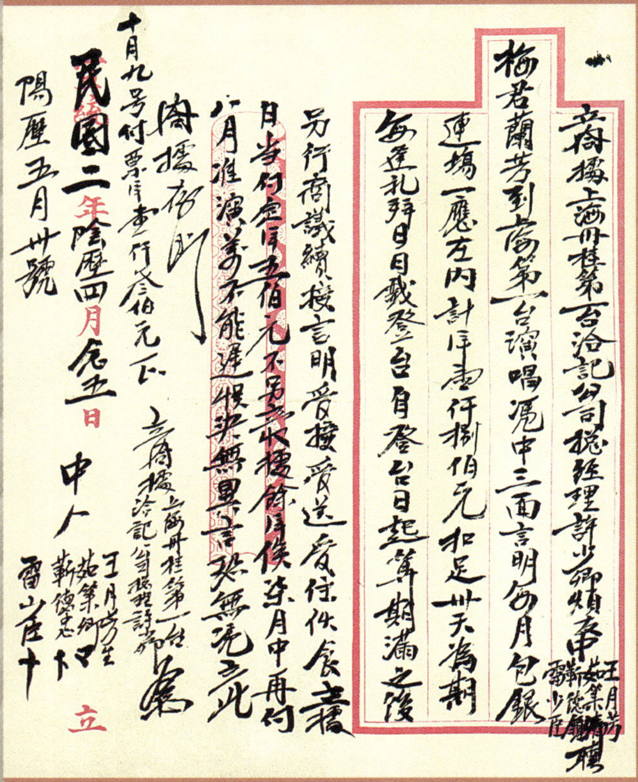

立議據上海丹桂第一台洽記公司總理許少卿煩中
梅君蘭芳到滬第一台演唱，憑中三面言明每月包銀
連場一應在內計洋壹仟捌佰元，扣足卅天為期
每逢禮拜日日戲登台，自登台日起算，期滿之後
另行商議續據，言明受接愛送，愛住供食，立據
月當付定洋五百元，不另立收據，餘洋俟本月中再付
八月准演，萬不能遲延，恐後無憑，立此
為據存照
十月九號付票洋壹仟叁佰元正
上海丹桂第一台洽記公司總理許少卿
民國二年陰歷四月念五日　立
中人
陽歷五月卅號

梅兰芳第一次赴上海演出时与戏院签订的合同（1913）

The contract with the theatre during Mei's first tour to Shanghai(1913)

1913年11月，梅兰芳随同驰名须生王凤卿赴上海丹桂第一台演出，首场演出剧目为《彩楼配》和《朱砂痣》，经王凤卿大力提携，16日改由梅兰芳主演大轴戏——茹莱卿亲授的《穆柯寨》。他出色地完成了“穆桂英”这一艺术人物的塑造，受到上海观众的交口称赞，遂崭露头角。此次上海之行也让梅兰芳更加自信，在京剧改革创新的道路上又向前迈进了一步。

Mei went to Shanghai as the supporting actor for the famous Sheng (male role)actor Wang Fengqing in November, 1913. The program of the premiere in Shanghai was *A Betrothal at the Colour Tower*. Later, as being recommended by Wang, Mei played the main role in the evening of November 16th. He portrayed Mu Guiying in the play *Mu's Village Fortress* and won applause. His name was soon spread all over Shanghai.

《汾河湾》，梅兰芳饰柳迎春，王凤卿饰薛仁贵
Mei Lanfang as Liu Yingchun and Wang Fengqing as Xue Rengui in *The Fen River Bend*

梅兰芳第一次演出大轴戏《穆柯寨》戏单（1913）
A program of Mei Lanfang's debut as the main role in *Mu's Village Fortress* in Shanghai(1913)

《穆柯寨》，梅兰芳饰穆桂英(1913)

Mei Lanfang as Mu Guiying in *Mu's Village Fortress*(1913)

1922年10月，梅兰芳29岁时，首次应香港太平戏院的邀请，率“承华社”140余人，经广州赴香港，演出了传统剧目、新编古装歌舞剧和现代时装戏20余出，多侧面地反映了他在表演艺术上的丰富多彩，受到香港各界人士和海外侨胞的高度评价。

In October 1922, Mei was invited by the Tai Ping Theatre of Hong Kong to present his performance for the Hong Kong audience. This was the first time he visited Hong Kong.

梅兰芳赴港时街头所搭的欢迎梅兰芳的彩牌楼（1922）

A decorated archway specially built to welcome Mei Lanfang on the street of Hong Kong(1922)

3280
302

此牌樓乃
是八和劇
員總工
会歡
迎
芳
全體
伶工友
影紀念

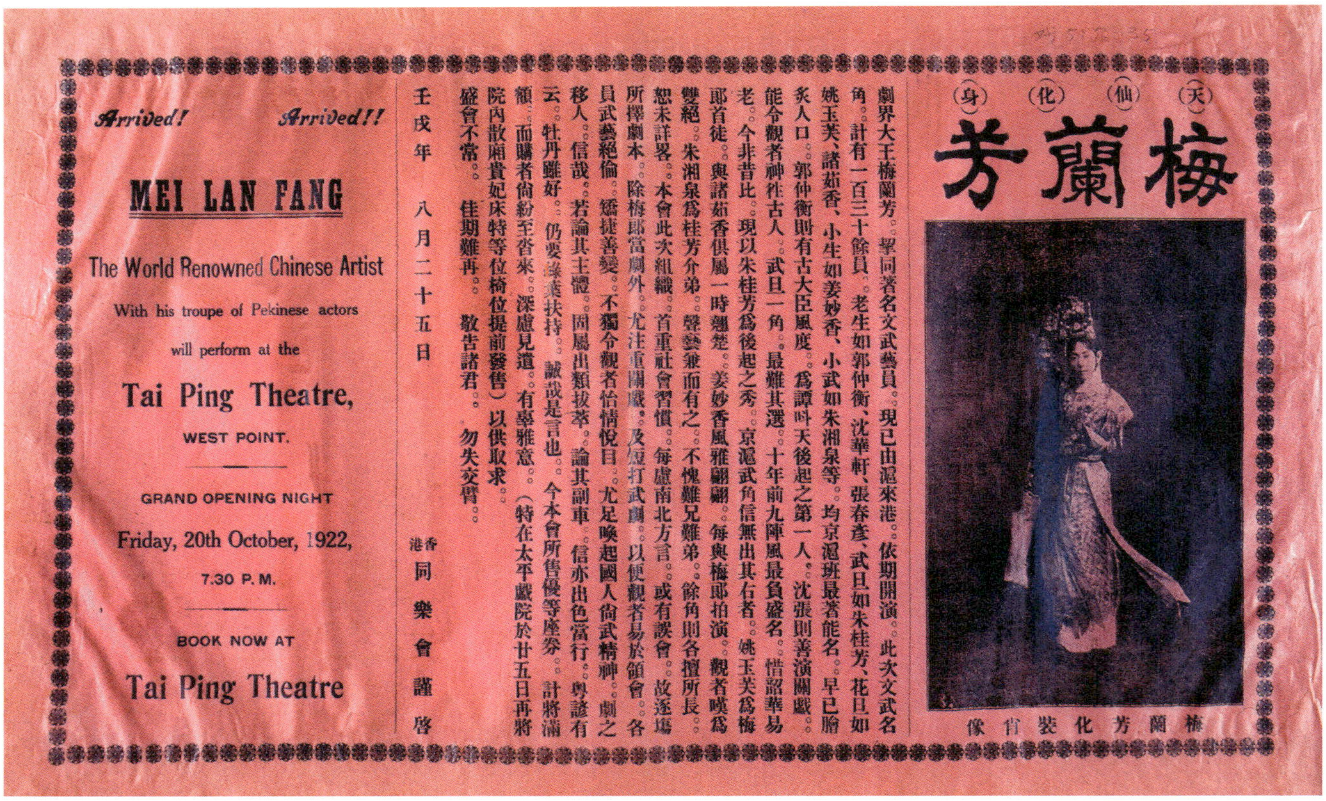

(天)(仙)(化)(身)

梅蘭芳

梅蘭芳化裝肖像

劇界大王梅蘭芳。挈同著名文武藝員。現已由滬來港。依期開演。此次文武名角。計有一百三十餘員。老生如郭仲衡、沈華軒、張春彥，武旦如朱桂芳、花旦如姚玉芙、諸茹香、小生如姜妙香、小武如朱湘泉等。均京滬班最著能名。早已膾炙人口。郭仲衡則有古大臣風度。爲譚叫天後起之第一人。沈張則善演關戲。能令觀者神往古人。武旦一角。最難其選。十年前九陣風最負盛名。惜韶華易老。今非昔比。現以朱桂芳爲後起之秀。京滬武角信無出其右者。姚玉芙爲梅郎首徒。與諸茹香俱屬一時翹楚。姜妙香風雅翩翩。每與梅郎拍演。觀者嘆爲雙絕。朱湘泉爲桂芳介弟。聲藝兼而有之。不愧難兄難弟。餘角則各擅所長。恕未詳畧。本會此次組織。首重社會習慣。每慮南北方言。或有誤會。故逐塲所擇劇本。除梅郎當劇外。尤注重關戲。及短打武劇。以便觀者易於領會。各員武藝絕倫。矯捷善變。不獨令觀者怡情悅目。尤足喚起國人尚武精神。劇之移人。信哉。若論其主體。固屬出類拔萃。論其副車。信亦出色當行。粵諺有云。牡丹雖好。仍要綠葉扶持。誠哉是言也。今本會所售優等座券。計將滿額。而購者尚紛至沓來。深慮見遺。有辜雅意。（特在太平戲院於廿五日再將院內散廂貴妃床特等位椅位提前發售）以供取求。盛會不常。佳期難再。敬告諸君。勿失交臂。

香港同樂會謹啓

壬戌年 八月二十五日

Arrived! Arrived!!

MEI LAN FANG

The World Renowned Chinese Artist

With his troupe of Pekinese actors

will perform at the

Tai Ping Theatre,

WEST POINT.

GRAND OPENING NIGHT

Friday, 20th October, 1922,

7.30 P. M.

BOOK NOW AT

Tai Ping Theatre

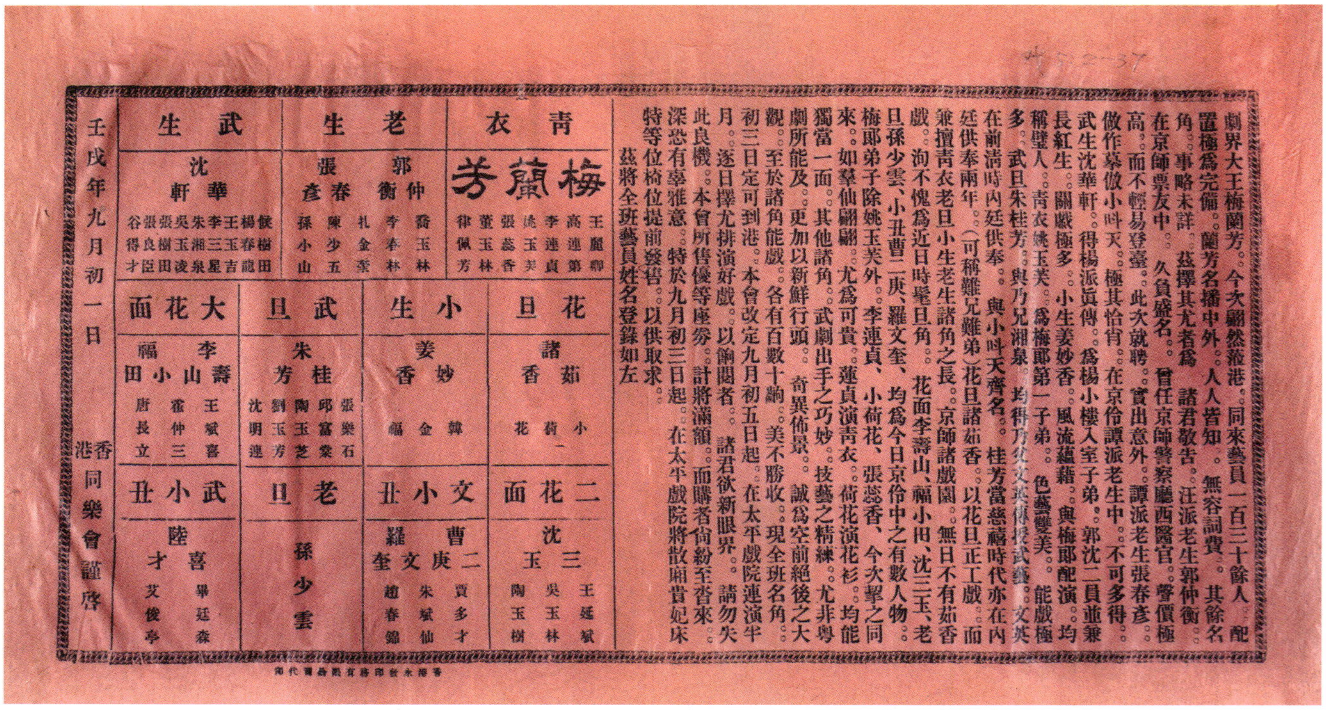

劇界大王梅蘭芳。今次翩然蒞港。同來藝員一百三十餘人。配置極爲完備。蘭芳名播中外。人人皆知。無容詞費。其餘名角。事略未詳。茲擇其尤者爲諸君敬告。汪派老生郭仲衡在京師票友中 久負盛名。曾任京師警察廳西醫官。聲價極高。而不輕易登臺。此次就聘。實出意外。譚派老生張春彥做作摹倣小叫天。極其恰肖。在京伶譚派老生中。不可多得。武生沈華軒。得楊派眞傳。爲楊小樓入室子弟。郭沈二員並兼長紅生。關戲極多。小生姜妙香。風流蘊藉。與梅郎配演。均稱璧人。青衣姚玉芙。爲梅郎第一子弟。色藝雙美。能戲極多。武旦朱桂芳。與乃兄湘泉。均得乃父文英傳授武藝。文英在前清時內廷供奉。與小叫天齊名。桂芳當慈禧時代亦在內廷供奉兩年。（可稱難兄難弟）花旦諸茹香。以花旦正工戲。而兼擅青衣老旦小生老生諸角之長。京師諸戲園。無日不有茹香戲。洵不愧爲近日時髦旦角。花面李壽山、福小田、沈三玉、老旦孫少雲、小丑曹二庚、羅文奎、均爲今日京伶中之有數人物。梅郎弟子除姚玉芙外。李連貞、小荷花、張蕊香、今次挈之同來。如羣仙翩翩。尤爲可貴。蓮貞演青衣。荷花演花衫。均能獨當一面。其他諸角。武劇出手之巧妙。技藝之精練。尤非粵劇所能及。更加以新鮮行頭。奇異佈景。誠爲空前絕後之大觀。至於諸角能戲。各有百數十齣。美不勝收。現全班名角初三日定可到港。本會改定九月初五日起。在太平戲院連演半月。逐日擇尤排演好戲。以餉閱者。諸君欲新眼界。請勿失此良機。本會所售優等座券。計將滿額。而購者尚紛至沓來。深恐有辜雅意。特於九月初三日起。在太平戲院將散廂貴妃床特等位椅位提前發售。以供取求。茲將全班藝員姓名登錄如左

行當	主角	其他
青衣	梅蘭芳	王麗卿 高連第 李連貞 姚玉芙 張蕊香 董玉林 律佩芳
老生	郭仲衡 張春彥	喬玉林 李春林 扎金奎 陳少五 孫小山
武生	沈華軒	餘樹田 楊春龍 王玉吉 李三星 朱湘泉 吳玉凌 張樹田 張良臣 谷得才
花旦	諸茹香	小荷花
小生	姜妙香	韓金福
武旦	朱桂芳	張樂石 邱富棠 陶玉芝 劉玉芳 沈明連
大花面	李壽山 福小田	王斌喜 霍仲三 唐長立
二花面	沈三玉	王廷斌 吳玉林 陶玉樹
文小丑	曹二庚 羅文奎	賈多才 朱斌仙 趙春錫
老旦	孫少雲	
武小丑	陸喜才	畢廷森 艾俊亭

壬戌年九月初一日

香港同樂會謹啓

上图 | 梅兰芳率团在香港演出时的海报

The poster regarding the arrival of Mei's performing troupe in Hong Kong

下图 | 梅兰芳率团在香港演出时各行演员的海报

The poster regarding the team member of Mei's performing troupe in the street of Hong Kong

梅兰芳（前排左三）与夫人王明华（前排左一）到香港后受到各界人士的欢迎

Mei Lanfang (left 3rd of front row)with his wife Wang Minghua(left 1st of front row) and other reception members during his arrival in Hong Kong

香港太平剧场（1922）
Tai Ping Theatre of Hong Kong(1922)

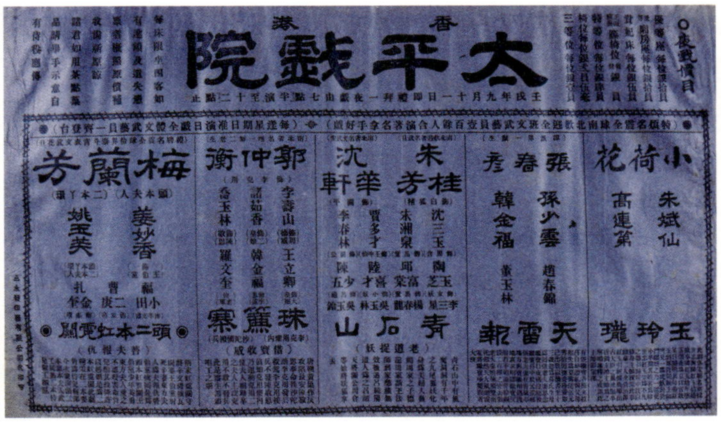

左图｜《虹霓关》（头本），梅兰芳饰东方氏，朱桂芳饰王伯党

Mei Lanfang as Lady Dongfang and Zhu Guifang as Wang Bodang in *Rainbow Pass*(1st part)

右图｜梅兰芳在香港演出头、二本《虹霓关》戏单（1922 ）

The program of *Rainbow Pass*(Part 1 and 2)performed by Mei Lanfang in Hong Kong (1922)

《虹霓关》（二本），梅兰芳饰丫环
Mei Lanfang as the Maid in *Rainbow Pass*(2nd Part)

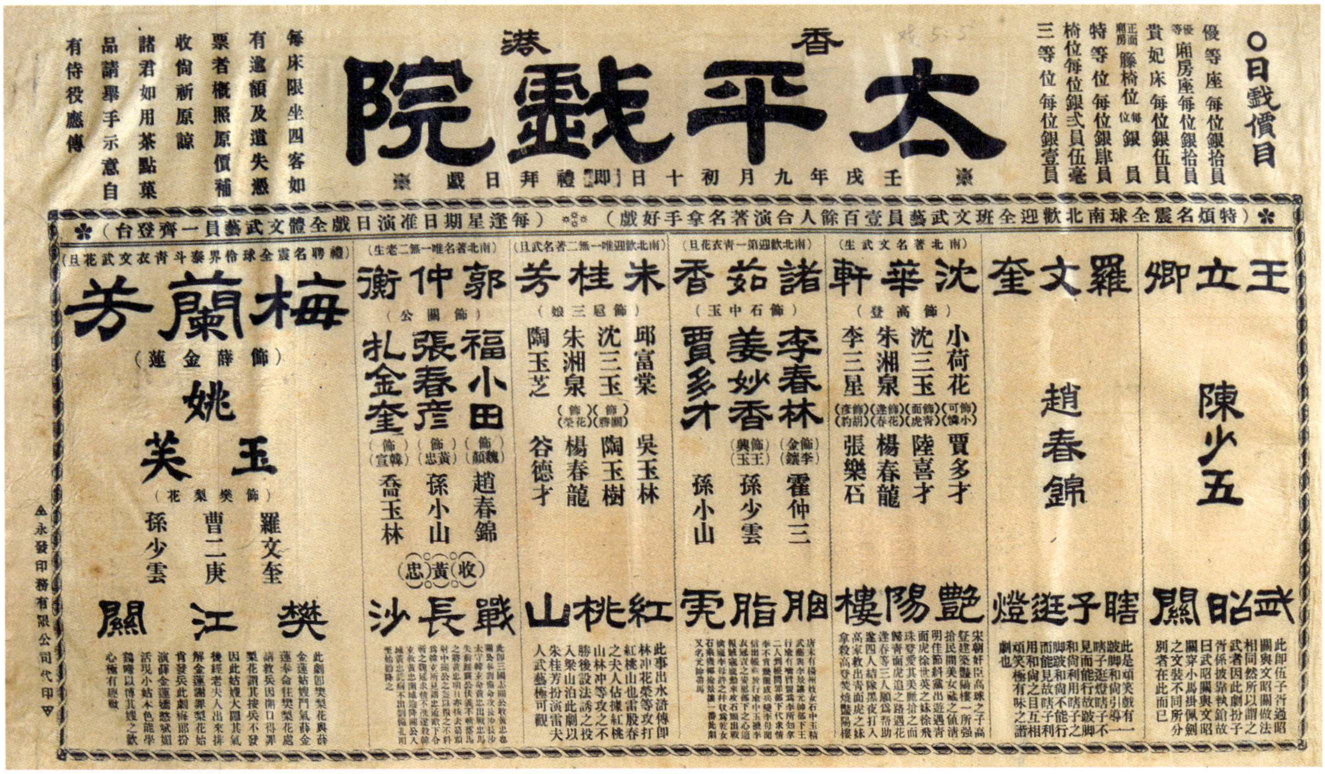

香港 太平戲院

壬戌年九月初十日【即】禮拜日戲

每床限坐四客如有逾額及遺失憑票者概照原價補收倘新原諒諸君如用茶點菓品請舉手示意自有侍役應傳

○日戲價目
優等座每位銀拾員
優等廂房座每位銀拾員
貴妃床每位銀伍員
正面廂房籐椅位每位銀員
特等位每位銀肆員
椅位每位銀弍員伍毫
三等位每位銀壹員

特煩名震全球南北歡迎全班文武藝員壹百餘人合演著名拿手好戲（每逢星期日准演日戲全體文武藝員一齊登台）

王立卿 陳少五
武昭關

羅文奎 趙春錦
瞎子逛燈

（南北著名文武生）沈華軒（飾高登）
小荷花 沈三玉 朱湘泉 李三星 賈多才 陸喜才 楊春龍 張榮石
艷陽樓

（南北歡迎第一青衣花旦）諸茹香（飾石中玉）
李春林 姜妙香 賈多才 霍仲三 孫少雲 孫小山
胭脂虎

（南北歡迎唯一無二著名武旦）朱桂芳（飾扈三娘）
邱富棠 沈三玉 朱湘泉 陶玉芝 吳玉林 陶玉樹 楊春龍 谷德才
紅桃山

（南北著名唯一無二老生）郭仲衡（飾關公）
福小田 張春彥 扎金奎 趙春錦 孫小山 喬玉林
戰長沙

（禮聘名震全球伶界泰斗青衣文武花旦）梅蘭芳（飾薛金蓮）
姚玉芙（飾樊梨花）
羅文奎 曹二庚 孫少雲
樊江關

永發印務有限公司代印

上左、上右 | 《樊江关》，梅兰芳饰薛金莲，朱桂芳饰樊梨花

Mei Lanfang as Xue Jinlian and Zhu Guifang as Fan Lihua in *Fanjiang Pass*

下图 | 梅兰芳在香港演出《樊江关》戏单（1922）

The program of *Fanjiang Pass* performed by Mei Lanfang in Hong Kong(1922)

戏剧前途的趋势是跟着观众的需要和时代而变化的。我不愿还是站在这旧的圈子里边不动，再受它的拘束。我要走向新的道路上去寻求发展。

The future trend of Chinese opera depends on the taste of audience and changes in time. I don't want to stand in the same old box, constrained and not moving. I want to walk my own path and search for new development.

——梅兰芳 *by Mei Lanfang*

贰

承前启后

Innovations in Performing Art

梅兰芳创造的梅派艺术风格及特点主要表现在其革新精神上。他在唱、念、做、舞、音乐、服装、扮相和剧目各个方面进行了全面、系统的创造与发展，达到了完美的境界，承前启后地将京剧旦行的演唱及表演艺术提高到了一个全新的水平，成为京剧旦行中影响极其深远的一个流派。

Throughout his life Mei progressed along with the time to adjust his stage art to meet the new taste of the audience. He reformed and developed the traditional Beijing Opera comprehensively and consistently. This was the reason why he became the great master of Beijing Opera.

With the help of relatives and friends, Mei adapted traditional plays and produced new plays. He enriched the performing art for the dan role, fulfilling his predecessor Wang Yaoqing's unfinished experiment to turn himself into a performer of multi-female roles, i.e., qingyi (quiet and gentle woman), huadan (vivacious young woman), guimendan (unmarried young girl) and daomadan (woman warrior), well versed not only in singing but also in dancing and acting as well, As a result, he reached the top level of the performing art of dan role, formed his own original style and developed what has become unanimously accepted as the "Mei Lanfang School" ——a school with unique characteristics and subtle dignity, which won high appraise both in China and abroad.

梅兰芳

《**女起解**》

梅兰芳饰苏三

Mei Lanfang as Su San in *Sending Criminal Su San Under Escort*

《**思凡**》

梅兰芳饰赵色空

Mei Lanfang as Zhao Sekong in *Longing for Worldly Pleasures*

佛 佛 佛

《**游园惊梦**》

梅兰芳饰杜丽娘，梅葆玖饰春香

Mei Lanfang as Du Liniang and Mei Baojiu as Chun Xiang in *The Peony Pavilion*

《春香闹学》

梅兰芳饰春香

Mei Lanfang as Chun Xiang in *Chun Xiang Upsets the Study*

改革创新

Reformation and Innovation

我曾经在新排的剧目当中，创造了京剧舞台上从来没有过的服装和化妆，这种尝试和我平时学习绘画有密切关系。

Previously in new shows, I created costumes and makeup that was first of its kind. The trials and experiments was mainly because I practice drawing during my free time.

——梅兰芳 *by Mei Lanfang*

1914年，梅兰芳21岁时在“翊文社”演出王瑶卿亲授的7本《儿女英雄传》等戏。7月，演出第一部时装新戏《孽海波澜》，从而拉开了编演新戏的序幕。梅兰芳在冯耿光、齐如山、吴震修、李释戡等各界友人及戏剧界同仁积极热心的协助下，依据京剧艺术的规律，改革唱腔，增添音色浑厚的“二胡”伴奏，设计新颖的舞蹈身段，改进化妆、服饰和人物造型，净化舞台，增添灯光布景装置等。正如他本人所言：“戏剧前途的趋势是跟着观众的需要和时代而变化的……我要走向新的道路上去寻求发展。”他先后编演了许多时装新戏和古装歌舞剧，其中不少剧目后来成为梅派艺术的精品。

In 1914, Mei was at 21, he played a seris of plays of seven volumn *Story of He Yufeng*. Then, in July of the same year, he played his first contemporary play in modern costumes *The Waves in Sea of Sin*. Later on, Mei had created quite a few new plays either in ancient costumes or in modern dresses. He reformed the melodies, increased musical instrument with Erhu. He enriched the dancing actions, improved the stage image designs and the stage sets. Mei reformed the Beijing Opera stage art totally but reasonably. Many of his new plays became the masterpieces of his school.

北京无量大人胡同寓所“缀玉轩”，梅兰芳经常在此与友人研究艺术革新问题（左起：梅兰芳、齐如山、罗瘿公）

The study at Mei Lanfang's house at Wuliang Daren Hutong (Mei Lanfang ,Qi Rushan and Luo Yinggong)

梅兰芳首次赴上海演出回京后，在化妆方面加以改革，包括画眼边，改变樱桃小口式的唇红

Returning from Shanghai, Mei improved the facial make-up

梅兰芳对传统京剧旦脚演员的化妆进行了大胆的革新。从前，北方的旦脚演员不讲究画黑眼圈，脸型也显得又高又宽，方方正正，这类扮相在今天看来非常死板和呆滞。梅兰芳改变了传统北方的旦脚化妆方法，结合南方化妆的方法，画上黑眼圈，吊起眉毛，显得眼睛格外好看有神。将演员的脸型通过“片子”（旦脚演员贴在两鬓的假头发）贴在不同位置来进行调整，以达到最美的效果，这为他的演出增添了光彩。

Mei Lanfang paid attention to the innovation of makeup, costumes, stage scenery and lighting. In every aspect, he treated beauty as a standard, making everything suitable for indoor theater performances.

左图 | 光绪年间，陈德霖等演《断桥》时将早年南府档案中所载白、青二人的“渔婆罩”改为戴“额子”。梅兰芳初期演出此戏时也戴“额子”，从20世纪30年代起进行了多次改革

The make-up of the Snake Ladies in The Legend of the White Snake Lady performed in the late years of the Qing Dynasty. Mei made improvement several times since 1930s

右图 | 梅兰芳后期演《白蛇传》头饰，梅兰芳饰白素贞，梅葆玖饰青儿

By Mei Lanfang in his later years. Mei Lanfang as Lady White and Mei Baojiu as Qing Er

梅兰芳演虞姬的如意冠是参考绘画《列女传》虞姬的小冕旒

The costume of Yuji in *The King's Parting with His Favourite*. The design of Yuji's crown was based on an an'cient illustrated book

梅兰芳研制的隔汗用竹衫

An underdress made of bamboo invented by Mei Lanfang to protect costume from perspiration

左上、左下｜梅兰芳演《四郎探母·坐宫》时所穿的旗袍

Cheongsam Mei wore in the role of Princess *Silang Visits His Mother*

右图｜梅兰芳演《四郎探母·盗令》时见母后所穿的蟒袍，俗称“旗蟒”

The costume Mei wore in the role of Princess *Silang Visits His Mother*

上图、右页下｜舞台上的门帘台帐和大帐

The back embroidered drop with the entrance and exit openings

右页上｜舞台上的“守旧”（门帘台帐）

The back embroidered drop on the stage is called *Shoujiu* in Chinese

左图 | 梅兰芳演《女起解》的服装
The costume in *Sending Crimimal Su San Under Escort*
右图 | 梅兰芳演《奇双会》的服装
The costume in *A Tale of Double Reunion*

左图｜梅兰芳演《霸王别姬》的服装和头饰
The costume and headdress Mei Lanfang worn in *The King's Parting with His Favorite*
右图｜梅兰芳演《洛神》的服装
The costume in The Goddess of *The River Luo*

梅兰芳与齐如山 Mei Lanfang and Qi Rushan

作为“梅派”幕后的重要人物齐如山（1875—1962），他醉心痴迷于京剧，对梅兰芳的表演表现出浓厚的兴趣。作为梅兰芳的编剧、幕后推手和策划人，齐如山为梅兰芳编写改编了几十出剧目，精心策划国外之行的前期宣传和制造声势，可以说他为梅派艺术所取得的成就立下了汗马功劳。梅兰芳始终把齐如山尊为长辈，两人不但是忘年之交，也是莫逆之交。1915年，齐如山为梅兰芳编排了一出旧式的新戏《牢狱鸳鸯》，演出后轰动京城。从此，齐如山便成了为梅兰芳编剧的主要人物，或者说是“贴身编剧”之一。随后，齐如山又从古画中得到启示，为梅兰芳设计了一套古装打扮，并且把古代各种不同舞姿安放到《嫦娥奔月》、《红线盗盒》、《天女散花》、《廉锦枫》等戏中。齐如山是一个具有现代意义的策划人，在剧目创作和导演方面都对中国戏曲起到了非常大的、建设性的作用。他排演的脍炙人口的《俊袭人》、《洛神》和连续上演的四本《太真外传》，使梅派新戏别具一格，长演不衰。在他与梅兰芳交往近20年的时间里，所编演的新剧达二十几出，再加上几出旧戏的改编，总计约有四十几出戏。尽管李释戡、罗瘿公也常参与出谋划策，但齐如山始终是其中功劳最大的一位。

Qi Rushan, an important person of "Mei Party", was addicted in Beijing Opera. And he showed a keen interest in Mei Lanfang's show. As Mei Lanfang's playwright, propagator and mastermind, Qi Rushan wrote dozens of plays for Mei Lanfang, carefully planned trip abroad, including the publicity and creating a momentum. It can say that he made a great contribution to Mei's art achievements. Mei Lanfang had always treated Qi Rushan as a senior. They were not only the friendship between generations, but also friends with complete mutual understanding. In 1915, Qi Rushan arranged an old-style new drama Prison Mandarin Duck for Mei Lanfang. After the show, it caused a sensation throughout Beijing. Since then, Qi Rushan became the main playwright, or one of the "personal playwrights" for Mei Lanfang. Then, Qi Rushan got inspiration from ancient paintings, designed a costume dress up for Mei Lanfang, and arranging various ancient dance adding to the opera of Lady Chang E Flies to the Moon, Hongxian Steals Box, The Heavenly Maids Scatter Blossoms, Lian Jinfeng. Qi Rushan was a modernism mastermind, who had a large effect on the Chinese Opera construction in writing and directing. He rehearsed the Beauty Xi Ren, The Goddess of the Luo River, which won universal praiseand and the The Legend of Yang Yuhuan made Mei Lanfang have his own style. These palys lasted for long and remained invincible. In his dealings with Mei Lanfang nearly twenty years, the new plays up to 20, plus a few old plays, a total of about forty plays. Although Li Shikan, Luo Yinggong also gave advice and suggestions, Qi Rushan was always a greatest credit. Mei Lanfang and Qi Rushan, one was a master of Beijing Opera, the other was a prominent opera literati, they each improved by association with the other cooperation and one's nobility last forever friendship, which became a model for study and admiration of later generations.

梅兰芳在上海与齐如山(左)、姚玉芙(右)
With Qi Rushan (left) and Yao Yufu (right) in Shanghai

梅兰芳与冯耿光

Mei Lanfang and Feng Gengguang

梅兰芳与琴师徐兰沅（右）、王少卿（左）合影（共同研究增加了二胡伴奏）（1937）

With his accompanists Xu Lanyuan (right) and Wang Shaoqing (left) [They decided to add an Erhu(Chinese fiddle) to the band](1937)

1923年，梅兰芳在北京排《西施》时感到旦脚单靠京胡伴奏过于单薄，就与徐兰沅商议，反复试验，最后决定加入二胡，利用京胡与二胡差八度的关系，又设计了不同的伴奏曲谱，这样合声伴奏演出效果更好，此次革新很快得到广大观众的认同。

In 1923, Mei Lanfang organized a group named "Chenghua Club". In order to well foil the singing style during rehearsing the new play *Beauty Xishi*, Wang Shaoqing and Xu Lanyuan made an effective reform on the problem of Jing ErHu and Jinghu differs from each other in one octave on the score scale, and the problem of how to make this two instruments coordinating played. Finally, they strengthened the effect of melody during the process of accompany by playing the two instruments more harmonious.

△國劇學會客廳外部之攝影▽

京劇之變遷（十）

·齊如山·

國劇學會附設 國劇傳習所章程

國劇學會附設 國劇傳習所章程

第一章 總則

第一條 定名 本所定名為國劇傳習所直隸於國劇學會理事會

第二條 宗旨 本所以研究國劇藝術發揚固有精神培植戲劇實地表演人才為宗旨

第三條 所址 本所暫設虎坊橋四十五號（電話南局二一一〇）遇必要時得另闢新所址

第二章 學員

第四條 學員不分性別但須具左列資格（以總社簡章先成立為憑）

一，身體健全品行端正

二，有普通常識

三，國文文理通順

第五條 報名手續

一，填寫報名表

二，繳最近四寸照像一張

三，繳試驗費一元（錄取與否概不退還）

第六條 試驗科目

一，口試

二，發音

三，常識測驗

四，國文

五，體格檢查

第七條 業經取錄學員須按入學手續來所報到並於每月授課前交納學費大洋四元

但以一系一組為單位如欲兼入他系之一組者加繳學費二元

第八條 本所學員除在本所受課時間外其他職業概不過問

第九條 本所學員須遵守本所一切規則

第十條 中途退學或犯規開除者已交各費概不退還

第三章 課程與分系

第十一條 課程以科學方法為教授之準則務使學者易於接受系分皮黃崑曲音樂三系

第十二條 皮黃崑曲兩系更分老生小生旦淨丑五組音樂系分文場武場兩組

各系各組專修課程如左

（皮黃系）

（老生）—唱工做工說白化裝習演

（小生）—唱工做工說白化裝習演

（旦）—唱工做工說白化裝習演

（淨）—唱工做工說白化裝習演

（丑）—唱工做工說白化裝習演

（老生）—唱工做工說白化裝習演

（小生）—唱工做工說白化裝習演

上图 | 国剧学会办公室

The office of the Society of National Chinese Opera

下图 | 国剧传习所章程

The Regulation of the Training Center of National Chinese Opera

国剧学会第二次集会时合影（前排左四为梅兰芳，前排左七为余叔岩）
At the 2nd meeting of the Society of National Chinese Opera (front left 4 : Mei Lanfang, front left 7: Yu Shuyan)

国剧学会 The Society of National Chinese Opera

1931年冬，梅兰芳在北京与余叔岩发起成立“国剧学会”，齐如山、溥绪（清逸居士）、张伯驹、傅惜华等人出任理事。学会成立之日，到会祝贺的有李石曾、胡适、袁守和、于学忠、刘天华、梁思成、焦菊隐、王梦白等各界人士。学会搜集、整理了大批京剧和地方戏的艺术资料，出版了《戏剧丛刊》和《国剧画报》，创办了国剧陈列馆。学会还附设国剧传习所，培养出刘仲秋、郭建英、高维廉等75名学员。梅兰芳亲自执教指导，并请徐兰沅、王泊生、余上沅、刘半农、徐凌霄和一些京剧演员及教师讲学传艺。国剧学会的建立对中国戏曲的研究和教学起到了很大的推动作用。

In 1931, Mei Lanfang and Yu Shuyan established the The Society of National Chinese Opera, published "Drama Journal" and "National Drama Illustrated", and founded the National Opera Gallery. the Institute of Chinese Theatre was played a significant role in promoting research and teaching Chinese opera.

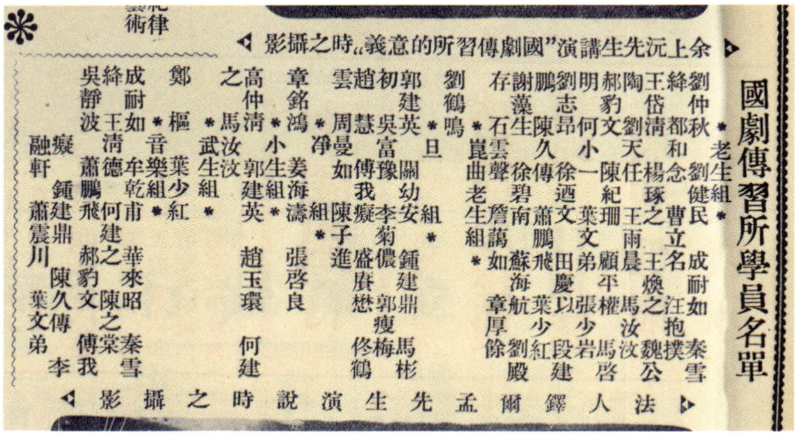

國劇傳習所學員名單

術律

余上沅先生講演"國劇傳習所的意義"時之攝影

劉絳王陶郝明劉鵬謝存 劉 郭初趙雲 章 高之 鄭 成絳吳
仲 岱 豹 志 藻 鶴 建 銘 仲 耐 靜
秋都清劉文何昂陳生石 鳴*英吳慧周*鴻*清馬* 樞*如王波
老 和 天 小 久 雲崑 旦 富 曼淨 小 汝武 音 清 癡融
生劉念楊任陳一徐傳徐聲曲 關豫傳如 姜生郭汝生 葉樂牟德蕭 軒
組健 琢 紀 迺 碧 老 幼 我 海組建 組 少組乾 鵬 鍾
*民曹之王珊葉文蕭南詹生 組安李癡陳組濤*英 *紅*市何飛 建蕭
立 雨 文 鵬 藹組 * 菊 子* 建 鼎震
成名王晨顧弟田飛蘇如* 鍾儂盛進 張 趙 華之郝 川
耐 煥 平 慶 海 建 賡 啓 玉 來 豹陳
如汪之馬權張以葉航章 鼎郭懋 良 環 昭陳文 久葉
抱 汝 少 少 厚 瘦 之 傳文
秦撲魏汝馬岩段紅劉徐 馬梅佟 何 秦棠傳 弟
雪 公 啓 建 殿 彬 鶴 建 雪 我李

法人鐸爾孟先生演說時之攝影

上图｜国剧传习所开学典礼时合影（前排左二为梅兰芳）
The Opening fumction of the Traing Centre of the Society of National Chinese Opera (left 2 of front row)

下图｜国剧传习所学员名单
The list of trainees of the Training Center

梅兰芳在国剧传习所成立时演讲
Mei Lanfang gave a speech at the opening ceremony of the Training Center of the Society of National Chinese Opera

国剧学会成员会见外宾时合影（前排右起：杨歇谷、梅兰芳、杜博恩、桥川时雄，后排右起：齐如山、张慎之、傅惜华、齐竺山、傅芸子、郑颖孙）（1934）

With foreign guests in the Society of National Chinese Opera (Front, from right to left: Yang Xiegu , Mei Lanfang , Du Bo'en , Hashikawa Saneo),(Back , from right to left: Qi Rushan, Zhang Shenzhi, Fu Xihua, Qi Zhushan, Fu Yunzi, Zheng Yingsun) (1934)

上图｜梅兰芳与乐咏西等在国剧学会会见外宾时合影
Mei Lanfang and Yue Rongxi with forign guests in the Society of National Chinese Opera
下图｜在国剧学会，梅兰芳操琴，余叔岩击鼓
In the Society of National Chinese Opera

时装新戏

New Plays in Modern Dresses

如果直接采取现代的事，编成新剧，看的人岂不更亲切有味，收效或许比老戏更大。

If we write new operas based on modern stories, I believe there will be more intimate connection between the audience, and the results may be better than old operas.

——梅兰芳 *by Mei Lanfang*

梅兰芳在京沪看过王钟声编演的文明新戏和欧阳予倩等组织的"春柳社"的话剧，从中得到很大启发。他初次由沪返京，在21岁至23岁时，先后以社会时事为题材，编演了反映妇女受压迫、婚姻不自由以及反对封建迷信的《孽海波澜》、《宦海潮》、《一缕麻》、《邓霞姑》和《童女斩蛇》等时装新戏，深受观众的欢迎和好评。

At the age of 21 to 23,Mei created some news plays based on the current events, such as Waves in the Sea of Sin, Tide in the Bureaucracy, Deng Xiagu and A Strand of Flax. These plays reflected the new thoughts of the contemporary society, protesting against the oppression on women, the restrained matrimony and the superstition, thus winning immediately the applause of the audience. Mei's creation was inspired by Ouyang Yuqian's modern spoken drama appeared in the 1910s and 1920s.

梅兰芳演时装戏的发式与服装

The dress and hair style in Mei's modern play

《一缕麻》，梅兰芳饰林纫芬

Mei Lanfang in the role of Lin Renfen with different dresses in *A Strand of Flax*

《一缕麻》，梅兰芳饰林纫芬

Mei Lanfang in the role of Lin Renfen with different dresses in *A Strand of Flax*

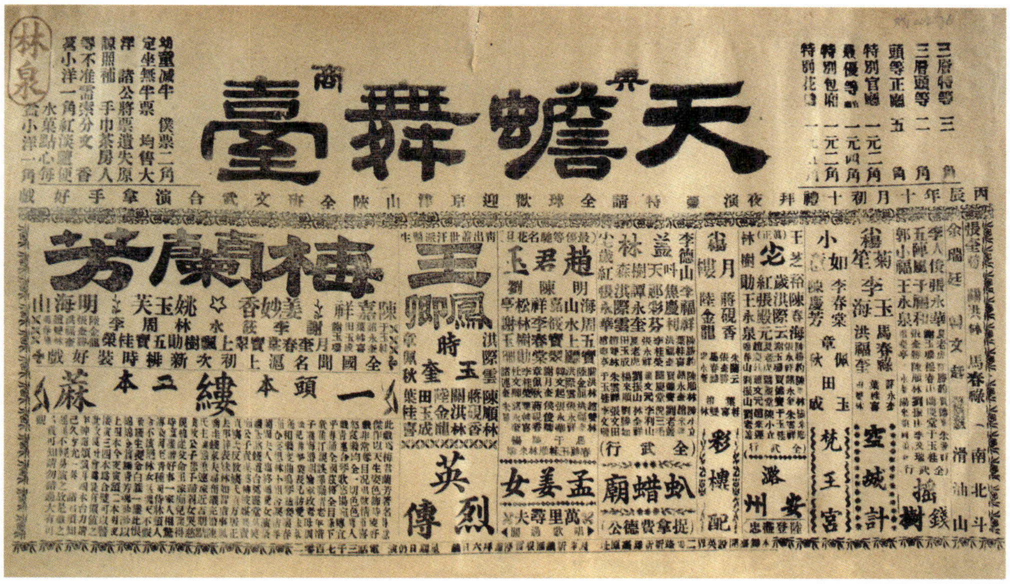

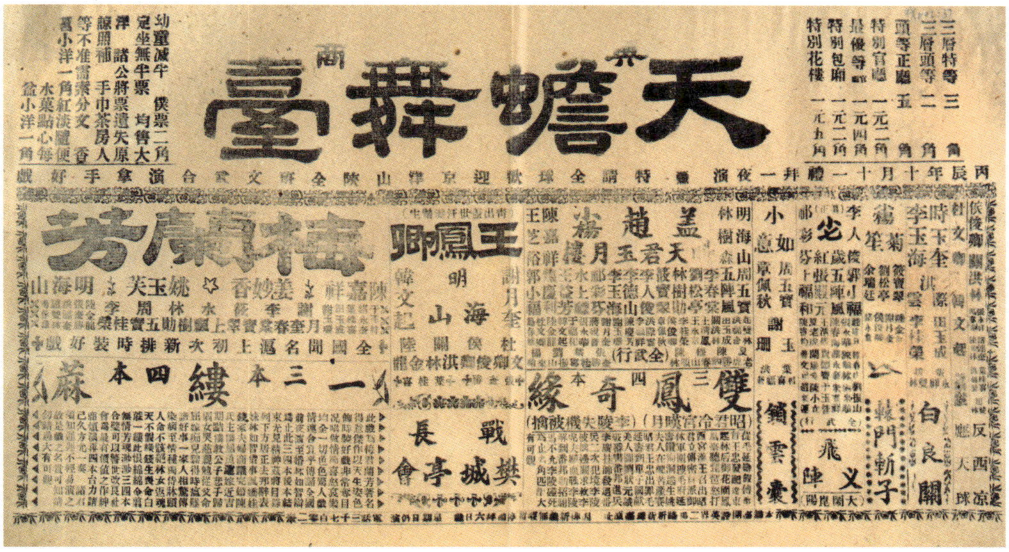

上图｜梅兰芳演出头、二本《一缕麻》戏单（1916）

The program of *A Strand of Flax*(Part 1 and 2)

下图｜梅兰芳演出三、四本《一缕麻》戏单（1916）

The program of *A Strand of Flax*(Part 3 and 4)

《邓霞姑》，梅兰芳饰邓霞姑
Mei Lanfang as Deng Xiagu in *Deng Xiagu*

文明茶園

禮拜五

男女分座

正陽門外(雙慶社)西珠市口路北

中華民國五年六月十六日(丙辰年五月十六日)

全社合演

永平安

草橋關

俞贊庭 惡虎村

許蔭棠 打金枝

俞振庭 豔陽樓

王鳳卿 捉放曹

俞振庭 梅蘭芳 姚玉芙 程繼仙 鄧霞姑

左图｜梅兰芳演出《邓霞姑》戏单（1916）

The program of *Deng Xiagu*(1916)

右图｜《邓霞姑》，梅兰芳饰邓霞姑

Mei Lanfang as Deng Xiagu in *Deng Xiagu*

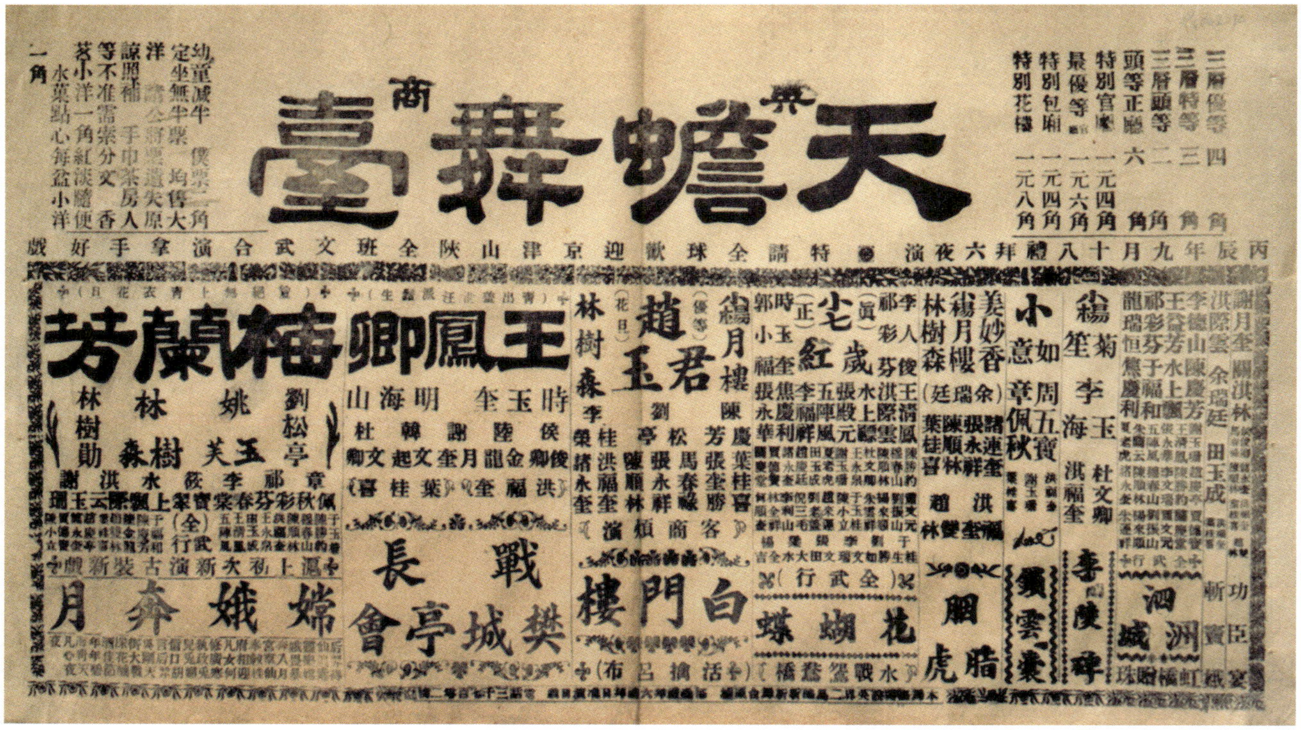

梅兰芳演出《嫦娥奔月》戏单（1916）
The program of *Lady Chang E Flies to the Moon by Mei Lanfang* (1916)

古装新戏 New Plays in Traditional Dresses

梅兰芳22岁时与齐如山、李释戡等人合作，首次编演了古装新戏《嫦娥奔月》，对传统的旦脚扮相做了改革，并增添了绚丽的歌舞表演和舞台装置，令观众耳目一新。而后又根据古典小说《红楼梦》编演了《黛玉葬花》、《千金一笑》（又名《晴雯撕扇》）和《俊袭人》等剧，首创京剧中的红楼戏。此后陆续编演了《天女散花》、《西施》、《洛神》、《麻姑献寿》、《霸王别姬》、《太真外传》等10余出剧目，开拓了古装歌舞剧的新路。梅兰芳的古装歌舞剧使中国优秀的传统民族舞蹈在京剧舞台上脱颖而出，大放异彩。

When Mei was 22,he produced and preformed a new play *Lady Chang E Flies to the Moon* in which the style of make-up of Chang E was different from the traditional form. Besides, many dance movements had been added. Mei also created some new plays on the basis of the classical novel *A Dream of Red Mansions*. They were *Daiyu Burying Flowers*, *Qingwen Tears the Fan* and others. Later on, he produced more than 10 new plays, including *The Heavenly Maid Showering Flowers*, *Goddess of the River Luo*, *Beauty Xi Shi*, *Ma Gu Wishing Wang Mu a Long Life*, *The Legend of Yang Yuhuan* and *The King's Parting with His Favourite*, in which many brilliant traditional dances of our nation were shown on the stage of Beijing Opera. Some of these plays became the masterpieces of Mei school.

梅兰芳创编的第一出古装戏《嫦娥奔月》

Lady Chang E Flies to the Moon, the first new play in ancient costume created by Mei Lanfang

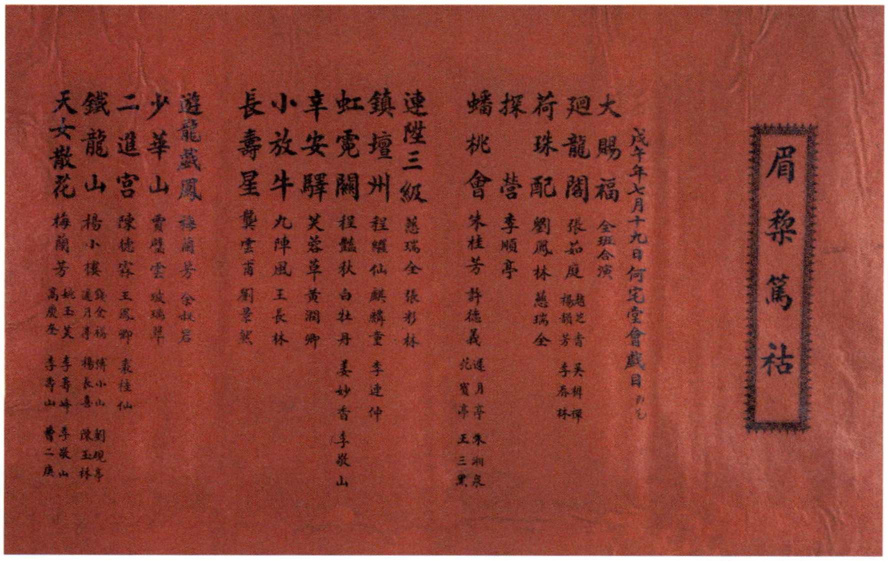

眉黎篤祜

戊午年七月十九日何宅堂會戲目

大賜福 全班合演
廻龍閣 張茹庭 趙芝青 楊韻芳 吳彩樑 李春林
荷珠配 劉鳳林 慈瑞全
探營 李順亭
蟠桃會 朱桂芳 許德義 遲月亭 范寶亭 朱湘泉 王三黑
連陞三級 慈瑞全 張彩林
鎮壇州 程繼仙 麒麟童 李連仲
虹霓關 程豔秋 白牡丹 姜妙香 李敬山
辛安驛 芙蓉草 黃潤卿
小放牛 九陣風 王長林
長壽星 龔雲甫 劉景然
遊龍戲鳳 梅蘭芳 余叔岩
少華山 賈璧雲 玻璃翠
二進宮 陳德霖 王鳳卿 裘桂仙
鐵龍山 楊小樓 錢金福 遲月亭 傅小山 楊長喜 劉硯亭 陳玉林
天女散花 梅蘭芳 姚玉芙 高慶奎 李壽峰 李壽山 李敬山 曹二庚

上图｜梅兰芳演《天女散花》舞台照
The stage scene of *The Heavenly Maid Showering Flowers*
下图｜梅兰芳演出《天女散花》戏单（1918）
The program of *The Heavenly Maid Showering Flowers*(1918)

《天女散花》，梅兰芳饰天女
Mei Lanfang as the Heavenly Maid in *The Heavenly Maid Showering Flowers*

左图｜《黛玉葬花》，梅兰芳饰林黛玉

Mei Lanfang as Lin Daiyu in *Daiyu Burying Flowers*

右图｜《黛玉葬花》，梅兰芳饰林黛玉，姜妙香饰贾宝玉

Mei Lanfang as Lin Daiyu and Jiang Miaoxiang as Jia Baoyu in *Daiyu Burying Flowers*

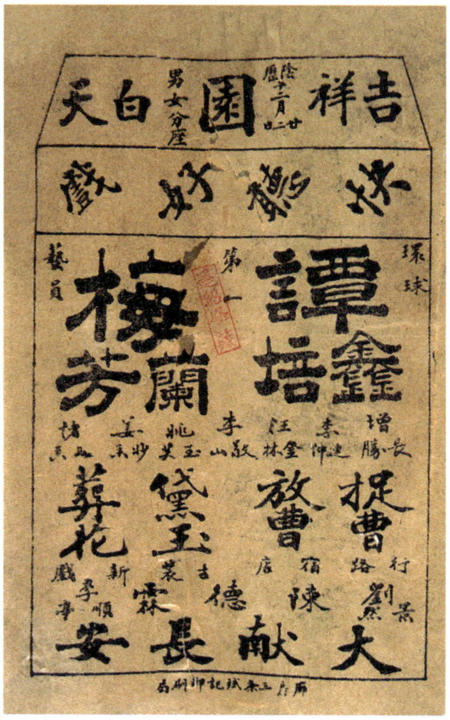
吉祥園 白天
陰曆十二月廿二日
男女分座
戲
環球第一 譚鑫培
藝員 梅蘭芳
提曹 放曹
黛玉 葬花 新戲
大 獻 長 安

上图 | 《黛玉葬花》，梅兰芳饰林黛玉试装照

Daiyu Burying Flowers, Mei Lanfang in the role of Lin Daiyu trying the new costume in his friend Mr. Feng Gengguang's house

下图 | 梅兰芳演出《黛玉葬花》戏单

The program of *Daiyu Burying Flowers*

《千金一笑》，梅兰芳饰晴雯

Qingwen Tearing the Fan, Mei Lanfang as Qingwen

上图 | 《千金一笑》，梅兰芳饰晴雯，姜妙香饰贾宝玉，姚玉芙饰麝月

Mei Lanfang as Qingwen, Jiang Miaoxiang as Jia Baoyu and Yao Yufu as Sheyue in *Qingwen Tearing the Fan*

左页 | 梅兰芳在沪第一次演《晴雯撕扇》时舞台上用的扇子撕毁后，重新裱成手卷并请名人题跋，这是装裱后的扇面（1916）

The fan torn on the stage in the first performance of *Qingwen Tearing the Fan* was repaired to be a souvenir and autographed by celebrities (1916)

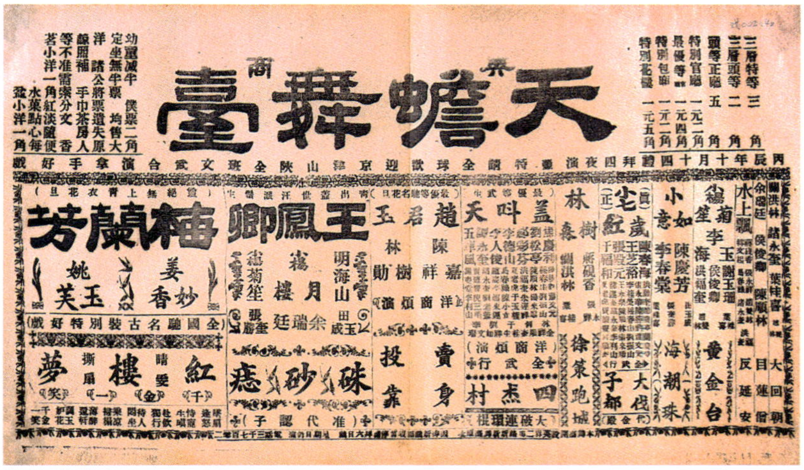

上图 |《千金一笑》，梅兰芳饰晴雯

Qingwen Tearing the Fan, Mei Lanfang as Qingwen

下图 | 梅兰芳演出《千金一笑》戏单（1916）

The program of *Qingwen Tearing the Fan* (1916)

《千金一笑》，梅兰芳饰晴雯

Qingwen Tearing the Fan, Mei Lanfang as Qingwen

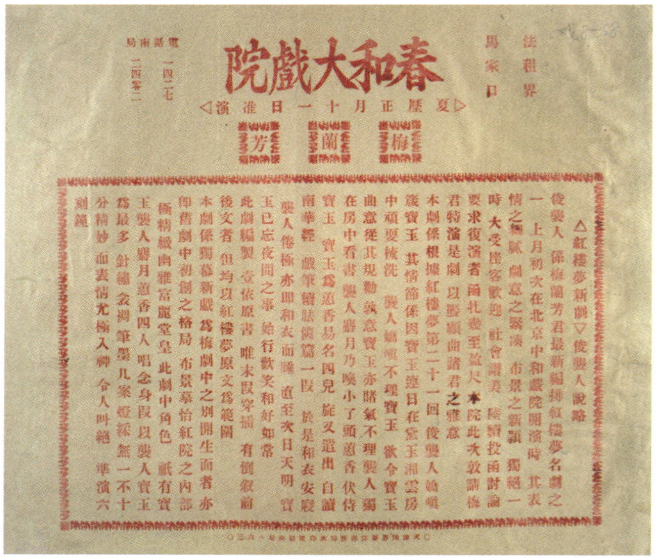

上左、上右｜《俊袭人》是一出以《红楼梦》为题材的独幕剧。只有此剧用完整的布景，全剧情节的地点不变，表演和布景没有丝毫矛盾

The pretty Xiren,a play based on *A Dream of Red Mansions*. This is an one act opera with a setting fitted for the performance

下图｜梅兰芳在天津演出《俊袭人》海报

The poster for *Pretty Xiren* in Tianjin

《俊袭人》，梅兰芳饰袭人

Mei Lanfang as Xiren in the *Pretty Xiren*

梅兰芳与朱桂芳（右）演《廉锦枫·刺蚌》剧照
Mei Lanfang and Zhu Guifang (right) in *Lian Jinfeng*

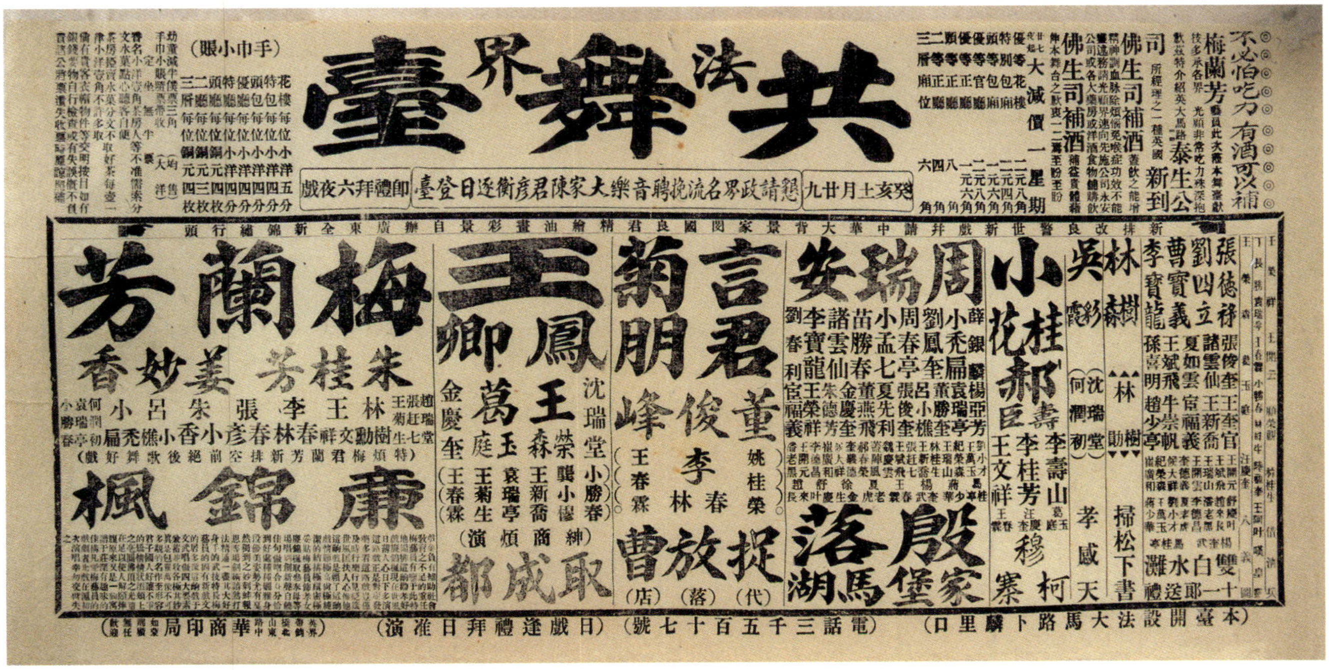

上图 | 《廉锦枫》，梅兰芳饰廉锦枫

Mei Lanfang as Lian Jinfeng in *Lian Jinfeng*

下图 | 梅兰芳演出《廉锦枫》戏单（1923）

The program of *Lian Jinfeng*(1923)

《木兰从军》剧照

Mei Lanfang as Hua Mulan in *Mu Lan , A Disguised Warrior Maiden*

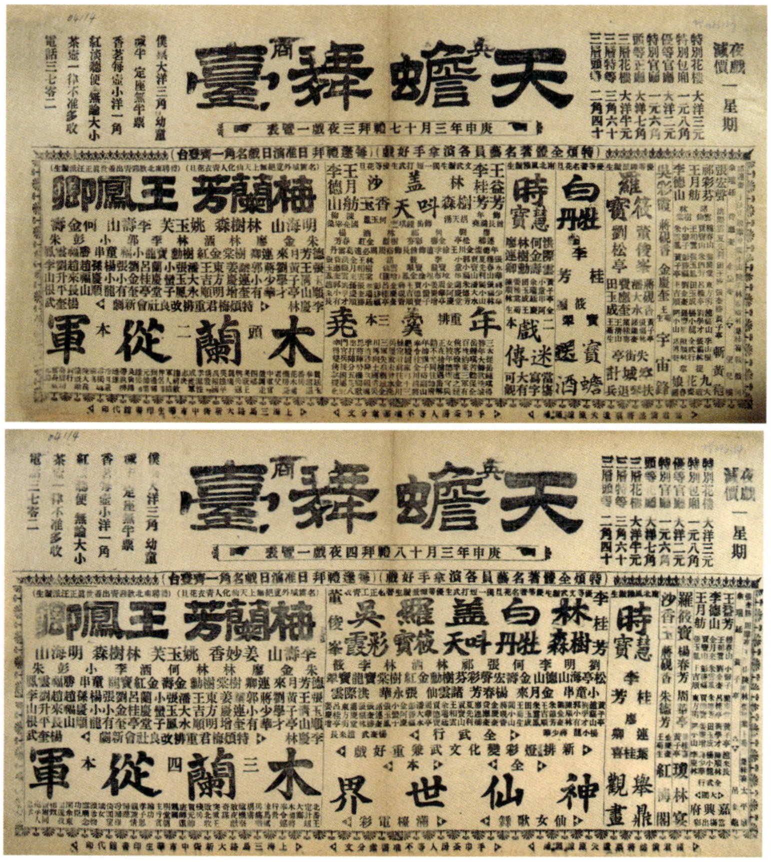

左图 | 梅兰芳演出一至四本《木兰从军》戏单（1920）

The program of *Mu Lan , A Disguised Warrior Maiden*

右图 | 《木兰从军》，梅兰芳饰花木兰

Mu Lan , A Disguised Warrior Maiden, Mei Lanfang as Hua Mulan

《木兰从军》，梅兰芳饰花木兰

Mu Lan, A Disguised Warrior Maiden, Mei Lanfang as Hua Mulan

这是梅兰芳早期演昆曲《红线盗盒》时饰红线女的头饰和服装。梅兰芳将此戏改为京剧古装戏，并在头饰、服装、化妆方面进行改革

Hongxian Stealing the Box was a play of Kunqu Opera in early years. Mei Lanfang changed it to Beijing Opera and made several improvements in make-up and costume

《红线盗盒》，梅兰芳饰红线女（“承华社”后期改为皮黄，头饰、服装也进行了改革）

Mei Lanfang as Hongxian in *Hongxian Stealing the Box*

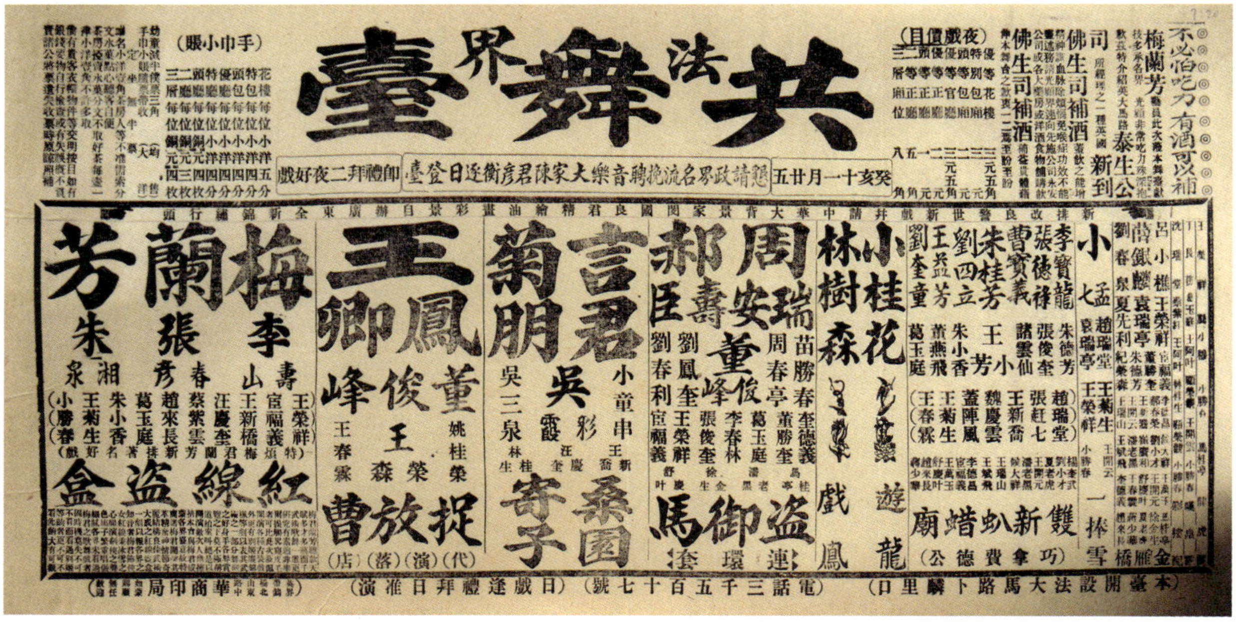

法界共舞臺

癸亥十一月廿五

懇請政界名流挽聘音樂大家陳君彥衡逐日登臺

即禮拜二夜好戲

夜戲價目

手巾小賬

佛生司補酒

梅蘭芳

新排改良警世新戲并請中華大青景家閣國良君精繪油畫彩景自辦廣東全新錦繡行頭

梅蘭芳 李壽山 張彥春 朱湘泉

紅線盜盒

王鳳卿 董俊峰

捉放曹（代演落店）

言菊朋 吳彩霞

桑園寄子

周瑞安 郝壽臣

盜御馬（連環套）

小桂花 林樹森

遊龍戲鳳

雙新八蜡廟（巧拿費德公）

一捧雪

金雁橋

本臺開設法大馬路卜鄰里口

電話三千五百七十號

日戲禮拜日準演

華商印局

左图｜梅兰芳演出《红线盗盒》戏单（1923）

The program of *Hongxian Stealing the Box*(1923)

右图｜梅兰芳等演《红线盗盒》剧照

Hongxian Stealing the Box on the stage

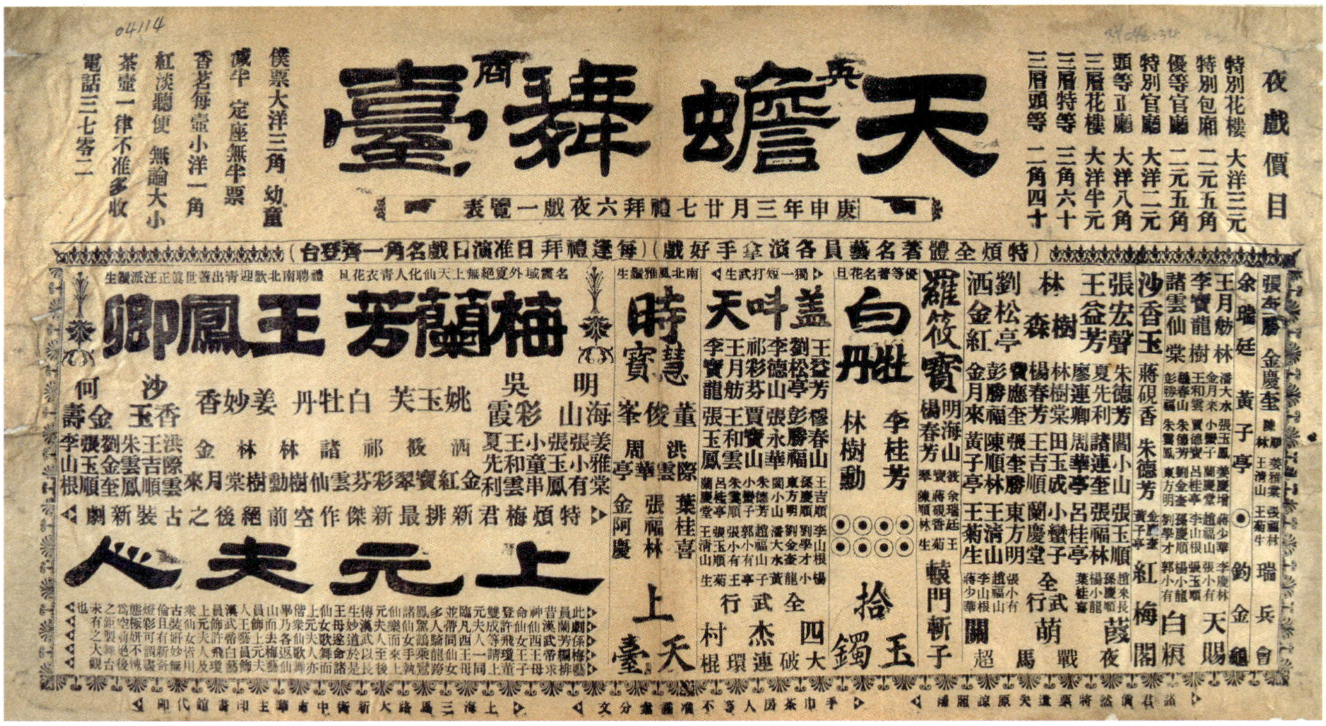

天蟾舞臺

庚申年三月廿七禮拜六夜戲一覽表

夜戲價目

特別花樓 大洋三元
特別包廂 二元五角
優等官廳 二元五角
特別官廳 大洋二元
頭等正廳 大洋八角
三層花樓 大洋半元
三層特等 三角六十
三層頭等 二角四十

僕票大洋三角 幼童減半 定座無半票
香茗每壺小洋一角
紅淡聽便 無論大小
茶壺一律不准多收
電話三七零二

特煩全體著名藝員各演拿手好戲

每逢禮拜日准演日戲名角一齊登台

梅蘭芳 王鳳卿

特煩梅君新排最新傑作空前絕後之古裝新劇

上元夫人

上图丨《上元夫人》，梅兰芳饰上元夫人

Stage photo of *Lady Shangyuan* on stage, Mei as Lady Shangyuan

下图丨梅兰芳演出《上元夫人》戏单（1920）

The program of *Lady Shangyuan*(1920)

《西施》中的梅兰芳(右)和朱桂芳(左)
Mei Lanfang and Zhu Guifen in *Beauty Xishi*

《西施》，梅兰芳饰西施
（左、右页）
Mei Lanfang as Xishi in *Beauty Xishi*

《西施》剧照
Stage photo of *Beauty Xishi*

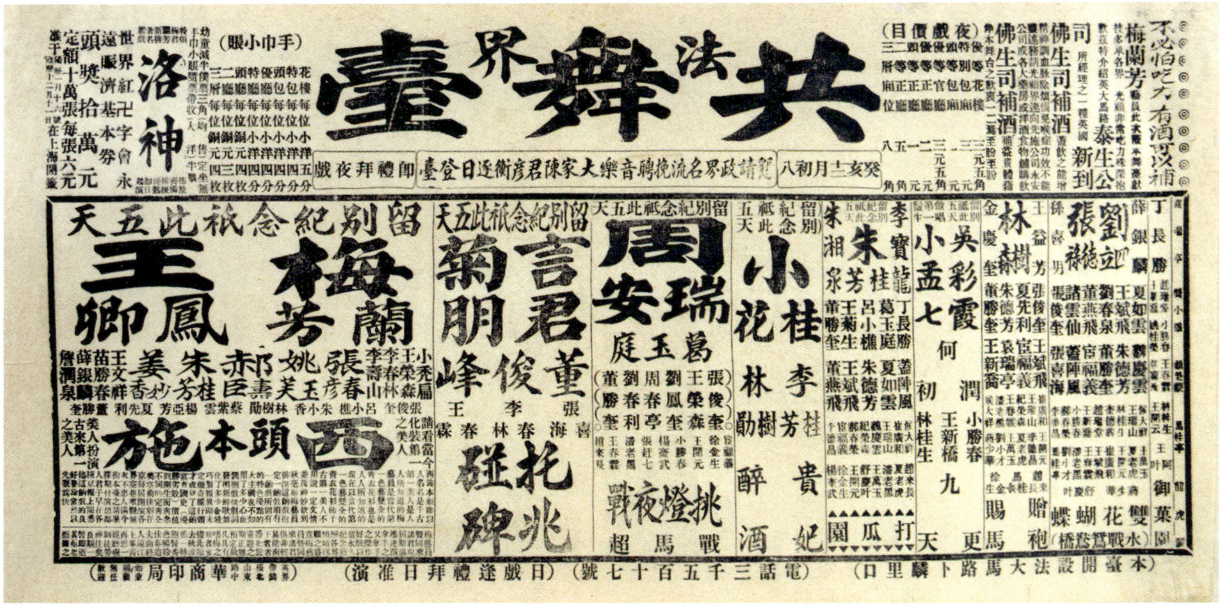

共舞臺 法界

留別紀念祇此五天

梅蘭芳 王鳳卿

頭本西施

言菊朋 董俊峰

周瑞安

小桂花

洛神

本臺開設法大馬路卜鄰里口 電話三千五百七十號 日戲逢禮拜日准演

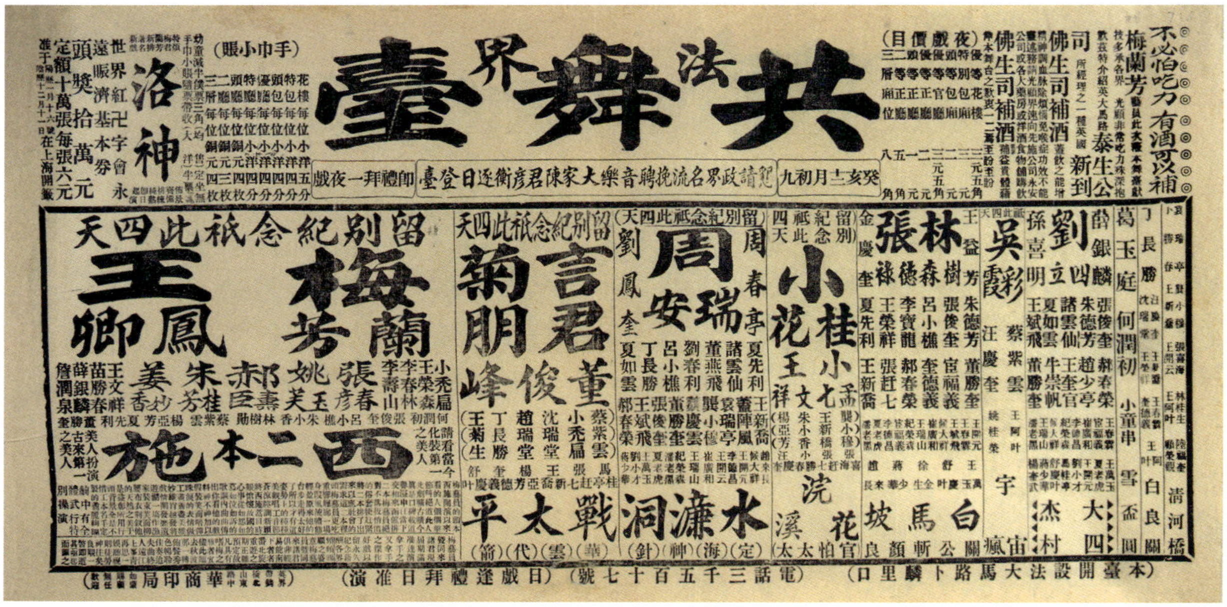

共舞臺 法界

留別紀念祇此四天

梅蘭芳 王鳳卿

二本西施

言菊朋 董俊峰

周瑞安

小桂花

洛神

本臺開設法大馬路卜鄰里口 電話三千五百七十號 日戲逢禮拜日准演

上图 | 梅兰芳演出头本《西施》戏单（1923）

The program of *Beauty Xishi*(Part 1) (1923)

下图 | 梅兰芳演出二本《西施》戏单（1923）

The program of *Beauty Xishi*(Part 2) (1923)

《西施》剧照

Stage photo of *Beauty Xishi*

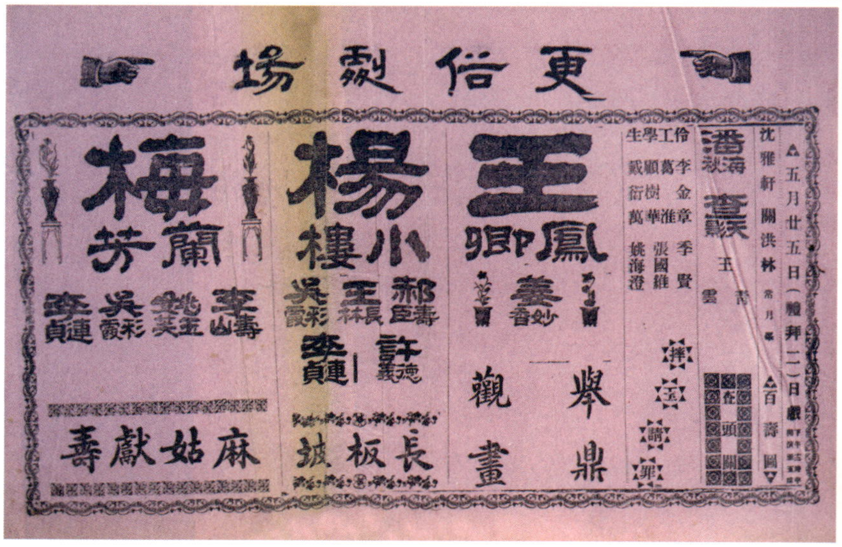

上图 | 《麻姑献寿》，梅兰芳饰麻姑
Mei Lanfang as Ma Gu in *Ma Gu Wishing Wang Mu a Long Life*

下图 | 梅兰芳在南通演出《麻姑献寿》戏单（1922）
Mei Lanfang as *Ma Gu Wishing Wang Mu a Long Life* performed by Mei Lanfang in Nantong (1922)

《麻姑献寿》，梅兰芳饰麻姑

Mei Lanfang as Ma Gu in *Ma Gu Wishing Wang Mu a Long Life*

《洛神》，梅兰芳饰洛神

Mei Lanfang as Goddess Luo in *Goddess of the River Luo*

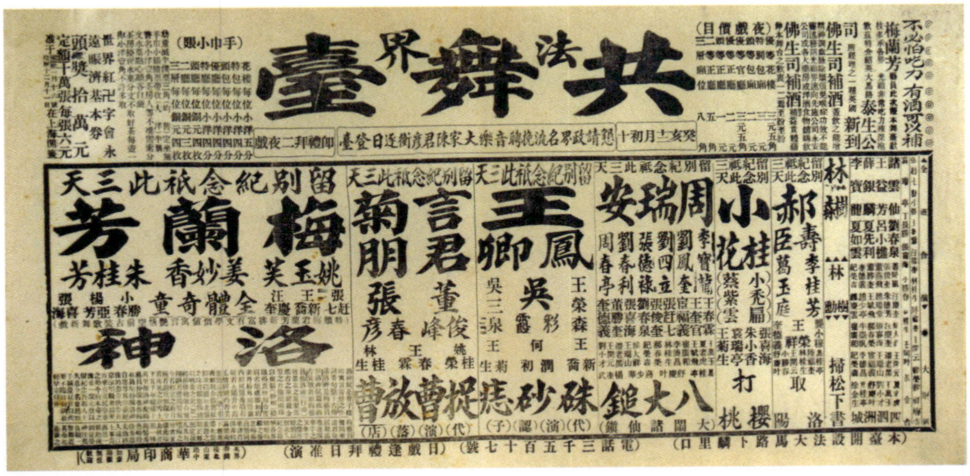

上图 | 梅兰芳演《洛神》剧照

Goddess of the River Luo on the stage

下图 | 梅兰芳演出《洛神》戏单（1923）

The program of *Goddess of the River Luo*(1923)

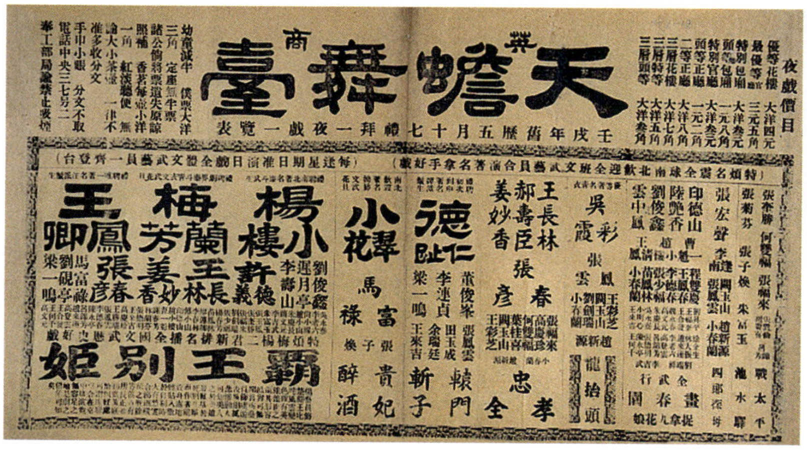

上左、上右｜《霸王别姬》，梅兰芳饰虞姬

Mei Lanfang as Yu Ji in *King's Parting with His Favorite*

下图｜梅兰芳演出《霸王别姬》戏单（1922）

The program of *King's Parting with His Favorite*(1922)

右页｜《霸王别姬》，梅兰芳饰虞姬

Mei Lanfang as Yu Ji in *King's Parting with His Favorite*

1922年，梅兰芳与杨小楼合作编演《霸王别姬》后，梅兰芳一生演出此剧数百场，先后有7名演员饰项羽，现列出4张剧照，分别为杨小楼（左页一）、金少山（左页二）、刘连荣（右页一）、袁世海（右页二）

King's Parting with His Favorite, Mei Lanfang as Yuji, Yang Xiaolou as King, Jin Shaoshan as King, Liu Lianrong as King, Yuan Shihai as King

《太真外传》，梅兰芳饰杨玉环（左、右页）

The Legend of Yang Yuhuan, Mei Lanfang as Yang Yuhuan

梅兰芳演《太真外传》剧照（左、右页）
Stage photo of *the Legend of Yang Yuhuan*

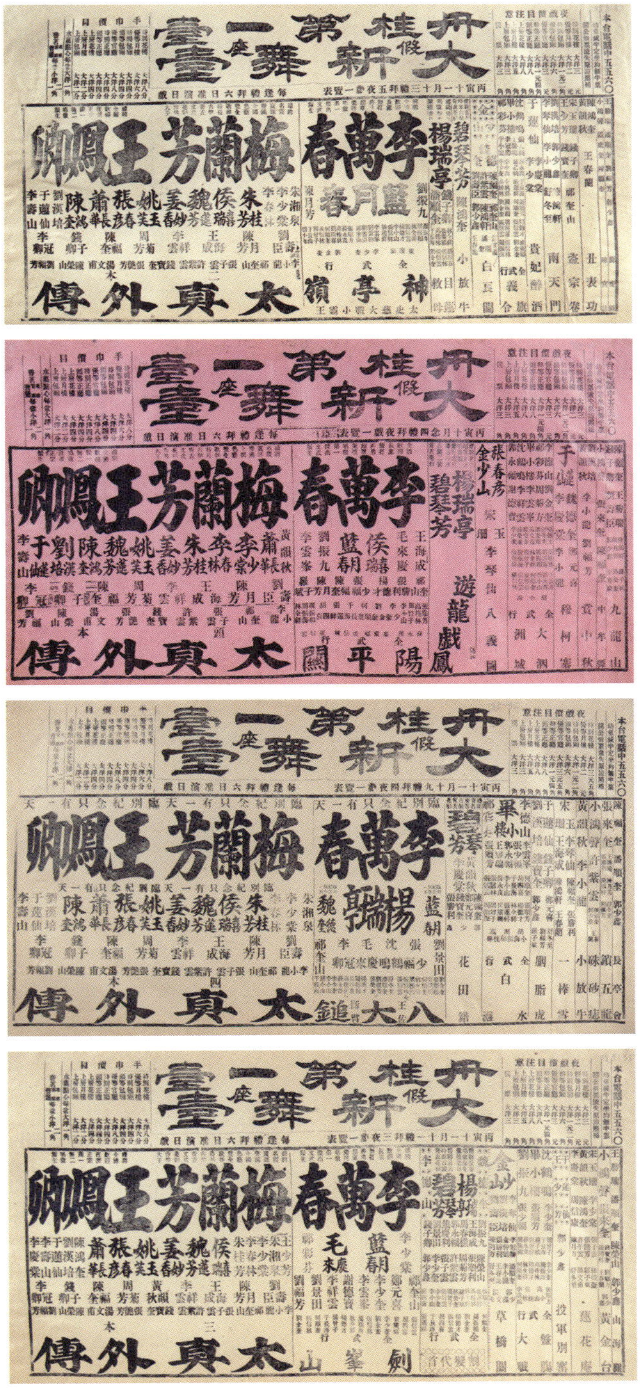

左页 | 梅兰芳演《太真外传》剧照

Stage photo of *the Legend of Yang Yuhuan*

右页 | 梅兰芳演出《太真外传》戏单（1926）

The program of *the Legend of Yang Yuhuan*(1926)

《佳期·拷红》，梅兰芳饰红娘
Mei Lanfang as Hongniang in *The West Chamber*

我提倡它（昆曲）的动机有两点：一、昆曲具有中国戏曲的优良传统，尤其是歌舞并重，可供我们采取的地方很多。二、有许多老辈们对昆曲的衰落失传，认为是戏剧界的一种极大的损失。

The two reasons why we are promoting Kunqu Opera are because Kunqu has a lot of positive Chinese Opera traditions especially the combination of singing and dancing. We can learn and use a lot from Kunqu. In addition, a lot of elders believe Kunqu's decline is a tremendous loss in Chinese opera.

—— 梅兰芳 *by Mei Lanfang*

提倡昆曲 Promoting Kunqu Opera

梅兰芳自幼就对昆曲怀有深厚感情，但时逢民国初期，昆曲日渐衰微。梅兰芳敏锐察觉到，昆曲衰落将是中国戏剧的一大损失，由此，他在学演皮黄剧目的同时，兼向多位师友学习昆曲剧目，并经常上演，借此提倡。他先后学演30余出昆曲剧目，不仅丰富了自己的上演剧目，而且也提高了演艺水平。正是“昆乱不挡”，使梅兰芳向艺术大师的道路更为扎实地迈进了一步。

Mei had shown great interest in Kunqu Opera since childhood and gradually learned more than 30 plays of Kunqu. This learning not only enriched his repertoire, but also improved his performing art. Besides, he did so in order to rescue the Kunqu Opera from its then declining condition in the theatrical field.

《春香闹学》，梅兰芳饰春香

Mei Lanfang as Chun Xiang in *Chun Xiang Upsets the Study*

左图 |《西厢记》，梅兰芳饰红娘，姚玉芙饰莺莺，姜妙香饰张生

Mei Lanfang as Hongniang,Yao Yufu as Yingying and Jiang Maoxiang as Zhangsheng in *the West Chamber*

右图 |《牡丹亭》，梅兰芳饰杜丽娘

Mei Lanfang as Du Liniang in *the Peony Pavilion*

右页 |《金雀记》，梅兰芳饰潘夫人

Mei Lanfang as Lady Pan in *A Tale of Golden Sparrow*

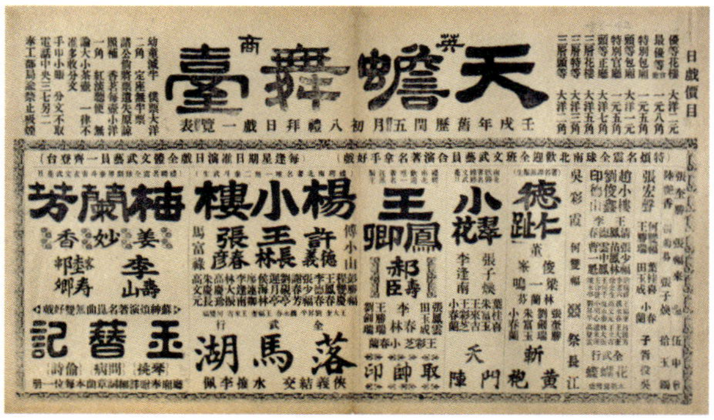

日戲價目

英商 天蟾舞臺

壬戌年舊曆閏五月初八禮拜日戲一覽表

特煩名震全球南北歡迎全班文武藝員合演著名拿手好戲

每逢星期日准演日戲全體文武藝員一齊登台

梅蘭芳 玉簪記

楊小樓 落馬湖

王鳳卿 取帥印

小翠花

左图｜梅兰芳演出《玉簪记》戏单

The program of *A Tale of Jade Hairpin*

右图｜《玉簪记》，梅兰芳饰陈妙常

Mei Lanfang as Chen Miaochang in *A Tale of Jade Hairpin*

上图 | 《思凡》，梅兰芳饰赵色空
Mei Lanfang as Zhao Sekong in *Longing for Worldly Pleasures*
下图 | 梅兰芳演出堂会戏《思凡》剧照
Stage photo of *the Longing for Worldly Pleasures*

上图 | 《金山寺》，梅兰芳饰青儿，王蕙芳饰白素贞
Mei Lanfang as Qing Er and Wang Huifang as Lady White in *the Legend of White Snake Lady*

下图 | 《断桥》，梅兰芳饰白素贞，姚玉芙饰青儿
Mei Lanfang as Lady White and Yao Yufu asQing Er in *the Legend of White Snake Lady*

《金山寺》，梅兰芳饰白素贞，路三宝饰青儿

Mei Lanfang as Lady White and Lu Sanbao as Qing Er in *the Legend of White Snake Lady*

梅舞芳歌

Mei Lanfang's Singing and Dancing

在编演新剧目的同时，梅兰芳在京剧已有的动作程式上，通过不断地总结与创新，编排了众多载歌载舞的京剧舞蹈，极大地丰富了京剧表演的内容。

Mei Lanfang arranged many singing and dancing performances in the play, which enriched the content of Beijing Opera.

梅兰芳演《廉锦枫》中的刺蚌舞

The dance of killing a clam in *Lian Jinfeng*

梅兰芳演《天女散花》中的绸舞

The silk dance in the *Heavenly Maid Showering Flowers*

梅兰芳与朱桂芳演《西施》中的佾舞
The feather dance in *Beauty Xishi*

梅兰芳演《麻姑献寿》中的杯盘舞

The cup and tray dance in *Ma Gu Wishing Wang Mu A Long Life*

上图 | 梅兰芳演《木兰从军》中的枪舞
The spear dance in *Mu Lan , A Disguised Warrior Maiden*
右页 | 梅兰芳演《红线盗盒》中的拂尘舞
The duster dance in *Hongxian Stealing the Box*

梅兰芳演《霸王别姬》中的剑舞

The sword dance in *King's Parting with His Favorite*

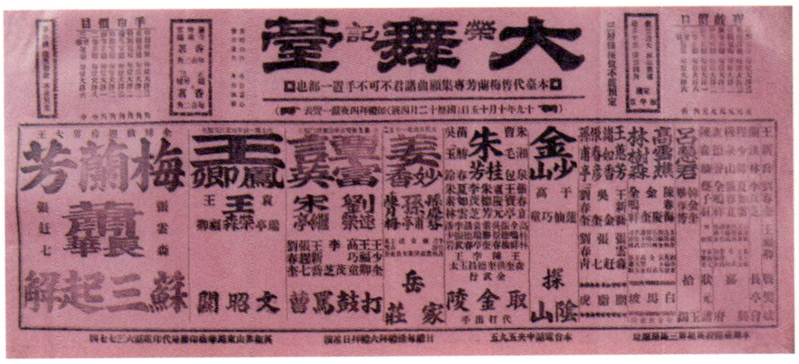

上图、下右 | 《苏三起解》，梅兰芳饰苏三，萧长华饰崇公道

Mei Lanfang as Su San and Xiao Changhua as the warder in *Sending Criminal Su San Under Escort*

下左 | 梅兰芳演出《苏三起解》戏单（1930）

Mei Lanfang as Lady White and Yao Yufu as Qing Er in The program of *Sending Criminal Su San Under Escort*(1930)

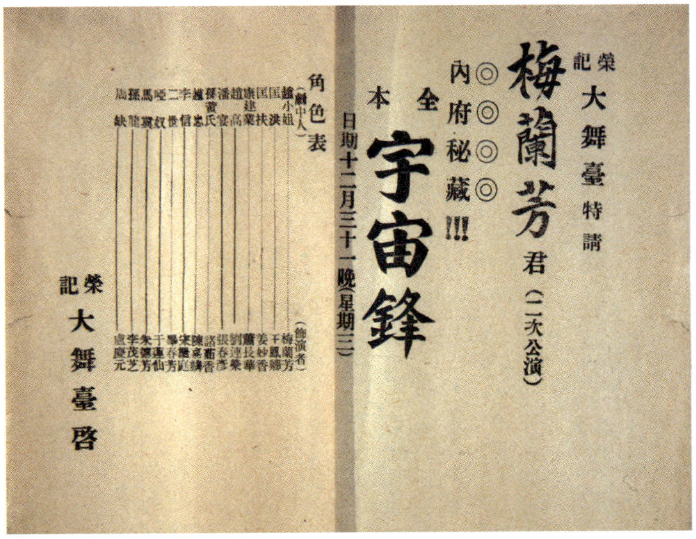

榮記大舞臺特請

梅蘭芳君（二次公演）

◎◎◎◎內府秘藏!!!

全本宇宙鋒

日期十二月三十一晚（星期三）

角色表

（劇中人）	（飾演者）
趙小姐	梅蘭芳
匡洪	[illegible]
匡扶	姜妙香
康建業	蕭長華
趙高	劉連榮
[illegible]	張春彥
[illegible]	[illegible]
[illegible]	[illegible]
[illegible]	宋繼庭
二世	[illegible]
啞奴	于連仙
[illegible]	朱傳芳
[illegible]	李茂芝
[illegible]	盧慶元

榮記大舞臺啓

上图、左页 | 《宇宙锋·装疯》剧照，梅兰芳饰赵艳容

Stage photo of *Beauty Defies Tyranny*

下图 | 梅兰芳演出《宇宙锋》说明书（1930）

The program of *Beauty Defies Tyranny*(1930)

上图、左页 | 《春灯谜》剧照，梅兰芳饰韦影娘

Stage photo of *A Riddle of the Spring Lantern*

下图 | 梅兰芳演出《春灯谜》（又名《错姻缘》）戏单（1930）

Stage Photot of *A Riddle of the Spring Lantern*(also named *A Mistaken Marriage*) (1930)

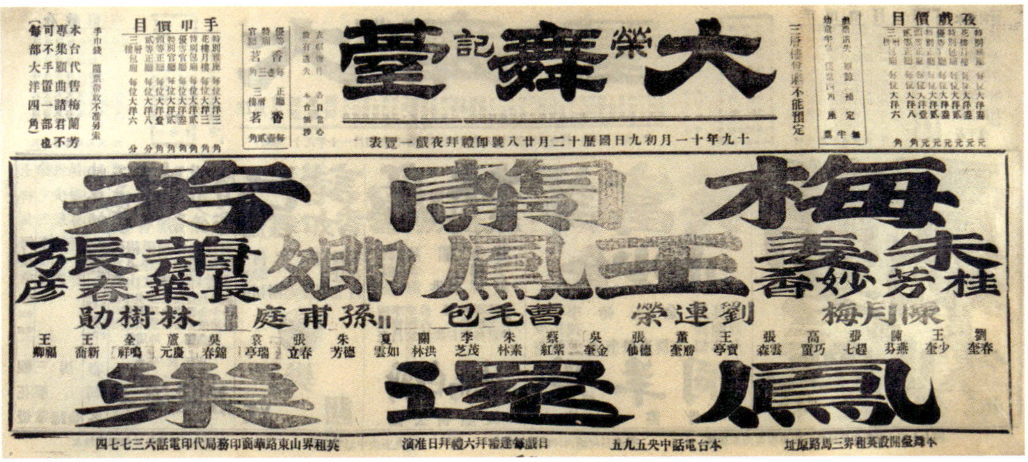

上图、左页 | 《凤还巢》剧照

Stage photo of the *Phoenix Returning to Its Nest*

下图 | 梅兰芳演出《凤还巢》戏单（1930）

The program of the *Phoenix Returning to Its Nest*(1930)

《御碑亭》剧照，梅兰芳饰孟月华，同台演出的还有王凤卿、萧长华等

Mei Lanfang as Meng Yuehua and Wang Fengqing and Xiao Changhua in *the Pavilion of Imperial Monument*

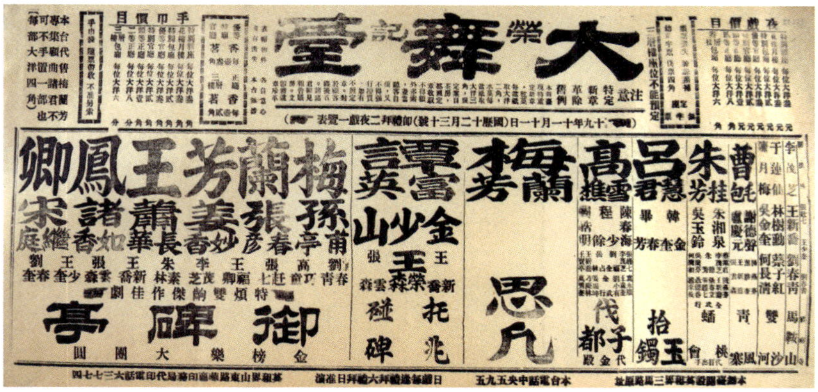

大舞臺 榮記

梅蘭芳 王鳳卿

孫甫亭 張春彥 姜妙香 蕭長華 諸如香 宋繼庭

特煩雙齣傑作佳劇

御碑亭

金榜樂 大團圓

譚富英 金少山

托兆碰碑

梅蘭芳

思凡

呂慧君 高雪樵

拾玉鐲

代子都

朱桂芳 曹毛包

左图 | 《御碑亭》，梅兰芳饰孟月华

Mei Lanfang as Meng Yuehua in *the Pavilion of Imperial Monument*

右图 | 梅兰芳演出《御碑亭》戏单（1930）

The program of *the Pavilion of Imperial Monument*(1930)

《审头刺汤》，梅兰芳饰雪艳，萧长华饰汤勤

Mei Lanfang as Xue Yan and Xiao Changhua as Tang Qin *in Killing Tang Qin*

梅兰芳与杨小楼合演《截江夺斗》剧照(1932)
Stage photo of Mei Lanfang as Lady Sun and Yang Xiaolou as Zhao Yun in *Grabbing Back the Son in the Middle of a River*(1932)

《霸王别姬》，梅兰芳饰虞姬，刘连荣饰项羽
Mei Lanfang as Yuji and Liu Lianrong as King in *the King's Parting with His Favorite*

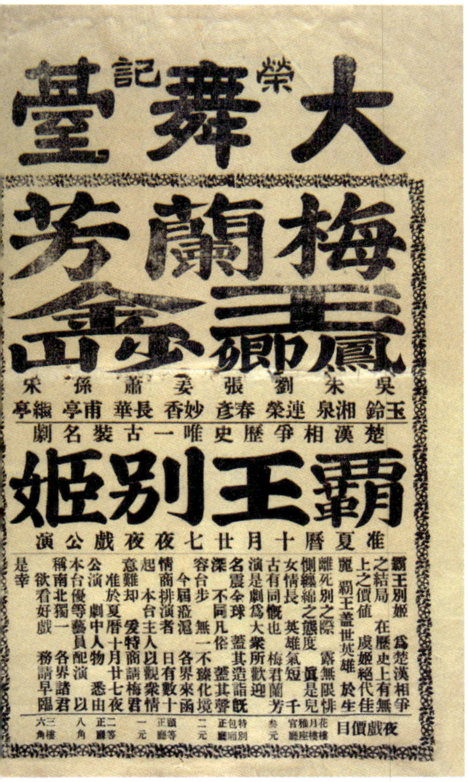

榮記 大舞臺

梅蘭芳

吳玉鈴 朱湘泉 劉連榮 張春彥 姜妙香 蕭長華 孫甫亭 宋繼亭

楚漢相爭歷史唯一古裝名劇

霸王別姬

准夏曆十月廿七夜夜戲公演

霸王別姬為楚漢相爭之結局在歷史上有無上之價值虞姬絕代佳麗霸王蓋世英雄於生離死別之際露無限悱惻纏綿之態度眞是兒女情長英雄氣短千古有同慨也梅君蘭芳演是劇爲大衆所歡迎名震全球蓋其造詣既深不同凡俗蓋其聲容台步無一不臻化境今届滬各界來函情商排演者日有數十起本台主人以觀衆情意難却爰特商請梅君准於夏曆十月廿七夜公演劇中人物悉由本台優等藝員配演以稱南北獨一各界諸君欲看好戲務請早臨是幸

夜戲價目 花樓月樓雅座官廳叁元 特別包廂正廳二元 頭等正廳一元 二等正廳八角 三樓六角

左图｜梅兰芳演出《霸王别姬》戏单

The program of *King's Parting with His Favorite*

右图｜《霸王别姬》，梅兰芳饰虞姬

Mei Lanfang as Lady Sun and Yang Xiaolou as Yuji in *King's Parting with His Favorite*

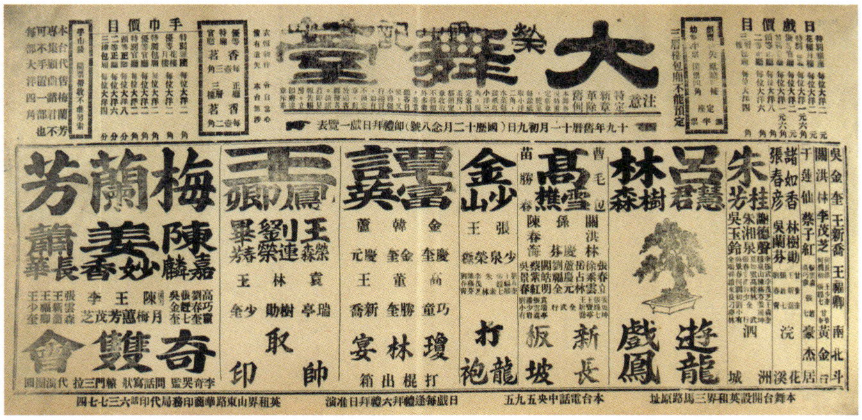

上图、左页 | 《奇双会》剧照，梅兰芳饰李桂

Stage photo of Mei Lanfang as Li Guizhi in *A Tale of Double Reunion*

下图 | 梅兰芳演出《奇双会》戏单（1930）

The program of *A Tale of Double Reunion*(1930)

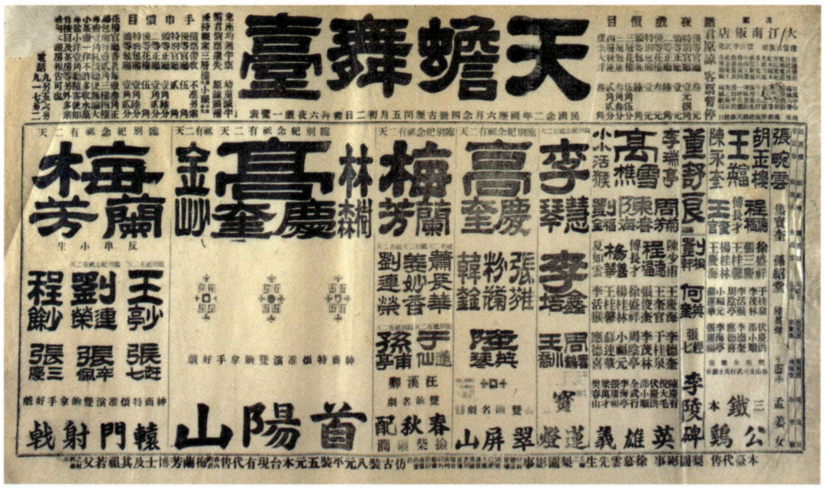

上图 | 《辕门射戟》，梅兰芳反串吕布

Mei Lanfang as Lu Bu in *Shooting Lance at the Camp Gate*

下图 | 梅兰芳演《辕门射戟》的戏单（1933）

The program of *Shooting Lance at the Camp Gate*(1933)

《黄鹤楼》，梅兰芳反串周瑜
Mei Lanfang as Zhou Yu in *Tower of Yellow Crane*

《贵妃醉酒》，梅兰芳饰杨玉环（左、右页）

Mei Lanfang as Yang Yuhuan in *Drunken Beauty*

《贵妃醉酒》，梅兰芳饰杨玉环（左、右页）
Mei Lanfang as Yang Yuhuan *in Drunken Beauty*

《玉堂春》剧照，梅兰芳饰苏三，同台演出的还有王凤卿、姜妙香等（左、右页）

Mei Lanfang as Su San in *Lady Magnolia*

《宝莲灯》剧照，梅兰芳饰王桂英，同台演出的还有王凤卿等（左、右页）
Stage photo of *Precious Lotus Lantern*, Mei Lanfang as Wang Guiying

《西施》，梅兰芳饰西施（左、右页）
Mei Lanfang as Xishi in *Beauty Xishi*

名旦之首

The Leading of Four Famous Dans

1921 年，28 岁的梅兰芳与杨小楼合作组织“崇林社”演出。次年，梅兰芳独挑大梁组织“承华社”演出。

1927 年，梅兰芳34岁，北京《顺天时报》发起读者评选京剧旦脚新戏的活动，梅兰芳、尚小云、程砚秋、荀慧生的新戏得票最多，自此“四大名旦”的称谓得到了社会公认。1931 年,《戏剧月刊》又对“四大名旦”进行评分，梅兰芳得分最多，按次序排列为梅、尚、程、荀，梅兰芳遂雄踞京剧旦行之首。

In 1927, When Mei was 34, the *Shun Tian Daily* of Beijing organized their readers to vote for great Dan actors. The final result was Mei being the top one. The other three were Shang Xiaoyun, Cheng Yanqiu, and Xun Huisheng. In 1931, the magazine *Theatre Monthly* held another ballot and confirmed the result of *Shun Tian Daily*.

梅兰芳（右二）、尚小云（左二）、程砚秋（左一）、荀慧生（右一）合影

Mei Lanfang (right 2nd), Shang Xiaoyun (left 2nd) , Cheng Yanqiu (left 1st)and Xun Huisheng(right 1st)

梅兰芳（前坐）、程砚秋（左）、尚小云（右）合影
Mei Lanfang (front),Cheng Yanqiu (left),Shang Xiaoyun (right)

《西厢记》，梅兰芳饰红娘，程砚秋饰崔莺莺（左），尚小云饰张生（右）
Mei Lanfang as Hongniang, Cheng Yanqiu as Cui Yingying(left) and Shang Xiaoyun as Zhang Sheng(right) in *The West Chamber*

《虹霓关》（二本），梅兰芳反串王伯党（右），程砚秋饰丫环（左），尚小云饰东方氏（中）

Mei Lanfang as Wang Bodang, Cheng Yanqiu as the Maid and Shang Xiaoyun as Lady Dongfang in *Rainbow Pass*

《六五花洞》，饰武大郎者左起：萧长华、曹二庚、慈瑞泉、罗文奎、高连峰、贾多才

Six Five Flowers Cave, Wu Dalang played by Xiao Changhua , Cao Ergeng , Ci Ruiquan , Luo Wenkui , Gao Lianfeng and Jia Duocai (from left to right)

《六五花洞》，饰真假潘金莲者左起：王幼卿、于连泉、尚小云、梅兰芳、程砚秋、荀慧生
Six Five Flowers Cave, Pan Jinlian portrayed by Wang Youqing ,Yu Lianquan, Shang Xiaoyun , Mei Lanfang , Cheng Yanqiu and Xun Huisheng (from left to right)

我出去的目的，一方面是想把中国戏曲介绍到国外，一方面是想借此观摩吸收外国戏剧艺术来丰富我们的民族艺术。

The reason why I toured abroad is because I want to introduce Chinese Opera to the world and also because I want to learn foreign theatre and adapt it to enrich our own cultural art.

——梅兰芳　*by Mei Lanfang*

叁

文化大使

Visiting Abroad Win Appraise from Overseas

1919年至1935年，梅兰芳先后到日本（1919、1924）、美国（1930）、苏联（1935）等国家演出，赴欧洲多个国家进行考察，结识了许多国际上各界知名人士，同他们建立了诚挚的友谊，获得了极高的国际声誉。他的这些活动不仅增进了各国人民对中国文化的了解，促进了国内外文化交流，也使我国的戏曲艺术跻身于世界戏剧之林。

Mei Lanfang was the most important Chinese to introduce and perform Chinese opera abroad. From 1919 to 1935, Mei Lanfang visited and performed in Japan (1919, 1924), United States (1930), the Soviet Union (1935) and other countries. During his tour, he formed many friendships with contemporaries of the literary and art circles. He gained international fame through his friendships and performances. He also popularized the Chinese classical drama among foreign audiences allowing them to better appreciate of Chinese art and culture. Through his performances, Beijing Opera obtained world recognition. The performing art of the Chinese theatre represented by Mei Lanfang is now recognized as one of the world's three contemporary main styles of performing art.

梅兰芳

《佳期·拷红》

梅兰芳饰红娘

Mei Lanfang as Hongniang in *The West Chamber*

《一缕麻》

梅兰芳饰林纫芬

Mei Lanfang as Lin Renfen in *A Strand of Flax*

《邓霞姑》

梅兰芳饰邓霞姑，姚玉芙饰周士普

Mei Lanfang as Deng Xiagu and Yao Yufu as Zhou Shipu in *Deng Xiagu*

梅兰芳创编的第一出古装戏《嫦娥奔月》

Lady Chang E Flies to the Moon, the first new play in ancient costume created by Mei Lanfang

民间外交

Meeting Foreign Guests

梅兰芳在国际上享有盛誉，来京的国际友人，包括文艺界、政商界的知名人士，大多要求一游长城，二观梅剧，三访梅宅。梅兰芳每月都会在无量大人胡同举行多次茶话会。借此机会，梅兰芳竭尽所能，为宣扬我国的民族传统戏曲艺术，促进国际间的文化交流作出了不可磨灭的贡献。

Since the establishment of fame at the age of 20, especially after the tour to Japan and America, Mei used to receive distinguished guests of literary and art circles from abroad, he met and entertained them in his house at Wuliang Daren Hutong in Beijing during the twenties and thirties.

梅兰芳在北京寓所与美国博物院驻华代表马尔智合影

With the representative of American Museums in China

梅兰芳在北京东城无量大人胡同寓所的客厅，梅兰芳经常在此处接待外宾

The drawing room in Mei's house at Wuliang Daren Hutong in Beijing. Mei usually received foreign guests here

梅兰芳（前排左三）在北京无量大人胡同寓所客厅会见瑞典王储古斯塔夫六世（前排左五）及夫人（前排左四）等（1926）
Mei Lanfang received Gustav VI(left 5th,front row), then the Crown Prince of Sweden, in his house at Wuliang Daren Hutong (1926)

梅兰芳等在北京与英国戏剧家罗伯特·罗兰合影
With British dramatist Robert Roland

上图｜梅兰芳（前排左六）、冯耿光等在北京寓所接待英国驻华公使时合影

With the company of Feng Gengguang and others, Mei Lanfang (front left 6) received the British Ambassador to China in his house in Beijing

下图｜梅兰芳（左六）在北京寓所接待美国教育家威廉·赫德·基尔帕特里克（右四）时合影，陪同会见的有张伯苓、齐如山等

With the company of Zhang Boling, Qi Rushan and others, Mei Lanfang (left 6) received the American educationist William Heard Kilpatrick at his home in Beijing

梅兰芳在北京寓所接待日本天华魔术团团长留影（1927）
Mei Lanfang meets the director of a Magic Performing Troupe of Japan at home (1927)

上图｜梅兰芳在北京寓所接待美国默片影帝范朋克（二排左四）时合影，在座的有齐如山等
Mei Lanfang received Douglas Fairbanks at home in Beijing together with Qi Rushan and others

下图｜梅兰芳（二排左三）在北京无量大人胡同寓所正房前与齐如山等会见范朋克（二排左四）时合影
Mei Lanfang met Douglas Fairbanks at home in Beijing together with Qi Rushan and others

梅兰芳在北京与夫人福芝芳等接待美国影星范朋克（化装为武松）时合影

Mei Lanfang hosted the American film star Douglas Fairbanks (disguised as Wu Song, a character of well known Beijing Opera based on the well-known novel the Water Margins)

左图｜梅兰芳与美国影星范朋克在北京合影
With American film star Douglas Fairbanks at home in Beijing
右图｜梅兰芳与化装为武松的范朋克合影
Mei Lanfang and Douglas Fairbanks (disguised as a Chinese stage character Wu Song)

上图 | 梅兰芳夫妇在北京寓所接待美国前总统威尔逊夫人时合影
Mei Lanfang and his wife Fu Zhifang received the wife of former American President Woodrow Wilson at home in Beijing
下图 | 梅兰芳在北京接待美国舞蹈先驱泰德·肖恩和露丝·圣·丹尼斯夫妇时合影（1926）
With American Denishawn dancers Ruth St. Denis and Ted Shawn in Beijing (1926)

梅兰芳在北京寓所庭院与来访的意大利女高音歌唱家嘉丽－古契等外宾合影（1929）
Mei Lanfang and his wife received the Italian soprano Amelita Galli-Curci in the courtyard of his house (1929)

上图｜梅兰芳（右十一）在北京寓所庭院与外宾们合影，在场的有郎静山（左六）父女及齐如山（左三）、冯耿光（左七）等人
Mei Lanfang(right 11th) with Feng Gengguang (left 7th), Qi Rushan and(left 3rd) Yao Yufu rece:ved foreign guests. Famous photographer Lang Jingshan(left 6th) and his daughter were also present

下图｜梅兰芳在北京寓所庭院与日本文艺界人士合影（1927）
Mei Lanfang received Japanese guests of literary and art circles in his house(1927)

梅兰芳夫妇在北京寓所庭院与外宾们合影，在场的有齐如山、李释戡等人

Mei Lanfang and his wife with foreign friends in the courtyard of his house. Qi Rushan , Li Shikan and others were present

上图 | 梅兰芳夫妇在北京寓所庭院与外宾们合影
Mei Lanfang and his wife received foreign guests at home
下图 | 梅兰芳在北京寓所接待各国出席太平洋会议的代表，图为茶话会后合影
Mei Lanfang held a tea party to entertain the delegates from various countries attending the Pacific Conference

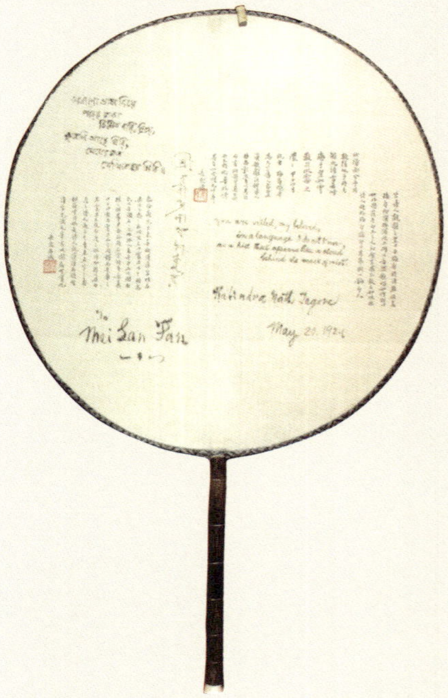

上左 | 梅兰芳（右三）在北京寓所与罗瘿公（右二）、姚玉芙（左二）、齐如山（左一）会见外宾时合影
Mei Lanfang met foreign guests with Luo Yinggong (right 2nd), Yao Yufu (left 2nd) and Qi Rushan (left 1st)

上右 | 1924 年，随著名诗人泰戈尔访问的印度著名画家南达拉尔・鲍斯观看梅兰芳演出《洛神》后，绘制此幅大型油画相赠
The Indian artist Nandalal Bose , who came to Chian with Tagore in 1924, painted a large oil painting of *Goddess* of the *River Luo* and presented it to Mei Lanfang

下图 | 1924 年，著名诗人泰戈尔来华访问时在观看梅剧后亲笔在纨扇上题词相赠
A silk fan presented to Mei Lanfang by Rabindranath Tagors after watching Mei's performance with the Indian poet's manuscript of a poem dedicated to Mei (1924)

梅兰芳在北京与音乐大师刘天华（后排右二）等人接待法国音乐学者拉劳义等外宾时合影

Mei Lanfang met French music scholars with musician Liu Tianhua (back ,right 2nd)

梅兰芳在汉口与谭小培（左九）、谭富英（左七）等会见外宾时合影

Mei Lanfang met foreign guests in Hankou ,together with Tan Xiaopei(left 9th), Tan Fuying(left 7th) and Nan Tiesheng

梅兰芳（二排左十一）在上海与马连良（二排左十三）、尚小云（二排左十）等会见外宾时合影

Mei Lanfang met foreign friends in Shanghai, together with Ma Lianliang, Shang Xiaoyun and others

出访日本

Visiting Japan Twice

梅兰芳在日本

Mei Lanfang in Japan

1919年，梅兰芳26岁时，应东京帝国剧场大仓男爵的邀请，偕夫人王明华率“喜群社”部分演员首次东渡扶桑，在东京、大阪和神户演出了《天女散花》、《御碑亭》、《贵妃醉酒》、《黛玉葬花》、《虹霓关》、《嫦娥奔月》、《春香闹学》、《游园惊梦》和《琴挑》等戏，这是他作为艺术使者向海外传播中国的文化艺术之行。1923年，日本遭到关东大地震的灾害，梅兰芳在北京主办了多场义演，捐献巨款赈灾。1924年，东京帝国剧场修复，再次邀请梅兰芳赴日参加隆重的开幕式演出。他先后在东京、大阪和京都演出《红线盗盒》、《贵妃醉酒》、《虹霓关》、《廉锦枫》、《麻姑献寿》、《审头刺汤》、《奇双会》、《御碑亭》、《黛玉葬花》和《洛神》，充分展示了他青衣、花旦、刀马旦等各个行当的表演艺术精华。日本观众和剧艺界对梅兰芳的多才多艺钦佩之至，梅兰芳的名字遂在日本家喻户晓。

In April-May, 1919, when Mei was 26, He went to Japan accompanied with his wife Wang Minghua and some members of his performing company. In Tokyo. Osaka and Kyoto, he presented *The Pavilion of Royal Monument*, *Chang E Flees to the Moon*,*Wu Jia Slope*, *Mei Long Town* and so forth. This was the first time Beijing Opera performed abroad.

In May and June 1924. Mei went to Japan again to present *The Goddess of River Luo*, *The Drunken Beauty*, *Qingwen Tearing the Fan*,*The Rainbow Pass*, *Lian Jinfong*, *Daiyu Burying Flowers*. His performances won great applause and extended his influnces in Japan.

上图 | 梅兰芳与夫人王明华在赴日轮船上留影

Mei Lanfang and his wife Wang Minghua on board

下图 | 梅兰芳（前排右二）与夫人王明华（后中）在赴日轮船上与工作人员合影

Mei Lanfang and his wife Wang Minghua(central of back row) on board ,with the staff of the steamer

左图｜梅兰芳在码头上接受日本记者采访
After arriving in Japan, Mei Lanfang accepted an interview by Japanese reporters

右图｜梅兰芳在日本留影
Mei Lanfang in Japan

梅兰芳与日本歌舞伎演员中村歌右卫门（五世）及其子合影
With Kabuki actor Nakamura Utaemon and his son

上图｜1919 年4 月26 日，梅兰芳应大仓男爵之邀在帝国剧场的东洋轩食堂用餐后与部分人员合影（右起：泽村宗之助、梅兰芳、大仓喜八郎、尾上梅幸、姚玉芙、松本幸四郎）

Mei Lanfang with Japanese Hosts after dining together on April 26th,1919

下左｜在日本东京演出时，梅兰芳（左二）与姚玉芙（左一）、齐如山（右二）、许伯明（左三）、沈亮超（右三）等合影

Mei Lanfang with his friends Yao Yufu, Qi Rushan, Xu Boming, Shen Liangchao

下右｜1919 年5 月9 日，梅兰芳一行参观东京第一绸缎杂货庄 —— 著名的三越吴服店时合影。（前排左起：沈亮超、姚玉芙、梅兰芳、齐如山，后排左起：笠原健一、仓知诚夫、村田乌江、许伯明、朝吹常吉）

Mei Lanfang with Japanese friends

梅兰芳与齐如山、张彭春、姚玉芙、沈亮超等合影

Mei Lanfang with Qi Rushan, Zhang Pengchun, Yao Yufu, Shen Liangchao and Japanese friends

上图 | 梅兰芳抵日时受到日本演员，板西中将（右一）、村田嘉久子（右三）、大仓喜七郎（右四）的欢迎
Mei Lanfang was welcomed by Japanese performers when he arrived in Japan

下图 | 在日本东京山雨楼留影（右起：王明华、梅兰芳、赵介卿、赵夫人等）
Mei Lanfang with his wife Wang Minghua and friends

梅兰芳（前排左三）、齐如山（后排左四）、许伯明（后排左三）、姚玉芙（前排左二）与日方欢迎人员合影
After arrival in Japan, Mei Lanfang(left 3rd, front row), Qi Rushan(left 4th, back row) and Yao Yufu(left 2nd, front row) with Japanese hosts

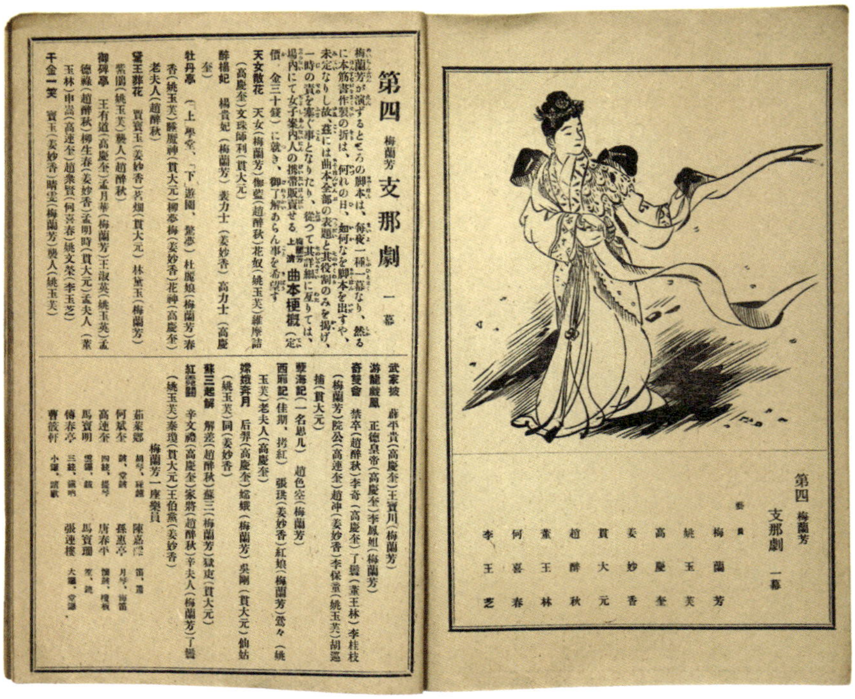

第四 梅蘭芳 支那劇 一幕

梅蘭芳が演ずるところの脚本は、毎夜一種一幕なり、然るに本脚書作製の折は、何れの日、如何なる脚本を出すや、未定なりし故、茲には曲本全部の表題と其役割のみを掲げ、一時の責を塞ぐ事となりたり、從つて其詳細に亙りては、場内にて女子案内人の携帶販賣せる梅蘭芳上演曲本梗概（定價金三十錢）に就き、御了解あらん事を希望す

天女散花 天女（梅蘭芳）伽藍（趙醉秋）花奴（姚玉芙）維摩詰（高慶奎）文珠師利（貫大元）

醉楊妃 楊貴妃（梅蘭芳） 裴力士（姜妙香） 高力士（高慶奎）

牡丹亭 （「上」學堂、「下」遊園、驚夢） 杜麗娘（梅蘭芳）春香（姚玉芙）睡魔神（貫大元）柳夢梅（姜妙香）花神（高慶奎）

老夫人（趙醉秋）

黛玉葬花 賈寶玉（姜妙香）茗烟（貫大元） 林黛玉（梅蘭芳）紫鵑（姚玉芙）襲人（趙醉秋）

御碑亭 王有道（高慶奎）孟月華（梅蘭芳）王淑英（姚玉英）孟德祿（趙醉秋）柳生春（姜妙香）孟明時（貫大元）孟夫人（董玉林）申嵩（高連奎）趙秉賢（何喜春）姚文榮（李玉芝）

千金一笑 寶玉（姜妙香）晴雯（梅蘭芳）襲人（姚玉芙）

武家坡 薛平貴（高慶奎）王寶川（梅蘭芳）

游龍戲鳳 正德皇帝（高慶奎）李鳳姐（梅蘭芳）

奇雙會 禁卒（趙醉秋）李奇（高慶奎）丁鑾（董玉林）李桂枝（梅蘭芳）院公（高連奎）趙冲（姜妙香）李保童（姚玉芙）胡巡捕（貫大元）

孽海記（一名思凡） 趙色空（梅蘭芳）

西廂記（佳期、拷紅） 張珙（姜妙香）紅娘（梅蘭芳）鶯々（姚玉芙）老夫人（高慶奎）

嫦娥奔月 后羿（高慶奎）嫦娥（梅蘭芳）吳剛（貫大元）仙姑（姚玉芙）同（姜妙香）

蘇三起解 解差（趙醉秋）蘇三（梅蘭芳）獄吏（貫大元）

紅霓關 辛文禮（高慶奎）家將（趙醉秋）辛夫人（梅蘭芳）丁鑾（姚玉芙）秦瓊（貫大元）王伯黨（姜妙香）

梅蘭芳一座樂員

茹萊卿 胡琴、笙 陳嘉樑 笛、簫

何斌奎 哨、堂鼓 孫惠亭 月琴、梅笛

高連奎 四鼓、板鼓 唐春平 胡鑼、堂鼓

馬寶明 雲鑼、鐃 馬寶珊 笙、哨

梅春亭 三鼓、鐃鈸 張連樓 大鑼、堂鼓

曹筱軒 小鑼、讀歌

第四 梅蘭芳 支那劇 一幕

藝員

梅蘭芳
姚玉芙
高慶奎
姜妙香
貫大元
趙醉秋
董玉林
何喜春
李玉芝

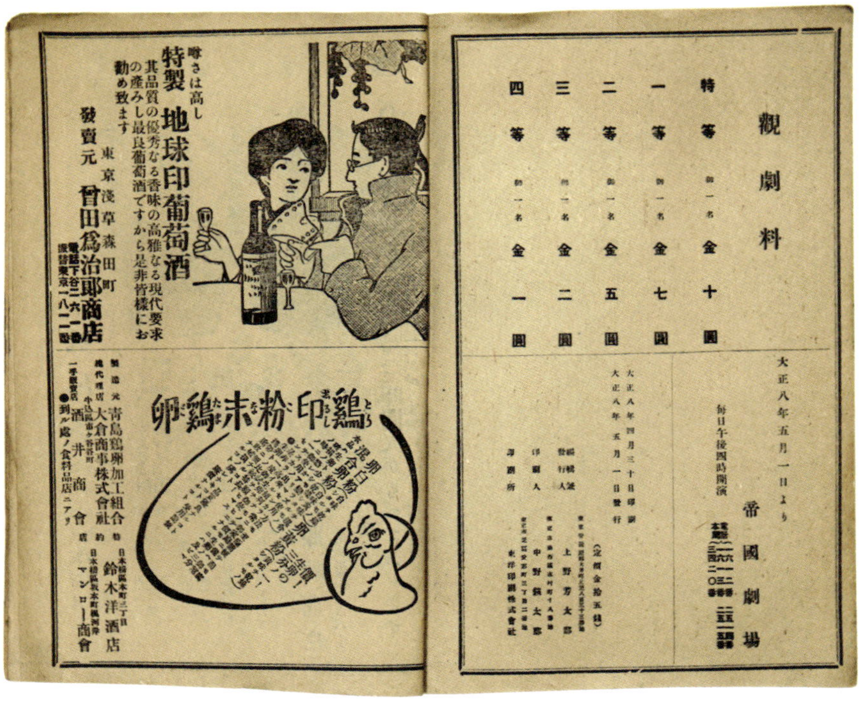

觀劇料

特等 御一名 金十圓
一等 御一名 金七圓
二等 御一名 金五圓
三等 御一名 金二圓
四等 御一名 金一圓

大正八年五月一日より
每日午後四時開演
帝國劇場

大正八年四月三十日印刷
大正八年五月一日發行
（定價金拾五錢）
編輯兼發行人 上野秀太郎
印刷人 中野鍛太郎
印刷所 東洋印刷株式會社

1919 年 5 月，歌舞伎和京剧演出说明书
The instructions to Beijing Opera and Kabuki

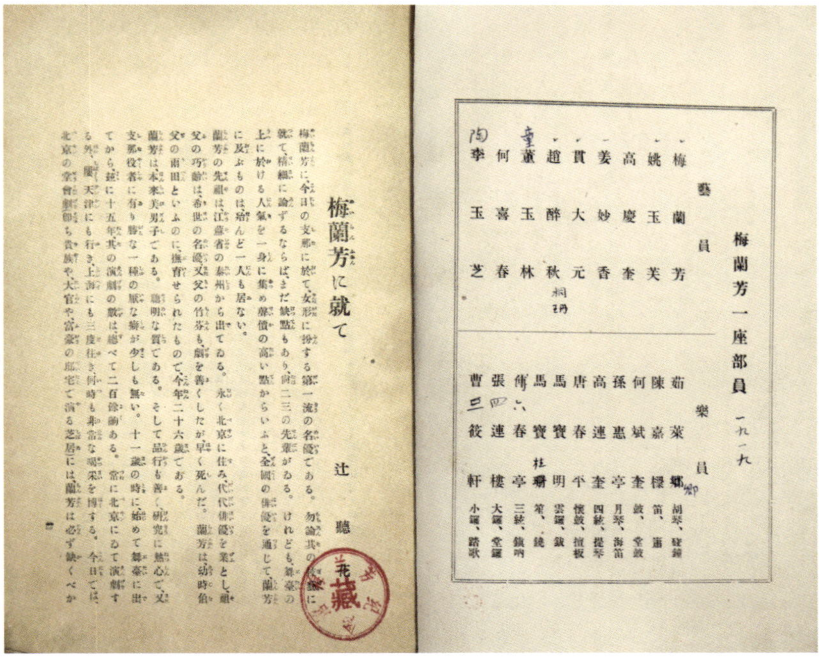

1919 年，梅兰芳在东京帝国剧场公演时的京剧说明《曲本梗概》封面和内页

The instruction to Beijing Opera in Japan

上图 | 梅兰芳第二次赴日演出前在北京与剧团全体人员21人合影（1924）（贯大元、高庆奎、茹莱卿、姚玉芙、姜妙香等）

Mei Lanfang with his tearmmates before his 2nd trip to Japan

下图 | 梅兰芳访日前与日方人员及齐如山等人合影（前排左起：许伯明、齐如山、沈亮超、村田、张謬子、李释戡、吴仲言，后排左起：罗瘿公、姚玉芙、梅兰芳、胡伯平、萧紫庭）

Before leaving for Japan, Mei Lanfang with Qi Rushan and others (Front, from left to right: Xu Boming, Qi Rushan, Shen Liangchao, Murata, Zhang Miaozi, Li Shikan, Wu Zhongyan, Back: Luo Yinggong, Yao Yufu, Mei Lanfang, Hu Boping, Xiao Ziting)

梅兰芳访日前在上海与冯耿光、吴震修、赵叔雍、李叔一等出席日本领事馆欢送会时合影（前排中为梅兰芳）

Mei Lanfang with Feng Gengguang , Wu Zhenxiu , Zhao Shuyong, Li Shuyi and others attending a Seeing-off Party at the Japanese Consulate in Shanghai before leaving for Japan

上图 | 中日人士欢送梅兰芳访日（前排左起：东日出子、坂东秀歌 、福芝芳 、村田嘉久子、梅兰芳、守田勘弥、尚小云、王琴侬）
Attending a seeing-off party in Beijing before visiting Japan

下图 | 1924 年10 月，梅兰芳抵达东京车站时受到帝国剧场演员的欢迎。（前排右起：村田嘉久子、尾上梅幸、东日出子、梅兰芳、延子）
Mei Lanfang with Japanese Kabuki performers

上图｜1924年11月，梅兰芳与大阪广珍园主人合影
Mei Lanfang with Japanese friends in Osaka(1924)
下图｜梅兰芳（前排右二）与村田嘉久子（前排右一）、长岛菊子（后排右一）等日本歌伎演员合影
Mei Lanfang with Japanese Kabuki actresses

梅兰芳抵日后出席村田嘉久子等在山水楼举行的茶话会（前排右起：村田嘉久子、梅兰芳、河野、速水、福地、坂西中将、冈田，后排右起：官田、佐佐木、李先生、川口、村松梢风、水岛尔杰布、泽田）（1924）
Mei Lanfang attended a welcome tea party held by Japanese actors and actresses

上图 | 梅兰芳（左四）、齐如山（左一）与日本歌舞伎演员长岛菊子（左三）、村田嘉久子（左五）等合影
Mei Lanfang (left 4), Qi Rushan (left 1) With Kabuki actors and actresses

下图 | 梅兰芳与日本歌舞伎演员中村雀右卫门
With Kabuki actor Nakamura Jakuemon

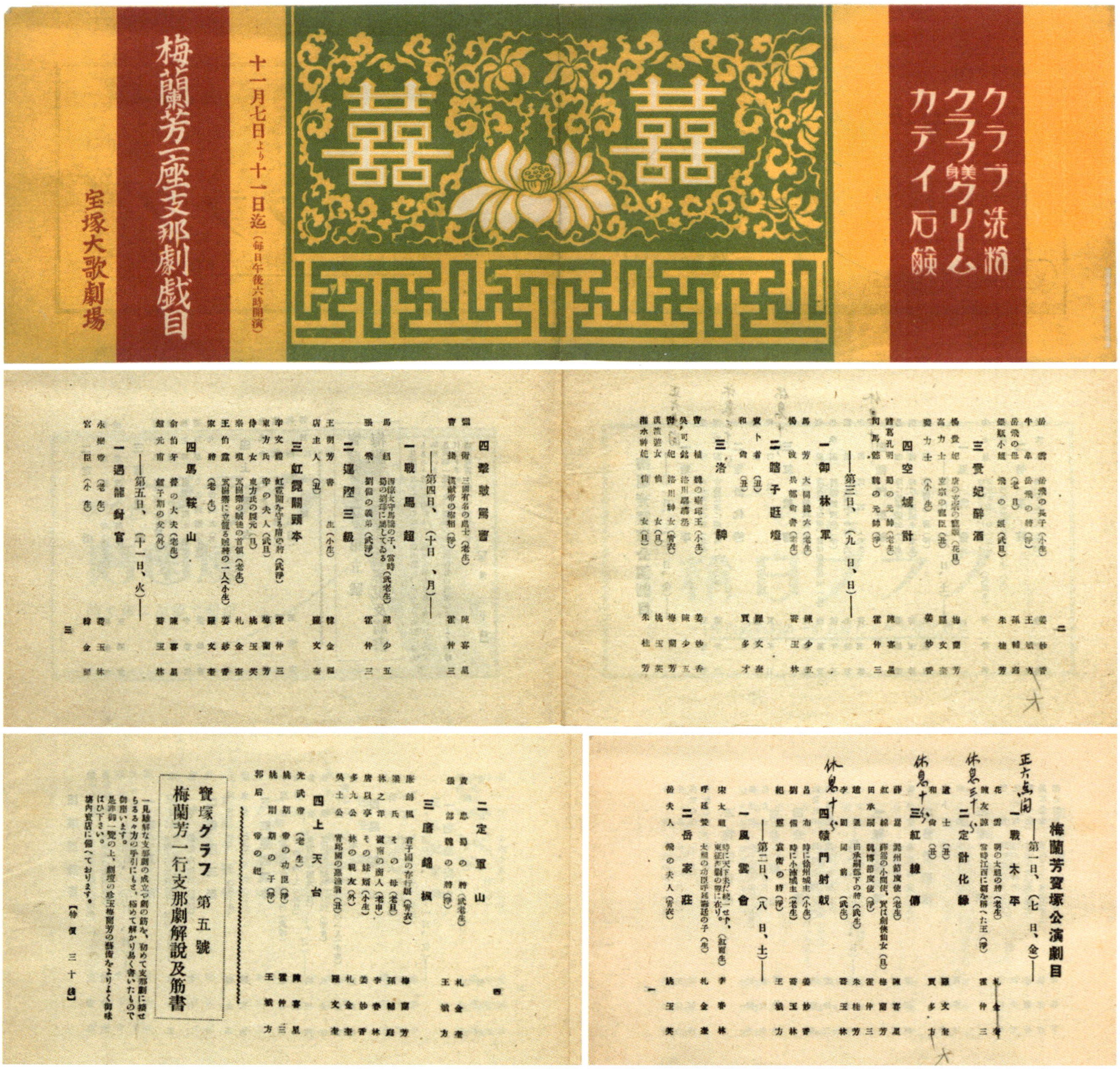

1924 年 11 月 7 日至 11 日，梅兰芳在日本宝塚大歌剧场演出的戏单

The programme of Mei's performance in Taka razuka Theatre, Japan from 7-11 November, 1924

上图 | 梅兰芳访日演出时的乐队
The Beijing Opera Band for Mei Lanfang
下图 | 帝国剧场全景
The Imperial Theatre in Japan

上左、上右｜在日本演出《天女散花》，梅兰芳饰天女
Mei Lanfang performed *The Heavenly Maid Showering Flowers* in Japan
下图｜在日本演出《贵妃醉酒》，梅兰芳饰杨玉环
Mei Lanfang performed *Drunken Beauty* in Japan

在日本演出《御碑亭》，梅兰芳饰孟月华
Mei Lanfang performed *The Pavilion of Imperial Monument* in Japan

上左 |《电影和舞台》月刊 1924 年第一卷第 4 号
Japanese magazine *Movie & Stage* (Vol.I,No.4 1924)

上中 |《戏剧和电影》1924 年 11 月号
Japanese magazine *Theatre & Movie* (November,1924)

上右 |《戏剧和电影》1924 年 8 月号
Japanese magazine *Theatre & Movie* (August,1924)

下图 |《戏剧和电影》1924 年 12 月号
Japanese magazine *Theatre & Movie* (December,1924)

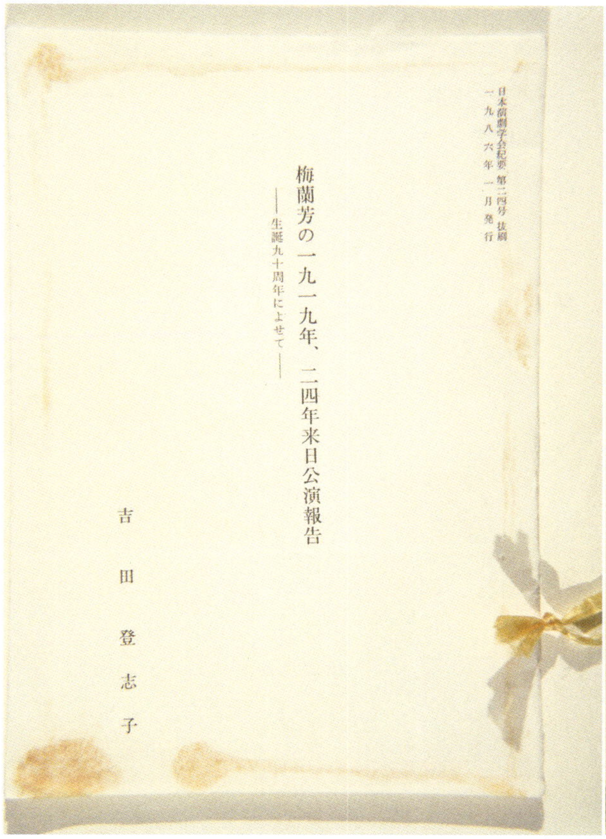

上左｜日本吉臣登志子撰写的《梅兰芳的一九一九年、二四年来日公演报告》之封面
The cover of a reportage on Mei's tours to Japan in 1919 and 1924 written by the Japanese writer Yoshida Toshiko (Published in January ,1986)

上右｜《朝日画报》封面（1924 年11 月12 日）
Japanese magazine *The Asahigraph* (November 12, 1924)

下图｜《时事新报》赠送梅兰芳的奖牌
The medal for Mei Lanfang presented by the Chinese newspaper *Time News*

美国之行

Successful U.S. Tour

1929年底，梅兰芳应邀赴美访问演出，齐如山和张彭春任剧团指导，全团24人，十分精干。当时正值美国经济大萧条时期，梅兰芳毅然访美，表现出了极大的胆识。他先后访问了华盛顿、纽约、芝加哥、旧金山、洛杉矶、圣地亚哥、西雅图和檀香山等城市，历时半年之久。上演的剧目有《贵妃醉酒》、《打渔杀家》、《霸王别姬》、《汾河湾》、《天女散花》、《刺虎》、《春香闹学》以及剑舞《红线盗盒》、羽舞《西施》、杯盘舞《麻姑献寿》、花镰舞《嫦娥奔月》、云帚舞《上元夫人》等舞蹈节目。他以中国戏曲艺术的巨大魅力和个人精湛的演技，赢得了美国民众以及艺术界、学术界的热情赞扬和高度评价，获得了南加州大学和波摩那学院颁发的荣誉文学博士学位，并结识了许多文艺界知名人士，同他们建立了诚挚的友谊。这是一次向海外传播东方艺术、影响极大的民间活动，不仅促进了中美两国人民之间的友谊，而且也沟通了东西方文化。

In the end of 1929, with the support and assistance of Dr. Zhang Pengchun and Qi Rushan, Mei led his performing troupe to visit the United States. He performed in New York, Washington, D.C., San Francisco, Chicago, Los Angeles, Seattle, San Diego and Honolulu. The plays he performed were *The Drunken Beauty*,*The Fisherman's Revenge*,*The King's Parting with His Favourite*, *Killing the Tiger General*, *By the Fen River Bend*, *Chun Xiang Upsets the Study* and *The Heavenly Maid Showering Flowers*,together with the sleeve dance in *Lady Shangyuan*, the feather dance in *Beauty Xishi*, the sickle dance in *Lady Chang E Flies to the Moon*, the cup and tray dance in *Ma Ku Wishing Wang Mu a Long Life* and the sword dance in *Hongxian Steeling the Box*.

His performances won great applause, University of Southern California and the Pomona College both conferred on him honorary doctorates of literature. Through his tour, he owned friendship with many luminaries of the literary and art circles. His American tour was an outstanding event of the people's cultural exchange, which introduced an art of the Orient to the West, with a result of not only promoting friendship between the peoples of China and the United States, but also removing the cultural barrier between the East and West.

梅兰芳赴美时所乘轮船由沪离开码头

The liner Mei Lanfang took was leaving Shanghai for America

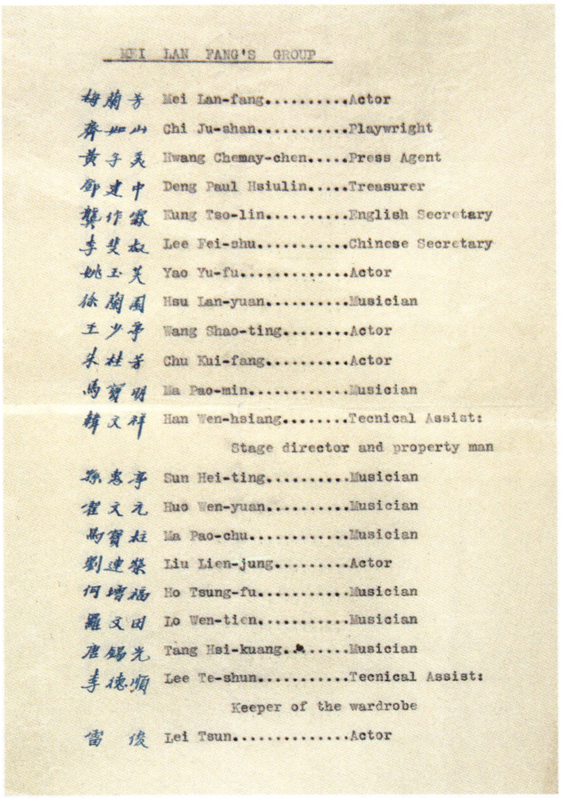

MEI LAN FANG'S GROUP

梅蘭芳 Mei Lan-fang..........Actor
齊如山 Chi Ju-shan...........Playwright
黄子美 Hwang Chemay-chen.....Press Agent
鄧建中 Deng Paul Hsiulin.....Treasurer
龔作霖 Kung Tso-lin..........English Secretary
李斐叔 Lee Fei-shu...........Chinese Secretary
姚玉芙 Yao Yu-fu.............Actor
徐蘭園 Hsu Lan-yuan..........Musician
王少亭 Wang Shao-ting........Actor
朱桂芳 Chu Kui-fang..........Actor
馬寶明 Ma Pao-min............Musician
韓文祥 Han Wen-hsiang........Tecnical Assist:
Stage director and property man
孫惠亭 Sun Hei-ting..........Musician
霍文元 Huo Wen-yuan..........Musician
馬寶柱 Ma Pao-chu............Musician
劉連榮 Liu Lien-jung.........Actor
何增福 Ho Tsung-fu...........Musician
羅文田 Lo Wen-tien...........Musician
唐錫光 Tang Hsi-kuang........Musician
李德順 Lee Te-shun...........Tecnical Assist:
Keeper of the wardrobe
雷 俊 Lei Tsun..............Actor

上左｜梅兰芳（左十）访美离沪时在轮船上与欢送人员合影
Mei Lanfang on the deck of the liner leaving the dock of Shanghai for America

上右｜1929 年 12 月 28 日，梅剧团访美离开北京时在前门火车站留影（左第二人为梅兰芳）
Mei Lanfang(left 2nd) and his performing troupe at Beijing Railway Station before leaving for America (December 28, 1929)

下图｜梅剧团访美时的人员名单
The list of members visiting America with Mei Lanfang

上图｜梅兰芳从上海赴美时与齐如山等人合影
Mei Lanfang with Qi Rushan and other friends before leaving for America
下图｜梅兰芳等在赴美的轮船上参加化装舞会时合影
Mei Lanfang attended a masquerade party on the liner sailing for America

左图｜梅兰芳访美时由北平乘车至天津换乘轮船，夫人福芝芳同船送行至上海，这是两人在轮船甲板上留影

Mei Lanfang and his wife on the deck of the steamer from Tianjin to Shanghai before leaving for America

右图｜梅兰芳在赴美时的“加拿大皇后号”轮船上

On the liner "Empress of Canada" to America

上左｜梅兰芳赴美演出，船经日本时与中日友人合影，中坐者梅兰芳、齐如山（照片背面写道：井山历太郎、川口市助、浅利龟田、冈刃有良、协西划八郎、末广久一，民国十九年一月二十一号于东京帝国剧场（1930）

Mei Lanfang with Chinese and Japanese friends during the US trip

上右｜梅兰芳赴美演出，船经日本时与中日友人合影，其中有齐如山（后排左一）、张学铭（后排左二）、梅兰芳（前中）及驻日公使汪荣宝、小村侯爵、李择一、坂西等（1930）

Mei Lanfang with Chinese and Japanese friend in Japan on the way to U.S.A

下图｜梅兰芳赴美演出时，梅兰芳（后立左二）、张彭春（后立左三）、黄子美（左四）与日本友人在船上合影

Mei Lanfang with Zhang Pengchun, Huang Zimei and Japanese friends on the liner sailing for America

左图｜梅兰芳赴美演出，船经日本，梅兰芳（前排右二）、张彭春（前排左一）、黄子美（后排左一）在东京帝国剧场与中日友人合影（1930）
Mei Lanfang with Japanese friends (1930)

右图｜梅兰芳、齐如山与日本名伶守田勘弥、村田嘉久子等合影（1930）
Mei Lanfang, Qi Rushan with well-known Japanese actors(1930)

梅兰芳在美国纽约设宴答谢各界人士

Mei Lanfang held a reciprocal banquet in New York

梅兰芳在美国纽约出席欢迎宴会

Mei Lanfang attended the welcome banquet in New York

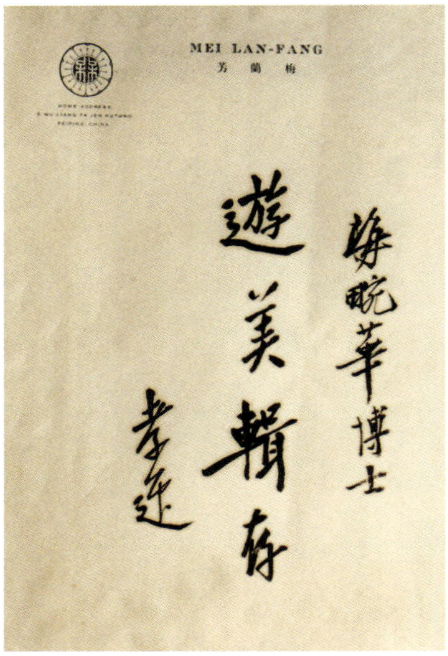
MEI LAN-FANG
梅蘭芳
梅畹華博士
遊美輯存

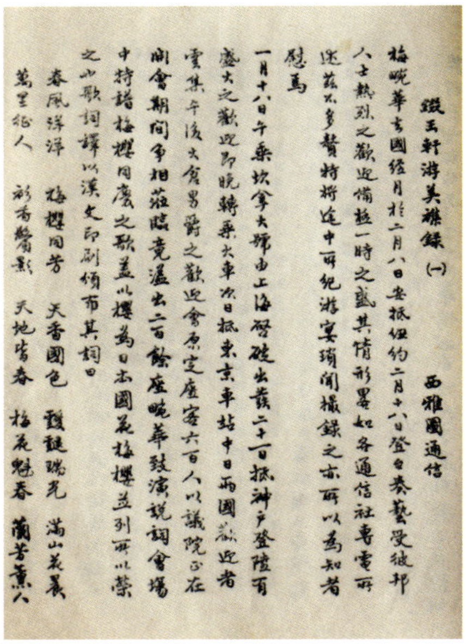
綴玉軒游美雜錄（一）　西雅圖通信
梅畹華去國經月於二月八日安抵紐約二月十八日登台奏藝受彼邦人士熱烈之歡迎備極一時之盛其情形略如各通信社專電所述茲不多贅特將途中所紀游宴瑣聞攝錄之亦所以為知者慰焉
一月十八日午乘坎拿大郵由上海啓碇出發二十日抵神戶登陸有盛大之歡迎即晚轉乘火車次日抵東京車站中日兩國歡迎者雲集午後大倉男爵之歡迎會原定座客六百人以議院正在開會期間爭相蒞臨竟溢出二百餘座畹華致演說詞會場中特諧梅櫻同慶之歌蓋以櫻為日本國花梅櫻並列所以繫之也歌詞譯以漢文印刷傾布其詞曰
春風洋洋　梅櫻同芳　天香國色　暨鏈瑞光　滿山花義
萬里伯人　形香鬱影　天地皆春　梅花魁春　蘭芳薰八

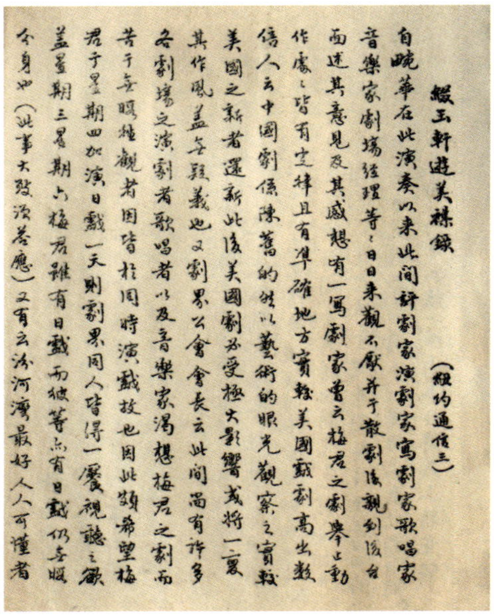
綴玉軒遊美雜錄　（紐約通信三）
自畹華在此演奏以來此間評劇家演劇家寫劇家歌唱家音樂家劇場經理等等日日來觀不厭並于散劇後親到後台而述其意見及其感想有一寫劇家曾云梅君之劇舉止動作處處皆有定律且有準確地方實較美國戲劇高出數倍人人云中國劇係陳舊的然以藝術的眼光觀察之實較美國之新者還新此後美國劇必受極大影響或將一變其作風蓋無疑義也又劇界公會會長云此間尚有許多各劇場之演劇者歌唱者以及音樂家渴想梅君之劇而苦于無暇往觀者因皆於同時演戲故也因此頗希望梅君于星期四加演日戲一天則劇界同人皆得一饜視聽之欲蓋星期三星期六梅君雖有日戲而彼等亦有日戲仍無暇分身也（此事大致設若應）又有云汾河灣最好人人可懂者

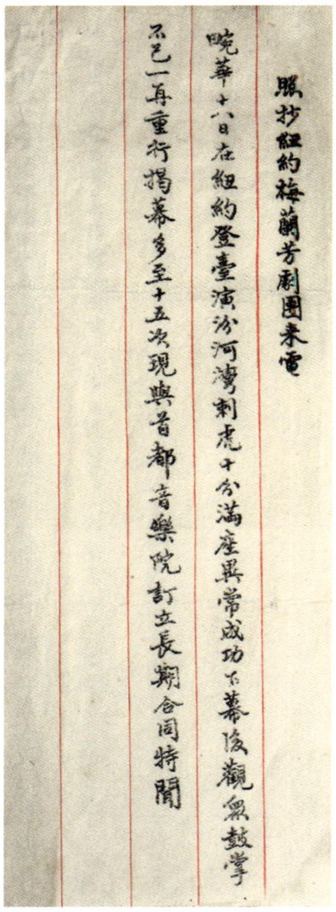
照抄紐約梅蘭芳劇團來電
畹華十八日在紐約登臺演汾河灣刺虎十分滿座異常成功下幕後觀眾鼓掌不已一再重行揭幕多至十五次現與首都音樂院訂立長期合同特聞

上图｜梅兰芳纪念馆藏《游美辑存》
America Trip Collection collected by Mei Lanfang Memorial Museum
下图｜梅兰芳纪念馆藏纽约梅兰芳剧团来电
The telegraph from New York collected by Mei Lanfang Memorial Museum

梅兰芳在美国纽约出席华侨举办的欢迎会

Mei Lanfang attended the welcome party held by the overseas Chinese in the U.S.

上图 | 梅兰芳、齐如山、张彭春、黄子美与美国著名戏剧家贝拉斯考在纽约合影
With dramatist David Belasco in New York, (Back, from right to left: Qi Rushan, Zhang Pengchun and Huang Zimei)

下图 | 美国雕塑家恩斯特・杜立格和克洛・杜立格为梅兰芳塑像
The American sculptor Ernest Durig was making a statue of Mei Lanfang

梅兰芳在纽约与著名戏剧家贝拉斯考合影
With the distinguished dramatist David Belasco in New York

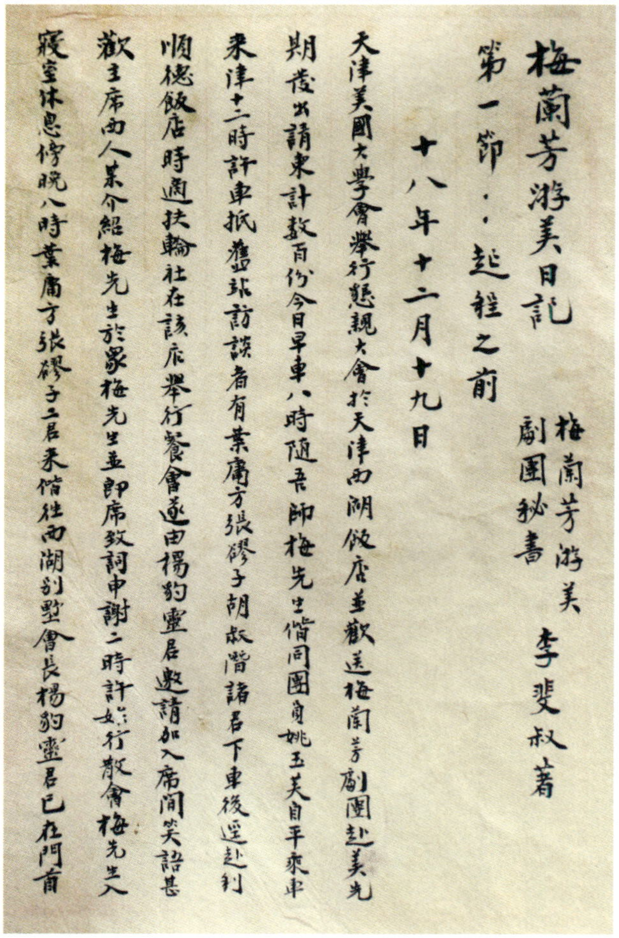

梅蘭芳游美日記

梅蘭芳游美劇團秘書 李斐叔著

第一節：起程之前

十八年十二月十九日

天津美國大學會舉行懇親大會於天津西湖飯店並歡送梅蘭芳劇團赴美先期發出請柬計數百份今日早車八時隨吾師梅先生偕同團員姚玉芙自平乘車來津十二時許車抵舊站訪談者有葉庸方張繆子胡叔僧諸君下車後逕赴利順德飯店時適扶輪社在該店舉行餐會遂由楊豹靈君邀請加入席間笑語甚歡主席西人某介紹梅先生於眾梅先生並即席致詞申謝二時許始行散會梅先生入寢室休息傍晚八時葉庸方張繆子二君來偕往西湖別墅會長楊豹靈君已在門首

上左、上右｜梅兰芳在旧金山市市长小卢尔夫陪同下乘车出席欢迎大会时受到民众夹道欢迎

Mei Lanfang's arrival in San Francisco during his U.S. tour in 1930. Mayor James Rolph Jr, escorted him from the railway station to the Capitor Theatre where a meeting of welcome was held

下图｜梅兰芳纪念馆藏李斐叔著《梅兰芳游美日记》手稿

Diary for Mei Lanfang U. S trip writter by Li Feishu

梅兰芳与旧金山市市长小卢尔夫
Mei Lanfang and Mayor James Rolph Jr. of San Francisco

上图 | 梅兰芳等在美国旧金山步入欢迎大会会场
Mei Lanfang entered the theatre where a meeting of welcome was held

下图 | 梅兰芳受到旧金山市市长小卢尔夫的欢迎
Mei Lanfang and Mayor James Rolph Jr. of San Francisco

欢迎梨园巨子梅兰芳大巡游
San Francisco welcomes Mei Lanfang

梅兰芳（前排左六）等出席中国驻美使馆的欢迎会时合影

Mei Lanfang (front, left 6) attended the welcome party held in the Chinese Embassy in Washington. D. C.

上图 | 1930 年4 月21 日，梅兰芳在美国旧金山与旅美广东粤剧演员合影

Mei Lanfang with Cantonese opera actors and actresses in San Francisco (April 21, 1930)

下左 | 梅兰芳在旧金山设宴答谢各界人士

Mei Lanfang held a reciprocal banquet in San Francisco (1930)

下右 | 梅兰芳在旧金山市出席梅氏家族欢迎宴会时合影

Mei Lanfang attended the banquet held by Mei Clansmen of overseas Chinese in San Francisco.

中華民國

上图 | 梅兰芳在洛杉矶举行宴会时合影（梅兰芳左侧为前美国财政部长麦克杜，梅兰芳右侧为张彭春）

Mei Lanfang held a banquet in Los Angeles. (Mr. William G. McAdoo, the former Minister of U.S. Treasury Department, at Mei's left side, and Zhang Pengchun at his right side)

下图 | 梅兰芳接受美国艺术家赠送的纪念品

American artists presented souvenirs

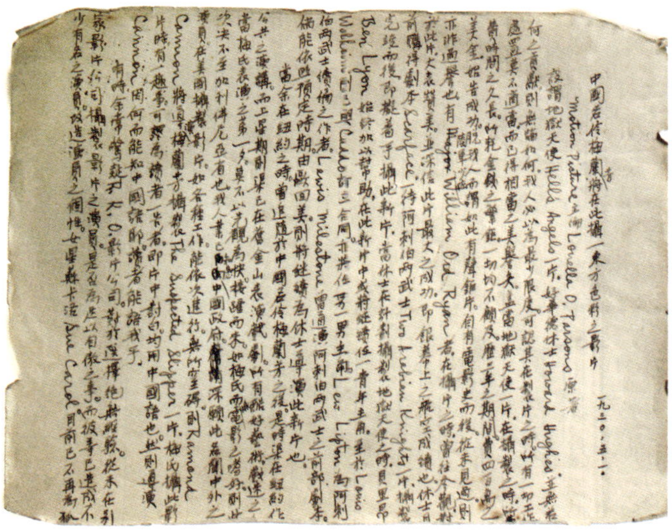

上左｜梅兰芳与洛杉矶博物院工作人员合影
Mei Lanfang and a staff member of the Los AngeLes Museum
上右｜梅兰芳在洛杉矶与博物院院长合影
Mei Lanfang and the curator of Los Angeles Museum
下图｜梅兰芳在美国拍摄彩色影片的手稿
Mei Lanfang's Script for shooting a colorful film

梅兰芳与电影大师卓别林

Mei Lanfang and Charlie Chaplin

上图｜梅兰芳（左四）在好莱坞与电影大师卓别林（左二）及三大戏院经理等合影

Mei Lanfang and Charlie Chaplin and three managers of American theatres in Hollywood

下图｜梅兰芳（左四）在好莱坞与电影大师卓别林（左三）等合影

Mei Lanfang With Charlie Chaplin and other film stars in Hollywood

梅兰芳与美国影星碧西劳馥等合影
Mei Lanfang With Bessie Love and other American film stars

上左｜梅兰芳与美国影星碧西劳馥
Mei Lanfang and American film star Bessie Love
上中、上右｜梅兰芳与美国影星玛丽·璧克福
Mei Lanfang and American film star Mary Burkfort

梅兰芳与美国艺术界人士合影
With American artists

上图｜梅兰芳在位于洛杉矶的美国影星范朋克、玛丽·璧克福夫妇的别墅中游泳

Mei Lanfang swimmed in Douglas Fairbanks' house

下左、下右｜梅兰芳在访问美国米高梅电影公司时与美国服装设计师吉尔伯特·A. 艾德里安

Mei Lanfang with American fashion designer Gilbert A. Adrian

上图｜梅兰芳在美国与歌舞演员合影
With Hula dancers in Hawaii. With American singers and dancers in several cities
下图｜梅兰芳在好莱坞与美国演员西奥·舍尔
Mei Lanfang with American actor Theo Scher

左图｜梅兰芳与电影名演员黛丽娥
With American film star Dolores Del Rio
右图｜梅兰芳与美国的戏院经理
With a manager of American theatre

Curatores
Collegii Pomonensis
OMNIBUS HAS LITERAS PERLECTURIS
Salutem in Domino
Notum sit quod Mei Lan-Fang pro meritis titulo graduque Doctoris in Litteris adornare nobis placuit eique concessimus honores dignitates jura et privilegia omnia quae ubique gentium ad gradum pertinent cujus sint testimonio collegii sigillum publicum atque nomina praesidis scribaeque literis hisce apposita Claremonti Californiae die Maii XXVIII annoque Salutis Humanae MCMXXX Reipublicae Americanae CLIV

University of Southern California
To all to whom these Letters shall come Greeting
The Trustees of the University on the recommendation of the President and by virtue of the Authority in Them vested have conferred on
Mei Lan-Fang
In recognition of distinguished achievement in the drama the degree of
Doctor of Humane Letters
with all the Rights Privileges and Honors thereunto appertaining
Given at Los Angeles in the State of California on the seventh day of June in the Year of our Lord One Thousand Nine Hundred and Thirty
President of the University
Secretary of the Board of Trustees

上左 | 美国波摩那学院授予梅兰芳的荣誉文学博士证书
The certificate of Litt. D. Diploma conferred on Mei Lanfang from the Pomona College

上右 | 美国南加利福尼亚大学授予梅兰芳的荣誉文学博士证书
The certificate of Litt. D. Diploma conferred on Mei Lanfang from the University of Southern California

下图 | 梅兰芳与美国波摩那学院院长晏文士
Mei Lanfang posed with Dr. Benjamin D. Scott, the President of Pomona College, after receiving an honorary doctorate from the College

右页 | 梅兰芳手持博士学位证书照
Mei Lanfang receieved the Litt.D.Diploma certificate from the Pomona College

梅兰芳（左五）在美国获波摩那学院授予的荣誉文学博士学位后与院长晏文士（右二）、齐如山（右二）、司徒宽（右三）等合影

Mei Lanfang posed with the President of Pomona College, together with Qi Rushan, Situ Kuan and others

梅兰芳参加美国波摩那学院同学会的欢迎会时与该院教授在宴会上合影

Mei Lanfang attended a welcome partys held by the alumni and professors of Pomona College

上图｜美国檀香山总督（前排右四）欢迎梅兰芳（前排左四）时合影，前排右三为齐如山，前排左三为张彭春，后排左二为黄子美
In Honolulu, the Honolulu Governor welcomed Mei Lanfang at the gate of his office
下图｜梅兰芳（左四）与檀香山总督（左二）等在庭院合影
With the Honolulu Governor in the courtyard of his office

左图｜梅兰芳与美国檀香山总督夫妇合影
Mei Lanfang and Governor of Honolulu and his wife
右图｜梅兰芳与檀香山总督
Mei Lanfang and Governor of Honolulu

上图｜梅兰芳（左二）、齐如山（左一）、张彭春（右一）等在美国檀香山合影
Mei Lanfang with Qi Rushan, Zhang Pengchun and other friends in Honolulu

下图｜梅兰芳（左六）在招待华侨的宴会上
Mei Lanfang at the reception held by the overseas Chinese

梅兰芳在美国与同行人员（左起：张彭春、齐如山、黄子美、梅兰芳、杨素）
With companions in the U. S. (From left to right: Zhang Pengchun, Qi Rushan, Huang Zimei, Mei Lanfang and Yang Su)

上图｜梅兰芳参观学校时与小朋友及老师合影
Mei Lanfang visited a primary school in Honolulu
下图｜梅兰芳与美国檀香山呼拉舞第一名家母女合影
Mei Lanfang with the best Hula dancer and her daughter in Honolulu

梅兰芳、齐如山、张彭春等在美国檀香山合影
Mei Lanfang with Qi Rushan, Zhang Pengchun and other friends in Honolulu

梅兰芳在美国与旅美华侨合影

Mei Lanfang was warmly welcomed by the oversea Chinese in the U.S.

梅兰芳在美国与歌舞演员合影

With Hula dancers in Hawaii and American singers and dancers in several cities

上图 | 梅兰芳在檀香山演出，歌舞演员上台献花时合影，其中有张彭春、齐如山等
In Honolulu, the hula dancing girls presented flowers to Mei Lanfang after the performance. Dr Zhang Pengchun and Qi Rushan were present

下左 | 梅兰芳在美国檀香山演出后，呼拉舞演员上台献花
In Hawaii, after Mei's performance, the hula girls presented flowers

下右 | 梅兰芳在檀香山留影
Mei Lanfang in Honolulu

梅兰芳到华侨家中拜访时合影

Mei Lanfang visited an overseas Chinese family

梅兰芳与旅美华侨合影

Mei Lanfang was warmly welcomed by the overseas Chinese in the U.S.

梅兰芳在美国受到各地华侨的欢迎
Mei Lanfang attended the welcome parties held by the overseas Chinese in the U.S.

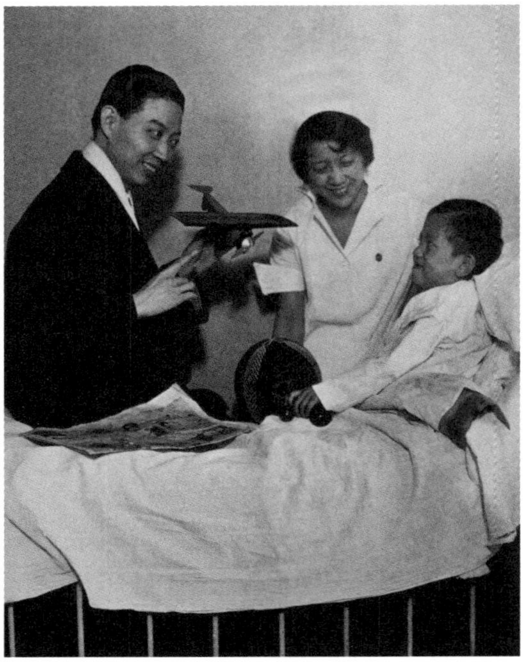

上左 | 梅兰芳与华侨儿童合影
Mei Lanfang with the overseas Chinese children

上右 | 梅兰芳到医院看望住院华侨儿童
Mei Lanfang showed loving care for an overseas Chinese boy in a hospital

下图 | 梅兰芳在当地火车站受到华侨的欢迎
With overseas Chinese at the railway station of an American city

梅兰芳在美国时，前往华侨住宅访问
Mei Lanfang visited overseas Chinese families

上图｜梅兰芳与中国驻美使馆人员合影

With officials of the Chinese Embassy in Washington. D. C.

下图｜梅兰芳在美国出席华侨欢迎会时合影

Mei Lanfang attended the welcome party held by the overseas Chinese in the U.S.

梅兰芳在美国访问当地华侨梅氏公所时受到欢迎并合影留念

Mei Lanfang visited the Hall of Mei Clansmen of oversea Chinese in the U.S.

梅兰芳在美国出席华侨欢迎会

Mei Lanfang attended the welcome party held by the overseas Chinese in the U.S.

梅兰芳在美国与旅美华侨在一起

Mei Lanfang was warmly welcomed by the overseas Chinese in the U.S.

上左、上右 | 梅兰芳在美国演出时的剧院

The theatre where Mei Lanfang gave performances in New York

下图 | 梅兰芳在美国纽约演出时的街头海报

The poster for Mei's performances on the street of New York

上图｜梅兰芳在美国演出时的剧场入口
The entrance of the theatre where Mei Lanfang gave performances in New York

下图｜梅兰芳在美国演出时的舞台装置
The stage setting of Mei's performance in the U.S.

梅兰芳在美国演出《天女散花》剧照（左、右页）

The Heavenly Maid Showering Flowers on the stage in the U.S.

梅兰芳在美国演出《虹霓关》剧照

Mei Lanfang as Lady Dongfang in *Rainbow Pass* performed in the U.S.

梅兰芳表演《霸王别姬》中的剑舞

Sword dance in *The King's Parting with His Favorite*

在美国演出《贞娥刺虎》剧照，梅兰芳饰贞娥，刘连荣饰一只虎，李斐叔、姚玉芙饰宫女
Mei Lanfang as Lady Fei and Liu Lianrong as Tiger General in *Killing the Tiger General* performed in the U.S.

梅兰芳在美国檀香山表演剑舞（左页）
Mei Lanfang performed sword dance in Honolulu of Hawaii

上图｜梅兰芳与刘连荣在美国演出《贞娥刺虎》中“刺虎”剧照
Mei Lanfang as Lady Fei and Liu Lianrong as Tiger General in *Killing the Tiger General* performed in the U.S.

下图｜梅兰芳与刘连荣在美国演出《贞娥刺虎》中饰贞娥
Mei Lanfang as Lady Fei and Liu Lianrong as Tiger General in *Killing the Tiger General* performed in the U.S.

在美国演出《汾河湾》，梅兰芳饰柳迎春，王少亭饰薛仁贵

Mei Lanfang as Liu Yingchun and Wang Shaoting as Xue Rengui in *By the Fen River Band* performed in the U.S.

在美国演出《汾河湾》，梅兰芳饰柳迎春
Mei Lanfang as Liu Yingchun in *By the Fen River Band* (also named *The Suspicious Slipper*) performed in the U.S.

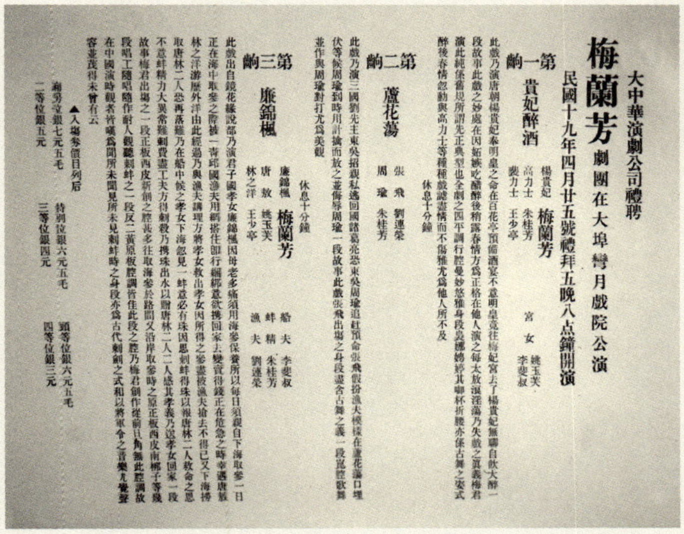

大中華演劇公司禮聘

梅蘭芳劇團在大埠彎月戲院公演

民國十九年四月廿五號禮拜五晚八点鐘開演

第一齣 貴妃醉酒

楊貴妃 梅蘭芳
高力士 朱桂芳
裴力士 王少亭
宮女 姚玉芙 李斐叔

此戲乃演唐朝楊貴妃奉明皇之命在百花亭預備酒宴不意明皇竟往梅妃宮去了楊貴妃無聊自飲大醉一段故事此戲之妙處在因妬嫉吃醋醉後稍露春情方為正格在他人演之每太放浪淫蕩乃失戲之真義梅君演此純係舊規所謂先正典型也全劇之四平調行腔曼妙悠雅身段裊娜婀娜其啣杯折腰亦係古舞之姿式醉後春情忽動與高力士等種種戲謔盡情而不傷雅尤為他人所不及

休息十分鐘

第二齣 蘆花蕩

張飛 劉連榮
周瑜 朱桂芳

此戲乃演三國劉先主東吳招親私逃回國諸葛亮恐東吳周瑜追赶預命張飛假扮漁夫模樣在蘆花蕩口埋伏等候周瑜到時用計擒而放之並侮辱周瑜一段故事此戲張飛出場之身段盡含古舞之義一段崑腔歌舞並作與周瑜對打尤為美觀

休息十分鐘

第三齣 廉錦楓

廉錦楓 梅蘭芳
唐敖 姚玉芙
林之洋 王少亭
船夫 李斐叔
蚌精 朱桂芳
漁夫 劉連榮

此戲出自鏡花緣說部乃演君子國孝女廉錦楓因母老多病須用海參保養所以每日須親自下海取參一日正在海中取參之際被一青邱國漁夫用網捞住即行綑綁意欲携回家去變賣得錢正在危急之時幸遇唐敖林之洋游歷外洋由此經過乃與漁夫講理方將孝女救出孝女因所得之參盡被漁夫搶去不得已又下海搏取唐林二人恐再落難乃在船中候之孝女下海忽見一蚌意必有珠因思刺蚌得珠以報唐林二人救命之恩不意蚌精力大異常雖刺費盡工夫方得刺殺乃携珠出水以贈唐林二人二人感其孝義乃送孝女回家一段故事梅君出場之一段正板西皮新創之腔甚多往取海參於路間又沿岸取參時之原正板西皮南梆子等幾段唱工隨唱隨作耐人觀聽刺蚌之一段反二黃原板腔調皆佳此段之腔乃梅君創作從前旦角無此腔調故在中國演時觀者皆嘖為聞所未聞見所未見刺蚌時之身段亦為古代刺劍之式和以將軍令之音樂尤覺聲容並茂得未曾有云

▲入場劵價目列后

廂房位銀七元五毛 特別位銀六元五毛 頭等位銀六元五毛
二等位銀五元 三等位銀四元 四等位銀三元

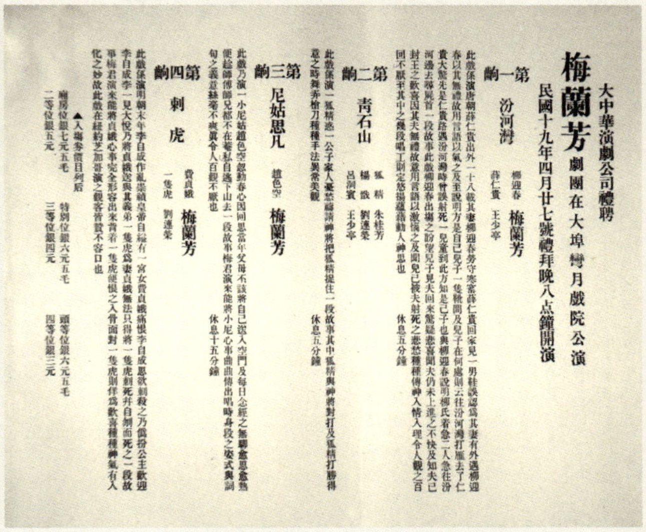

大中華演劇公司禮聘

梅蘭芳劇團在大埠彎月戲院公演

民國十九年四月廿七號禮拜晚八点鐘開演

第一齣 汾河灣

柳迎春 梅蘭芳
薛仁貴 王少亭

此戲係演唐朝薛仁貴出外一十八載其妻柳迎春苦守寒窰薛仁貴回家見一男鞋誤認為其妻有外遇柳迎春以其無禮故用言語以氣之及至說明方是自己兒子一隻耕問及兒子在何處則云往汾河灣打雁去了仁貴大驚先是仁貴路過汾河灣時曾誤射死一兒童到此方知是己子也與柳迎春說明柳氏著急二人急往汾河邊去尋屍首一段故事此戲柳迎春出場之盼望兒子見夫回來驚疑悲喜聞夫仍未上進之不快及知夫已封王之歡喜因其夫無禮故意用言語以激憤之及聞兒已被夫射死之悲愁種種傳神入情入理令人觀之百回不厭至其中之幾段唱工則完愁揚蘊藉動人神思也

休息五分鐘

第二齣 青石山

狐精 朱桂芳
楊戩 劉連榮
呂洞賓 王少亭

此戲係演一狐精迷一公子家人憂愁請神將把狐精捉住一段故事其中狐精與神將對打及狐精打勝得意之時舞弄槍刀種種手法異常美觀

休息五分鐘

第三齣 尼姑思凡

趙色空 梅蘭芳

此戲乃演一小尼姑趙色空忽動春心因回思當年父母不該將自己送入空門及每日念經之無聊意甚煩悶便趁師傅師兄都不在菴私自逃下山去一段故事梅君演來能將小尼心事曲曲傳出唱時身段之姿式與詞句之義意絲毫不爽真令人百觀不厭也

休息十五分鐘

第四齣 刺虎

費貞娥 梅蘭芳
一隻虎 劉連榮

此戲係演明朝末年李自成作亂崇禎皇帝自縊有一宮女費貞娥痛恨李自成思欲刺殺之乃偽扮公主歡迎李自成李一見大悅乃將貞娥送與其義弟一隻虎為妻貞娥無法只得將一隻虎刺死并自刎而死之一段故事梅君演來能將貞娥心事完全形容出來背着一隻虎則仇恨之入骨面對一隻虎則佯為歡喜種種神氣有入化之妙故此戲在紐約芝加哥演之觀客皆贊不容口也

▲入場劵價目列后

廂房位銀七元五毛 特別位銀六元五毛 頭等位銀六元五毛
二等位銀五元 三等位銀四元 四等位銀三元

上图 | 梅兰芳访美时印制的《梅兰芳歌曲谱》书影（音乐大师刘天华首次用五线谱为梅兰芳演出唱词谱曲）

The volume of the *The Music Score of Mei's Songs* arranged by Liu Tianhua, specially printed for Mei's U.S. tour

下图 | 梅兰芳在旧金山演出时的戏单

The program of Mei's performance in San Francisco

上图｜梅兰芳在访美回国的轮船上与张彭春、李斐叔合影
On the liner returning to China with Zhang Pengchun and Li Feishu
下图｜梅兰芳在访美回国的轮船上与张彭春、齐如山合影
On the liner returning to China with Zhang Pengchun and Qi Rushan

梅兰芳在访美返回国的轮船上

On the liner returning to China

轮船抵达码头时，梅兰芳在船上向欢迎人群招手致意

Mei Lanfang on the deck of the liner waved to the welcoming people

梅兰芳访美归来到达上海码头时受到民众的热烈欢迎
The liner was arriving at the dock of Shanghai

访苏旅欧

Visiting the Soviet Union

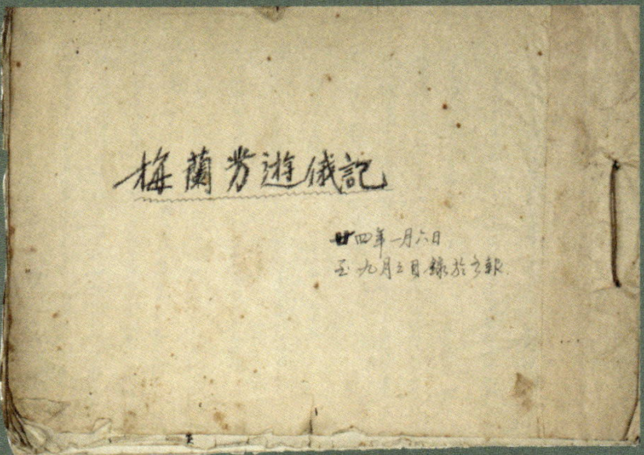

梅兰芳纪念馆藏《梅兰芳游俄记》手稿

1935年，梅兰芳应苏联对外文化协会的邀请，率团赴苏访问，张彭春和余上沅两位教授任正、副艺术指导。当时苏方由于梅兰芳拒绝通过伪“满洲国”前往，特派“北方号”专轮至沪迎接他直赴海参崴，然后再转乘穿越西伯利亚火车去莫斯科。在莫斯科和彼得格勒两地，梅兰芳先后演出了《打渔杀家》、《虹霓关》、《汾河湾》、《宇宙锋》、《刺虎》和《贵妃醉酒》以及《红线盗盒》、《西施》、《麻姑献寿》、《木兰从军》、《思凡》和《抗金兵》中的舞蹈部分，受到苏联民众和文艺界人士的热烈欢迎。观看梅兰芳演出的斯坦尼斯拉夫斯基、丹钦柯、梅耶荷德、爱森斯坦、泰伊洛夫、特里杰亚考夫与德国的皮斯卡托和布莱希特等艺术大师和戏剧家，高度赞扬中国戏曲艺术和梅兰芳卓越的表演。访苏期间，梅兰芳以篆书写下“沟通文化，促进邦交”的题词赠给苏方留念。这是由于面对当时日寇霸占东北，窥视华北的严峻局势，加强与邻国苏联的友好往来实属必要，梅兰芳毅然担当了促进邦交的民间使者的重任。

At the invitation of the All-Union Society for Cultural Relations with Foreign Countries(VOKS), Mei went to perform in Moscow and Leningrad in March and April. 1935, The programmes included *Beauty Defies Tyranny*,*The Fisherman's Revenge*,*The Rainbow Pass*,*The Drunken Beauty*, *By Fen River Bend* and *Killing the Tiger Generla*, together with several dance parts of other plays. Mei's performances won warm applause and his performing art was highly praised by Konstantin Stanislavsky. Nemirovich-Danchenko, W.E.Meyerhold, S.M.Eisenstein and German dramatists Erwin Piscator and Bertolt Brecht. The words Mei wrote as a parting souvenir for VOKS were:"Facilitate the cultural exchange and promote the diplomatic relation."

梅兰芳抵达海参崴后，中国驻该地领事权世恩举行欢迎宴会时与梅兰芳等合影
The banquet given by the Chinese Consul Quan Shien when Mei Lanfang arrived at Vladivostok

梅兰芳抵达莫斯科时受到各界人士的热烈欢迎，同行的有张彭春、余上沅等

Mei Lanfang received flowers at the station of Moscow, together with Dr. Zhang Pengchun and Prof. Yu Shangyuan

梅兰芳抵达莫斯科时，在火车站受到苏方代表的欢迎

Welcome by the Soviet representative when Mei Lanfang arrived in Moscow

上图｜梅兰芳抵达莫斯科后在火车站与东方外交部东方司副司长包罗弗爱（Borovoy）、中国大使馆代办吴南如、鄂山荫秘书等合影

Mei Lanfang with Borovoy, the deputy director of Oriental Foreign Ministry and Chinese lonsal Wu Nanru, Secretary E shanyin

下图｜梅兰芳抵达莫斯科后在火车站与铁提可夫、鄂山荫等合影

Mei Lanfang with Toetyakov, Cherniavsky and E shanyin

上图｜梅兰芳与苏联艺术大师斯坦尼斯拉夫斯基合影
Mei Lanfang and Konstantin Stanislavsky in Moscow
下图｜梅兰芳与苏联戏剧家梅耶荷德合影
Mei Lanfang and W. E. Meyerhold

上图｜梅兰芳与苏联文化界人士爱森斯坦、铁提可夫、泰伊洛夫等合影

Mei Lanfang With Eisenstein, Tetykov, Tairov and other members of Soviet cultural circle

下图｜梅兰芳与苏联美丽剧院院长泰伊洛夫亲切交谈

Mei Lanfang talked with the president Tairov of Beauty Theater

梅兰芳与中国驻苏大使颜惠庆及苏联导演爱森斯坦、道其可夫、施尼代洛夫、实验剧院院长阿罗可夫等合影
Mei Lanfang with Chinese Ambassador to Soviet Union Yan Huiqing, film director Eisenstein and others friends

上图 | 梅兰芳与苏联著名电影导演铁提可夫等在座谈会上合影

With Soviet film director Tetykov and others at a symposium

下图 | 梅兰芳在苏联拍电影时与张彭春、余上沅及苏联导演爱森斯坦、剧作家特里杰亚考夫等合影

Pictures taken when the film was being shot. Mei Lanfang, Zhang Pengchun, Yu Shangyuan, Eisenstein,Tretyakov and other Soviet dramatists

梅兰芳访苏时观看了瓦赫坦戈演出的《杜兰朵》后与剧组人员合影
（右二为瓦赫坦戈夫人，左六为英国戏剧家戈登·克雷）
Mei Lanfang with the Soviet drama actors of *Turandot*

上图 | 梅兰芳与苏联第一艺术剧院经理及该剧院演员合影
With the manager of The First Art Theatre and the actors and actresses
下图 | 梅兰芳与苏联戏剧界人士亲切交谈
Mei Lanfang with Soviet dramatists

上图｜梅兰芳与苏联电影导演爱森斯坦及戏剧家梅耶荷德

With S. M. Eisenstein and W. E. Meyerhold

下图｜梅兰芳与苏联戏剧家梅耶荷德及演员瑞阿区女士、鲍高洛夫、科西可夫等合影

With W. E. Meyerhold and Soviet Union actors and actresses

梅兰芳与苏联对外文化协会人员、余上沅及苏联演员在宴会上

Mei Lanfang attended a banquet held by the VOKS, together with Yu Shangyuan and Soviet Union actors and actresses

上图｜梅兰芳在苏联对外文化协会举办的欢迎会上致辞
Mei Lanfang attended the banquet held by VOKS
下图｜梅兰芳在苏联对外文化协会主办的欢迎午宴上致辞
Mei Lanfang was giving a speach at the barquet held by the VOKS

上图｜梅兰芳在苏联出席招待会时留影
Mei Lanfang at the reception held by VOKS
下图｜梅兰芳即兴清唱
Mei Lanfang was singing without costume

梅兰芳与挪威公使考兰台
Mei Lanfang with the Minister of Norway Kollantai

梅兰芳在苏联拍电影时与张彭春、余上沅及苏联导演爱森斯坦、剧作家特里杰亚考夫等合影

Pictures taken when the film was being shot. Mei Lanfang, Zhang Pengchun, Yu Shangyuan, Eisenstein, Tretyakov and other Soviet dramatists

上图｜梅兰芳在瓦格坦果夫剧院观看《人间喜剧》剧后与演员合影

Mei Lanfang with the actors of *Human Comedy at* Vahgtangov Theatre

下图｜梅兰芳与瓦格坦果夫剧院著名演员西门诺夫合影

Mei Lanfang with the famous actor Simonov of Vahgtangov Theatre

上图｜梅兰芳（左一）与中国驻苏大使颜惠庆（左三）及苏联对外文化协会会长阿洛塞夫合影

With Yan Huiqing, Chinese Ambassador to the Soviet Union, and Alexandre Arosseff, Chairman of the All- Union Society for Cultural Relations with Foreign Countries (VOKS)

下图｜梅兰芳与苏联戏剧家梅耶荷德及余上沅、张彭春等在一起

Mei Lanfang talked with Meyerhold, together with Zhang Pengchun and Yu Shangyuan

梅兰芳在苏联拍电影时与张彭春、余上沅、苏联导演爱森斯坦、剧作家特里杰亚考夫等合影

Pictures taken when the film was being shot. Mei Lanfang, Zhang Pengchun, Yu Shangyuan, Eisenstein, Tretyakov and other Soviet dramatists

梅兰芳在莫斯科向列宁墓献花圈

Mei Lanfang laid a wreath at Lenin's Tomb

上图｜1935 年，梅兰芳（左一）在赴苏联的轮船前与电影明星胡蝶（中）合影，右一为余玉清

In 1935, Mei Lanfang went to the Soviet Union before the cruise with film star Hu Die and Yu Yuqin in Mocow

下图｜梅兰芳与梅剧团成员同苏联文艺界人士爱森斯坦、特里杰亚夫等人合影

Mei Lanfang and his colleagues with Eisenstein, Tretyakov and members of Soviet literary and art circles

梅兰芳在莫斯科演出时，剧场门前观众踊跃入场

The Moscow audiences were entering the theatre where Mei Lanfang gave performance

梅兰芳在莫斯科演出时的海报

The poster for Mei Lanfang's performance in Moscow

五十萬人渴望觀劇

梅蘭芳今日起在俄京公演

劇票於十日前銷空盛況可知

列寗格勒表演後再來莫斯科

中央莫斯科廿二日電　今日下午梅蘭芳劇團在音樂廳舉行試演、蘇聯戲劇界到會者座爲之滿、首由蘇聯文化協會藝術部長邱蘭斯基介紹張彭春教授演說　中國劇團來俄之目的、次由梅氏表演汾河灣、費貞娥刺虎、及紅綫盜盒三劇、其他演員亦表演兩劇、觀衆熱烈鼓掌表示歡迎、明日首次公演戲目、與今日預演者相同、梅劇團在莫斯科列寗格勒兩地表演戲票、已於十日前銷售一空、蘇聯文化協會會長阿羅西夫因此請梅氏於列寗格勒表演後、再來莫斯科表演、據文化協會估計、現足有五十萬人渴望購票觀劇云、

上图 | 苏联剧场舞台及观众席

The stage setting of Mei's performance in the Soviet Union

下左 | 苏联剧场门前

The entrance of the theatre where Mei Lanfang gave performance in Soviet Union

下右 | 梅兰芳赴苏演出的报道

The news of Mei Lanfang performed in Moscow

梅兰芳在《宇宙锋》中饰赵艳容，同台演出的有刘连荣、王少亭等

Mei Lanfang as Zhao Yanrong, Liu Lianrong as her father and Wang Shaoting as the Emperor in *Beauty Defies Tyranny* performed in Moscow

上图｜梅兰芳在苏联拍摄《虹霓关》电影片断，导演为爱森斯坦（中）
S. M. Eisenstein directed and filmed a few scenes from Mei's per formance *Rainbow Pass*

下图｜《虹霓关》（头本），梅兰芳饰东方氏
Mei Lanfang as Lady Dongfang in *Rainbow Pass* performed in Moscow

右页｜《虹霓关》，梅兰芳饰东方氏剧照，同台者为朱桂芳（右）
Rainbow Pass performed in Moscow, Mei Lanfang as Lady Dongfang and Zhu Guifang as Wang Bodang

《打渔杀家》，梅兰芳饰萧桂英，王少亭饰萧恩

Mei Lanfang as Xiao Guiying and Wang Shaoting as Xiao En in *The Fisherman's Revenge* performed in Moscow

梅兰芳在招待会上表演剑舞
The sword dance performed by Mei Lanfang at a reception party in Moscow

《打渔杀家》，梅兰芳饰萧桂英
Mei Lanfang as Xiao Guiying in *The Fisherman's Revenge*

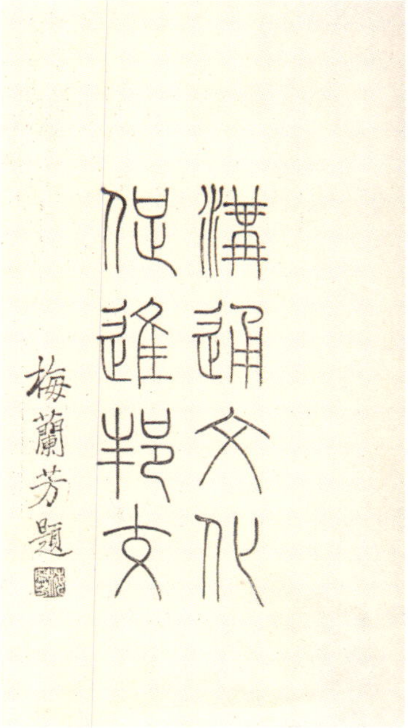

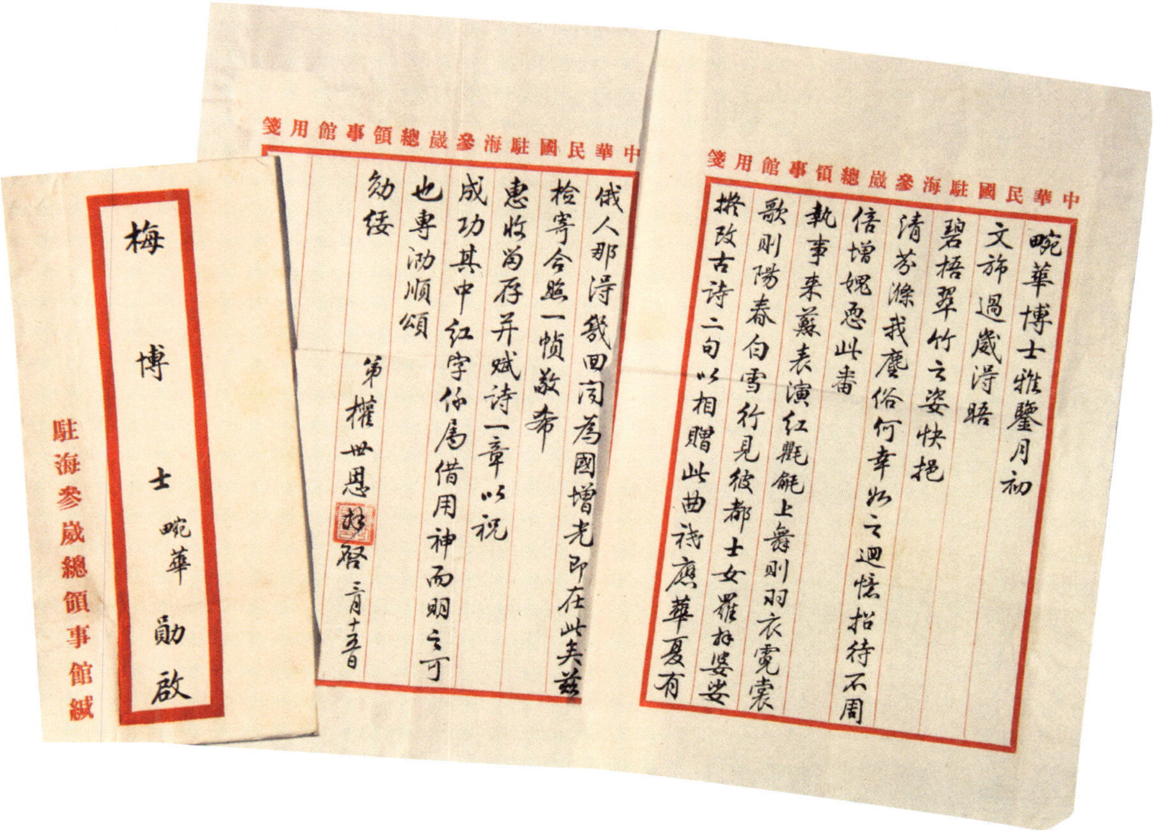
中華民國駐海參崴總領事館用箋

畹華博士雅鑒月初
文旆過崴得睹
碧梧翠竹之姿快挹
清芬滌我塵俗何幸如之迴怯招待不周
倍增媿恧此書
執事來蘇表演紅氍毹上舞則羽衣霓裳
歌則陽春白雪行見彼都士女羅拜婴妥
捃改古詩二句以相贈此曲祗應華夏有

中華民國駐海參崴總領事館用箋

俄人那得幾回聞為國增光即在此矣茲
檢寄合照一幀敬希
惠收尚存并賦詩一章以祝
成功其中紅字係局借用神而明之可
也專泐順頌
勛綏
弟權世恩拜啓 三月十五日

梅博士 畹華 勛啟
駐海參崴總領事館緘

上左 | 梅兰芳访苏时赠送给苏联对外文化协会的题词
The calligraphy written and presented to the VOKS by Mei Lanfang in 1935

上右 | 梅兰芳剧团出国演出证
The Certificate of Mei Lanfang's group

下图 | 梅兰芳访苏后，中国驻海参崴领事权世恩致梅兰芳的信件，盛赞在苏演出成功
A letter to Mei Lanfang from Quan Shien, the Chinese Consul atVladivostok, highly praising Mei's success in the Soviet Union

上左｜梅兰芳在德国与中国驻德公使刘崇杰夫妇等合影
In Berlin, Mei Lanfang with Chinese Ambassador to Germany Mr. Liu Chongjie, Mrs. Liu and other friends

上右｜1935 年4 月21 日，梅兰芳在华沙出席中国驻波公使举办的宴会时合影
Mei Lanfang attended the banquet held by Chinese Ambassador to Poland(1935) in Warsaw

下图｜梅兰芳、余上沅、刘崇杰（左前三）等在宴会上
Mei Lanfang with his friends in Europe

梅兰芳在欧洲留影

Photos taken in Europe

梅兰芳、余上沅与旅馆人员在日内瓦合影
With Yu Shangyuan and the staff of a hotel in Geneva

梅兰芳、余上沅、吴邦本及接待人士在欧洲一火车站合影
Mei Lanfang, Yu Shangyuan, Wu Bangben and some local persons at a station in Europe

梅兰芳在欧洲与友人合影

Mei Lanfang with friends in Europe

上左｜梅兰芳（左四）与友人在欧洲

Mei Lanfang (left 4th)in Europe

上右｜梅兰芳在伦敦与美国黑人歌唱家罗伯逊（左一）及黄柳霜（左二）、熊式一（左四）、余上沅（右一）等合影

Mei Lanfang and Paul Robesen in London

下图｜梅兰芳（左二）在伦敦与熊式一（左一）、黄柳霜（右二）、余上沅（右一）合影

With Professor Xiong Shiyi(left 1st), Huang Liushuang(right 2nd) and Professor Yu Shang yuan(right 1st) in London

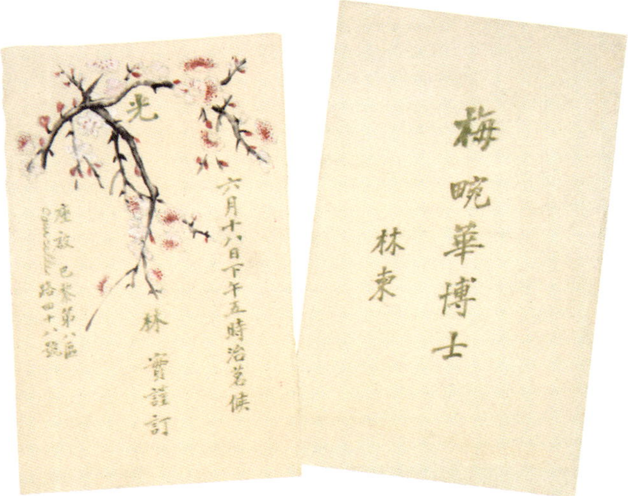

左图｜梅兰芳旅法时收到巴黎一位华侨的邀请帖
The invitation card to a welcome party from an overseas Chinese in Paris

右图｜梅兰芳等在欧洲旅行时合影（前排左起：林德良、吴闻天、曾炯之、蒋廷黻、余上沅、朱子清、郑 x 叶（不详），二排左起：张肖松、邱伟真、伦次珊、郑雪玫、小孩顾达夫、陈士华、外国妇女、陆传纹、郎焦学娴、江周菁柏，三排左起：萧瑞勋、刘思职、冯宣、杨 x 治（不详）、梁瑞寅、林时清、郭翘野、黄锦昌、王锋露，后排左起：冯锡庠、周生、吴国原、黄文彬、王修家、吴作人、李启颐、郎奎第、尹光宇、张枚新、邓鄂、何新文、曾匪石、王超、佴鸾、林继庸、杨武之、陆 x（不详），倒数二排右一为梅兰芳）
Mei Lanfang and his friends in Europe

CONTE VERDE
TRIESTE

国家出版基金项目
NATIONAL PUBLICATION FOUNDATION

一代宗师

梅兰芳

The Master
Mei Lanfang

【下】

名誉主编／梅葆玖
主　编／王文章
副主编／秦华生

文化艺术出版社
Culture and Art Publishing House

肆

德艺双馨

Excellence in Both Performing Skills and Moral Integrity

说起梅兰芳先生的高尚品德，首先要谈到他的祖父梅巧玲。梅巧玲是清末同治、光绪年间世称"同光十三绝"之一的著名京剧旦脚演员，为人豪爽，仗义疏财，经常照顾贫苦同行，当时亦享有"义伶"之称。梅兰芳虽未见过祖父，但继承了祖父的风范。

梅兰芳在生活中始终待人热情和蔼，谦虚恭让；在艺术上，坚持择善而从，兼收并蓄，尊重长者，扶植新秀，与同行配合默契，毫无名人架子。

梅兰芳每次演出，总是准时从容地到后台，向在场的人员打招呼问候，对龙套演员、演奏员、检场、服装等工作人员更是热情，道声"辛苦"后自己才化装。同班老演员因病不能登台，梅兰芳仍照常给"开份"（报酬）。如有演员在舞台上无意中出现错误，梅兰芳总是安慰他们，从不苛责。平时同行和朋友遇有困难时，梅兰芳也亲往慰问并毫不吝惜地给予经济补贴。抗战时期，梅兰芳蓄须明志，息影舞台，曾以鬻画和典物度日，但仍不忘接济剧团更为困难的人员。

梅兰芳大师一生具有的谦虚朴素、宽厚待人、急公好义、济贫扶危等高尚品德，至今受到人们的称颂和追思。

Mei Lanfang was very gentle and humble in his life and got recognition from art circle. Although Mei Lanfang already rose to fame when he was young, he got along well with people all along, always amiable and easy of approach, refined and courteous. Some people were attracted to, he always grant whatever was requested, answered all the questions. Relatives and friends to come to his house, he must be neatly dressed to meet; he would personally hold tea to guests. He had never look fierce and talk boisterously, even friends or students was at fault, he was with a sincere attitude, euphemistic words of advice, but also to all the audience make no exception, equal respect.

All contact with Mei Lanfang of the people know, he has no temper, he was humble and kind hearted. In the aspect of the show, when Mei Lanfang acting on the stage, no matter who comes out of the accident, he was always the first to review his own shortage. When accompaniment errors occured, some main actors often stared at them, and it was called "Fanchang" (internal conflict) in jargon. Mei Lanfang never did, but to find out accident people after walking off the stage, and then said softly: "It's my fault that didn't rehearse with you before got on the stage, or not out of this accident!"

In his daily life, Mei Lanfang cared his theatrical colleagues meticulous. Regardless of whether they are actors, accompaniment or back stage staff, who had run into financial difficulties in life, he would to assist financially. Mei Lanfang not only gave the theatre people enthusiastically help, for the other acquaintances, or even know but not familiar with Mei, no matter who had difficulties in life, old, disease, death, marriage, or funeral matters, Mei also immediately to help.

梅兰芳

《黛玉葬花》

梅兰芳饰林黛玉

Mei Lanfang as Lin Daiyu in *Daiyu Burying Flowers*

《天女散花》

梅兰芳饰天女

Mei Lanfang as Heavenly Maid in *The Heavenly Maid Showering Flowers*

《洛神》

梅兰芳饰洛神

Mei Lanfang as Goddess Luo in *The Goddess of the River Luo*

《西施》

梅兰芳饰西施

Mei Lanfang as Xishi in *Beaury Xishi*

抗战剧目

Patriotic Plays

《抗金兵》，梅兰芳饰梁红玉

Mei Lanfang as Liang Hongyu in *Fighting against the Chins*

早在1916年，梅兰芳就编演过《木兰从军》，激发人们的爱国主义精神。1932年，他南迁上海后，又于1933年和1936年编演了以反侵略为主题的《抗金兵》和《生死恨》，鼓舞民众抗敌救国，两剧对当时的爱国抗战情绪起了很大的激励作用。

Early in1916 Mei had staged a play *Mulan, the Disguised Warrior Maiden* to inspire people's patriotic spirit. In 1933 and 1936, he created and performed another two new plays *Fighting Against the Chins* and *A Wedding in the Dream* both reflected the strong patriot feeling of Chinese people against aggressors.

《抗金兵》，梅兰芳饰梁红玉（右页）

Mei Lanfang as Liang Hongyu in *Fighting against the Chins*

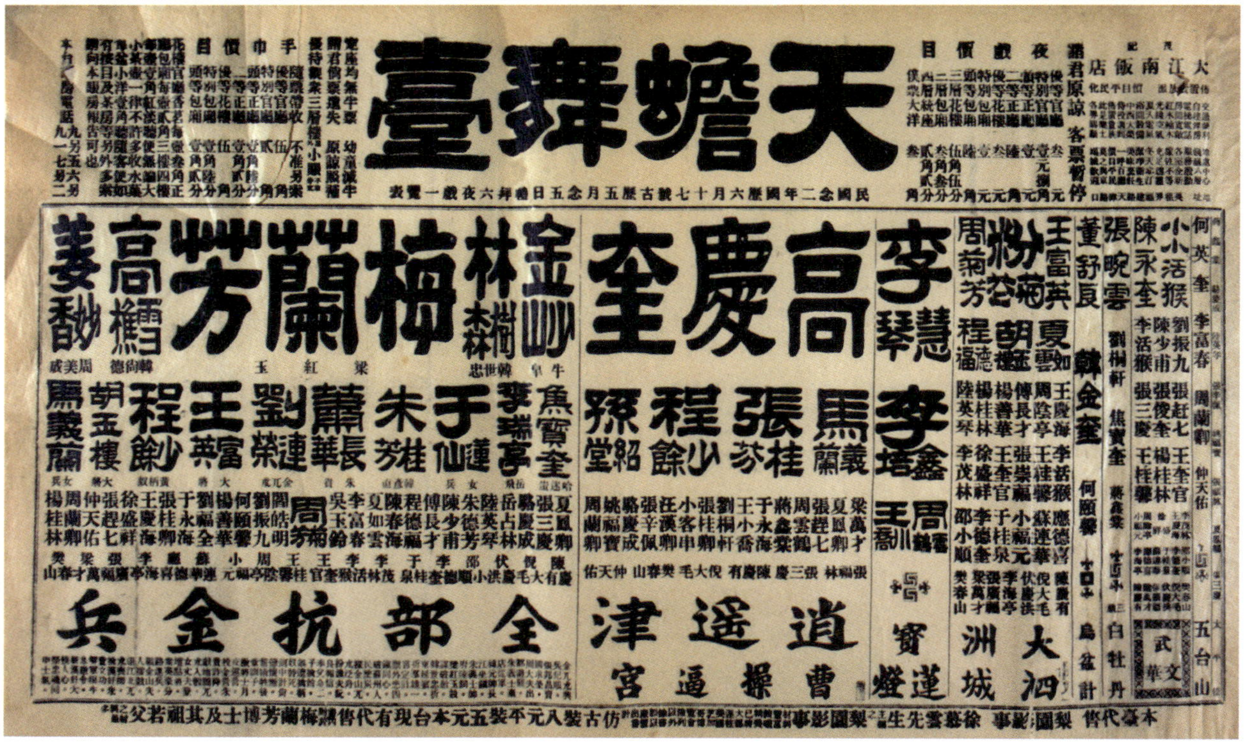

上左 | 梅兰芳演《抗金兵》时使用的道具 —— 战鼓、帅旗

The props used by Mei Lanfang in the role of Liang Hongyu in *Fighting against the Chins*

上右 | 《抗金兵》，梅兰芳饰梁红玉

Mei Lanfang as Liang Hongyu in *Fighting against the Chins*

下图 | 梅兰芳演《抗金兵》的戏单（1933）

The program of *Fighting against the Chins* (1933)

《抗金兵》，梅兰芳饰梁红玉，刘连荣饰金兀术

Mei Lanfang as Liang Hongyu and Liu Lianrong as Jin Wuzhu in *Fighting against the Chins*

《抗金兵》，梅兰芳饰梁红玉（左、右页）

Photos taken when the play *Fighting against the Chins* was being performed by Mei Lanfang on the stage

梁

梁

《生死恨》，梅兰芳饰韩玉娘（左、右页）

Mei Lanfang as Han Yuniang in *A Wedding in the Dream*

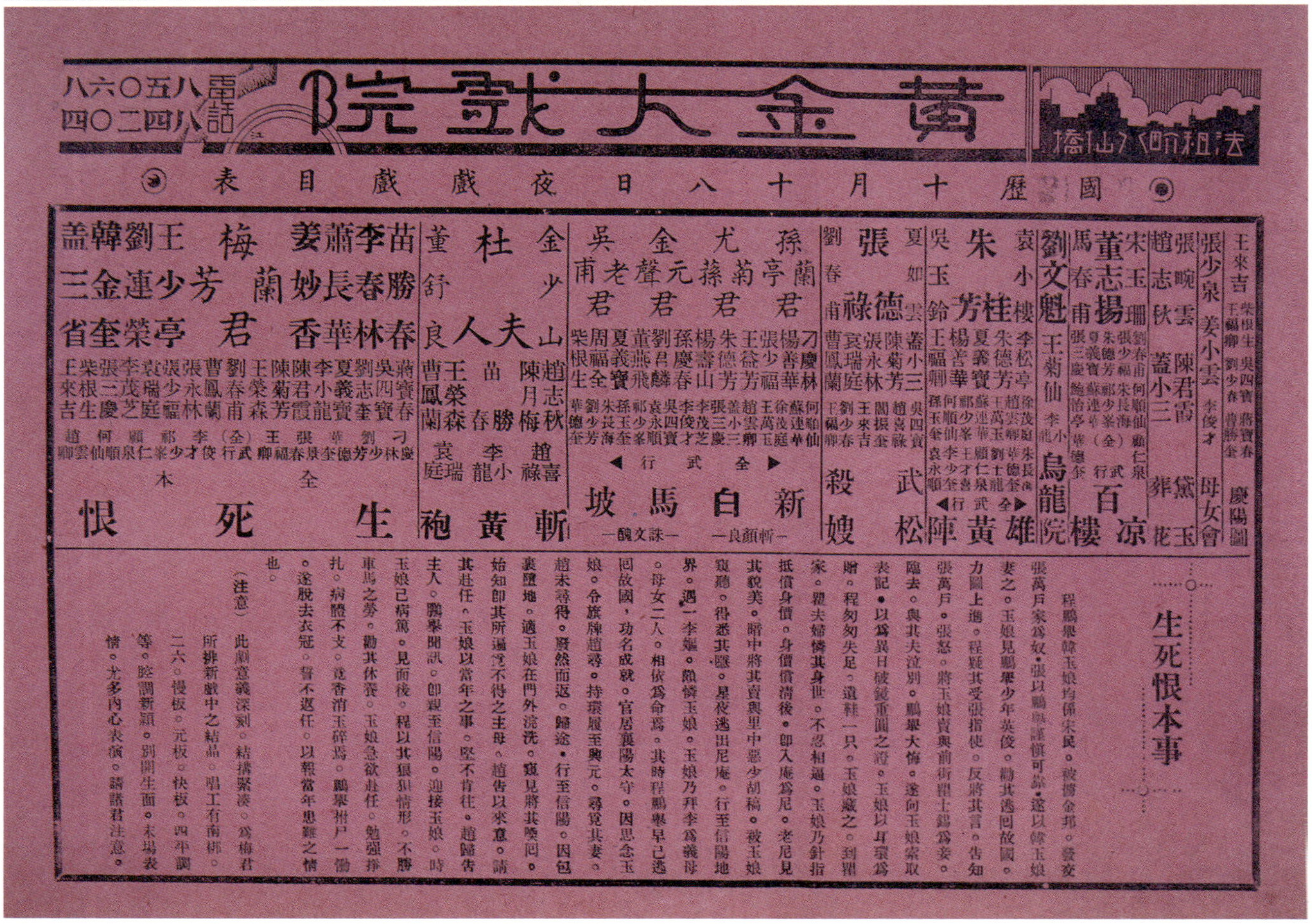

黃金大戲院

電話 八六〇五八 四〇二四八

法租界八仙橋

國曆十月十八日夜戲戲目表

慶陽圖　母女會　黛玉葬花　百涼樓　烏龍院　雄黃陣　武松殺嫂　新白馬坡（一斬顏良一　一誅文醜一）　斬黃袍

梅蘭芳　全本　生死恨

生死恨本事

程鵬舉韓玉娘均係宋民。被擄金邦。發交張萬戶家爲奴。張以鵬舉謹愼可嘉。遂以韓玉娘妻之。玉娘見鵬舉少年英俊。勸其逃回故國。力圖上進。程疑其受張指使。反將其言。告知張萬戶。張怒。將玉娘賣與前街瞿士錫爲妾。臨去。與其夫泣別。鵬舉大悔。遂向玉娘索取表記。以爲異日破鏡重圓之證。玉娘以耳環爲贈。程匆匆失足。遺鞋一只。玉娘藏之。到瞿家。瞿夫婦憐其身世。不忍相逼。玉娘乃針指抵償身價。身價償清後。即入庵爲尼。老尼見其貌美。暗中將其賣與里中惡少胡稿。被玉娘窺聽。得悉其隱。星夜逃出尼庵。行至信陽地界。遇一李媼。頗憐玉娘。玉娘乃拜李爲義母。母女二人。相依爲命焉。其時程鵬舉早已逃回故國，功名成就。官居襄陽太守。因思念玉娘。令旗牌趙尋。持環履至興元。尋覓其妻。趙未尋得。廢然而返。歸途。行至信陽。因包裹墮地。適玉娘在門外浣洗。窺見將其喚回。始知即其所遍覓不得之主母。趙告以來意。請其赴任。玉娘以當年之事。堅不肯往。趙歸告主人。鵬舉聞訊。即親至信陽。迎接玉娘。時玉娘已病篤。見面後。程以其狼狽情形。不勝車馬之勞。勸其休養。玉娘急欲赴任。勉强掙扎。病體不支。竟香消玉碎焉。鵬舉撫尸一慟。遂脫去衣冠。誓不返任。以報當年患難之情也。

（注意）此劇意義深刻。結構緊湊。爲梅君所排新戲中之結晶。唱工有南梆。二六。慢板。元板。快板。四平調等。腔調新穎。別開生面。末場表情。尤多內心表演。請諸君注意。

上左、上右丨梅兰芳演《生死恨》剧照

A Wedding in the Dream on the stage

下图丨梅兰芳演《生死恨》的戏单

The program of *A Wedding in the Dream*

梅兰芳演《生死恨》剧照

A Wedding in the Dream on the stage

蓄须明志

Grew Moustache to Keep Himself Away From the Stage

梅兰芳蓄须照

Mei Lanfang grew a moustache to keep himself away from the srage during the Japanese occupation of Shanghai

1937年7月7日，我国展开全面抗战。日本帝国主义侵略军侵占上海后，1938年初，为摆脱敌伪骚扰，梅兰芳借第4次赴香港演出之机，逃出樊笼。演出后，他便居留香港，息影舞台，深居简出，一住就是4年。1941年末，太平洋战争爆发，香港沦陷，敌寇多次逼迫他演出，他蓄起唇髭坚决抵制。1942年夏，他返回上海，与家人共患难，敌伪又多次要挟他登台庆祝所谓的“大东亚战争胜利”，他威武不屈，断然拒绝。正如他在抗战胜利后对著名作家柯灵先生所说：“他们要庆祝的，就是我们的耻辱；他们要笑的，我们该哭。我怎么能唱这个戏呢？”1943年，拒不登台的梅兰芳经济拮据，生活日益困难，遂把北平无量大人胡同寓所卖掉以维持生计，并接济穷困的同行。此后他又与叶恭绰先生在上海合办画展，以出售自己的画作度日。尽管生活困顿，但梅兰芳依然在家中授徒传艺，对抗日胜利充满了信心。

In the winter of 1937,when Shanghai was occupied by Japanese invaders, Mei found a chance to give performances in Hong Kong and then stayed there. After the Pacific War began, he was forced to go back to Shanghai in the summer of 1942, but he refused to give any performances to entertain the enemies. For this sake, he grew his moustache as a weapon. After the victory of the War of Resistance Against Japan, he once said to the well-known writer Mr.Ke Ling,"What they want to celebrate is our shame, and while they laugh we should cry. How can I perform for them!" He supported his family and impoverished colleagues by selling his Beijing house and his painting works. Although life was hard, Mei had full confidence on the final victory over the Japanese aggress ion, and taught his students at home with dignity.

梅兰芳在上海寓所作画（1943）
Mei Lanfang was painting at home in Shanghai (1943)

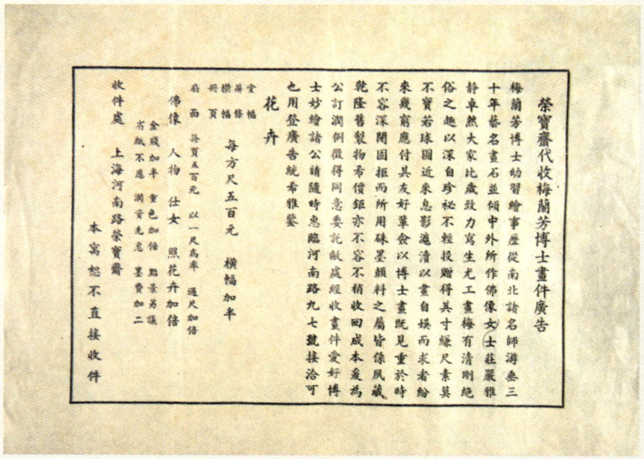

榮寶齋代收梅蘭芳博士畫件廣告

梅蘭芳博士幼習繪事歷從南北諸名師游垂三十年藝名畫石並傾中外所作佛像女士莊嚴雅靜卓然大家比歲致力寫生尤工畫梅有清剛絕俗之趣以深自珍秘不輕投贈得其寸縑尺素莫不寶若球圖近來息影滬濱以畫自娛而求者紛來幾窮應付其友好輩僉以博士畫既見重於時不容深閉固拒而所用硃墨顏料之屬皆係夙藏乾隆舊製物希價鉅亦不容不稍收回成本爰為公訂潤例徵得同意委託敝處經收畫件愛好博士妙繪諸公請隨時惠臨河南路九七號接洽可也用登廣告統希雅鑒

花卉

堂幅 屏條 橫幅 冊頁 每方尺五百元 橫幅加半

扇面 每頁五百元 以一尺為率 過尺加倍

佛像 人物 仕女 照花卉加倍

金箋加半 重色加倍 點景另議

劣紙不應 潤資先惠 墨費加二

收件處 上海河南路榮寶齋

本寓恕不直接收件

左图 | 梅兰芳绘《春消息》

Mei Lanfang's painting *The News of Spring*

右上 | 梅兰芳绘扇面

Mei's painting on the covering of a fan

右下 | 荣宝斋代收梅兰芳画件广告

The advertisement of Rong Baozhai Gallery for Dr. Mei Lanfang's painting works

梅兰芳在上海寓所作画（1943）
Mei Lanfang was painting at home in Shanghai (1943)

梅兰芳在上海寓所看剧本和剧照（1942）
Reading script and watching album at home in Shanghai (1942)

1941 年夏，福芝芳携子女由上海来香港拍摄的全家合影
（前排左起：梅葆玥、福芝芳、梅葆玖、梅兰芳，后排左起：梅绍武、梅葆琛）
Mei Lanfang and his wife with their children in the summer of 1941 in Hong Kong
(From left to right in front: Mei Baoyue. Fu Zhifang. Mei Baojiu. Mei Lanfang. From left to right in 2nd row: Mei Shaowu. Mei Baochen)

左图｜梅兰芳及夫人福芝芳携子女在香港合影（1938）
（前排左起：梅葆玖、梅葆玥，二排左起：梅葆琛、梅绍武）
Mei Lanfang and his wife Fu Zhifang with their children in Hong Kong(1938)
右图｜梅兰芳与儿子梅葆琛在香港留影
Mei Lanfang and his eldest son Baochen in Hong Kong

梅兰芳由港回沪后与夫人福芝芳合影（1942 ）
Me: Lanfang and his wife when he went back to Shanghai from Hong Kong(1942)

左图｜1932 年，梅兰芳全家迁居上海，图为马斯南路的住宅门首
The house in whick Mei Lanfang moved to Shanghai to stay in 1932
右图｜梅兰芳在上海寓所阳台上与夫人福芝芳合影
Mei Lanfang and his wife Fu Zhifang at the balcony of their house in Shanghai

梅兰芳在上海
Mei Lanfang in Shanghai

上图｜梅兰芳与夫人福芝芳及子女和名旦朱琴心（后排右一）、弟子顾正秋（前排左五）等在沪寓所院内合影（1944）

Mei Lanfang, his wife and children ,together with his disciple Miss Gu Zhengqiu (left 5th,front row)and Dan actor Zhu Qinxin(right 1st,back row) in the garden of his house(1944)

下图｜梅兰芳为弟子言慧珠（左三）说戏后，与夫人福芝芳（左二）及子女梅葆玥（右一）、梅葆玖（左一）在上海寓所合影

After teaching his disciple Yan Huizhu, Mei Lanfang(left 4th) with Yan Huizhu (left 3rd), Mrs. Mei (left 2nd), Baoyue (right 1st) and Baojiu (left 1st) at his house in Shanghai

梅兰芳在上海寓所花园内教弟子李世芳上马和舞剑姿势

Teaching his disciple Li Shifang the conventional gesture of riding on horse and sword dance in the garden of his house in Shanghai

剃须登台

Came Back on Stage Again

梅兰芳在沪寓所由琴师王少卿为其调嗓，准备重返舞台（1945）

Mei Lanfang practised his voice with his accompanist Wang Shaoqing at home in Shanghai (1945)

1945年8月15日，日寇投降，梅兰芳当即剃掉唇髭，两个月内便在上海美琪大戏院重返舞台，庆祝抗日战争的伟大胜利。他与俞振飞合作演出了昆曲《断桥》、《游园惊梦》、《奇双会》等剧目，受到上海人民的欢迎。随后，他又与杨宝森、王琴生等合作演出。1948年，他拍摄了由费穆执导的我国第一部彩色戏曲影片《生死恨》。

On hearing the news of Japanese surrender on August 15,1945. Mei shaved off his moustache at once, and after no more than 2 months, he performed *The Broken Bridge*, *The Peony Pavilion* and *A Tale of Double Reunion* with Yu Zhenfei at the Majesty Theatre in Shanghai to celebrate the victory of the War of Resistance Against Japan. They were rapturously welcomed by the audience. In 1948, *A Wedding in the Dream*, the first Chinese Technicolor film of Beijing Opera, directed by Fei Mu, with Mei as the main role, was completed.

上图｜抗战胜利，梅兰芳重返舞台时演出的剧场——上海“美琪大戏院”
The Majesty Theatre in Shanghai. Mei Lanfang reappeared on stage in this theatre after the war

下图｜梅兰芳在上海寓所的书房——“梅花诗屋”
Mei Lanfang was reading in his study in Shanghai

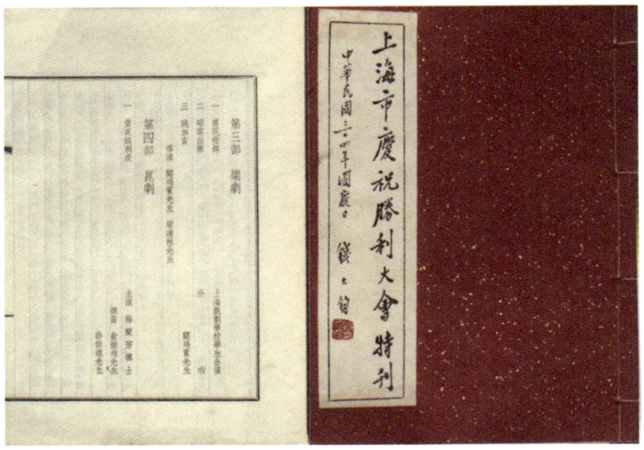

上图 | 《贞娥刺虎》，梅兰芳饰费贞娥

Mei Lanfang as Lady Fei in *Killing the Tiger General*

下图 | 抗战胜利后，梅兰芳首次登台演出《贞娥刺虎》的说明书（1945）

The program of the performance *Killing the Tiger General* given by Mei Lanfang in Shanghai after the war (1945)

《贞娥刺虎》，梅兰芳饰费贞娥

Mei Lanfang as Lady Fei in *Killing the Tiger General*

《游园惊梦》，梅兰芳饰杜丽娘，俞振飞饰柳梦梅（左、右页）
Mei Lanfang as Du Liniang and Yu Zhengfei as Liu Mengmei in *The Peony Pavilion*

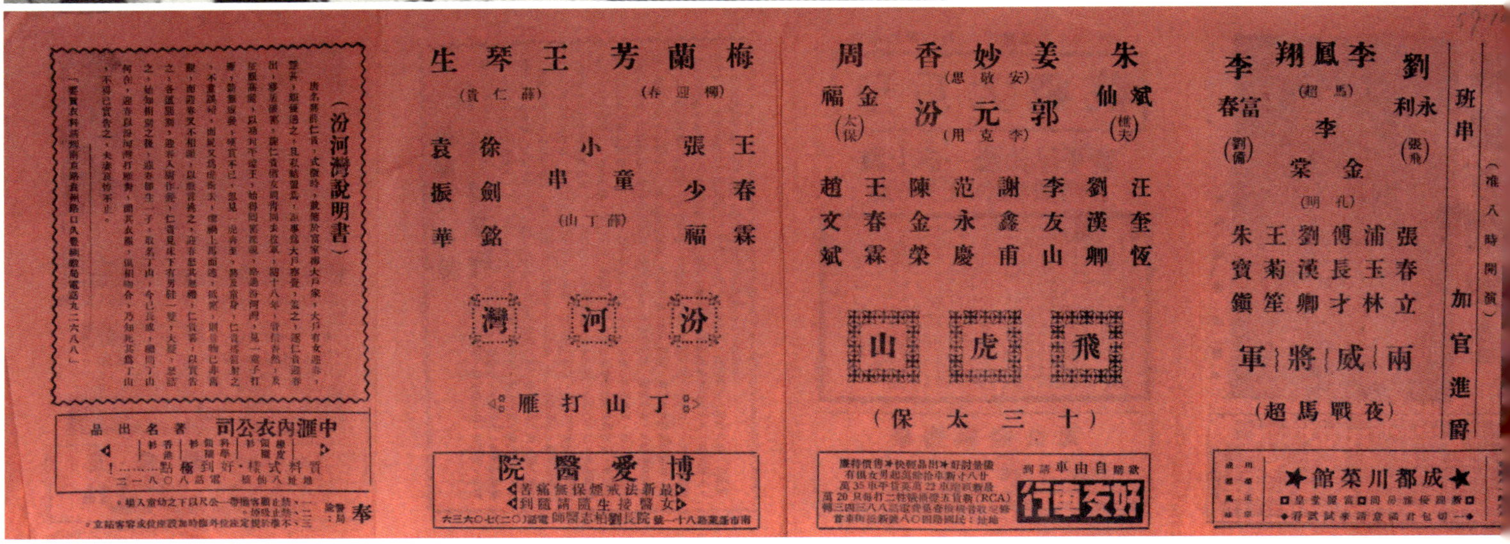
班串 （准八時開演）
加官進爵
劉永利（張飛） 李鳳翔（馬超） 李富春（劉備） 李金棠（孔明）
張春立 浦玉林 傅長才 劉漢卿 王菊笙 朱寶鏞
兩威將軍（夜戰馬超）
朱斌仙（樵夫） 姜妙香（安敬思） 周金福（太保） 郭元汾（李克用）
汪奎恆 劉漢卿 李友山 謝鑫甫 范永慶 陳金榮 王春霖 趙文斌
飛虎山（十三太保）
梅蘭芳（柳迎春） 王琴生（薛仁貴）
王春霖 張少福 小童串（薛丁山） 徐劍銘 袁振華
汾河灣（丁山打雁）
（汾河灣說明書）
博愛醫院
好友車行
成都川菜館
中滙內衣公司

上图 |《武家坡》，梅兰芳饰王宝钏
Mei Lanfang as Wang Baochuan in *The Meeting at Wujiapo*

下图 | 抗战胜利后，梅兰芳首次演出《汾河湾》的说明书（1945）
The program of the performance of *The Fen Rierbend* given by Mei Lanfang in Shanghai after the war (1945)

右页 |《汾河湾》，梅兰芳饰柳迎春，王琴生饰薛仁贵
Mei Lanfang as Liu Yingchun in *The Fen RiverBend*

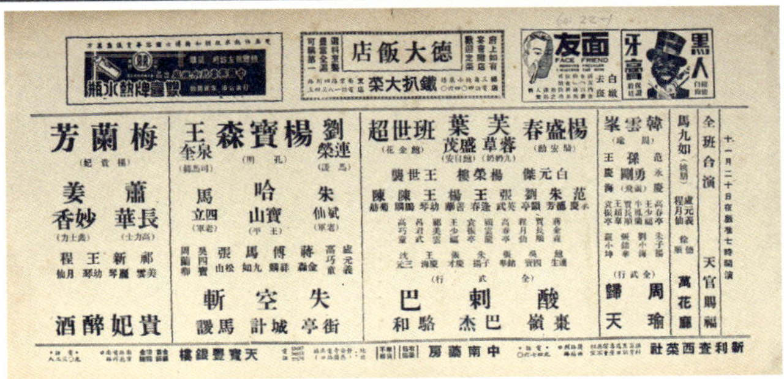

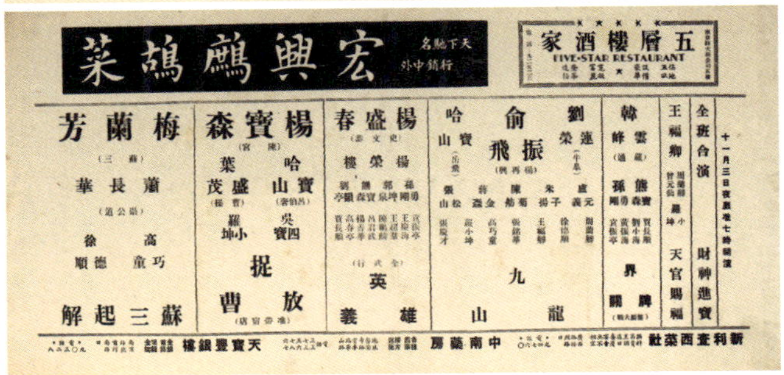

左页｜《苏三起解》，梅兰芳饰苏三，萧长华饰崇公道
Mei Lanfang as Su San and Xiao Changhua as the warder in *The Extradition of Su San*

上图｜《贵妃醉酒》，梅兰芳饰杨玉环，孙盛武饰高力士
Mei Lanfang as Yang Yuhuan and Sun Shengwu as Gao Lishi in *The Drunken Beauty*

中图｜梅兰芳演《贵妃醉酒》的戏单
The program of *The Drunken Beauty*

下图｜梅兰芳演《苏三起解》的戏单
The program of *The Extradition of Su San*

《三娘教子》，梅兰芳饰王春娥
Mei Lanfang as Wang Chun E in *Mother Educates Her stepson*

《宇宙锋》，梅兰芳饰赵艳容
Mei Lanfang as Zhao Yanrong in *Beauty Defiles Tyranny*

《宇宙锋》，梅兰芳饰赵艳容
Mei Lanfang as Zhao Yanrong in *Beauty Defiles Tyranny*

《四郎探母》，梅兰芳饰铁镜公主，马连良饰杨延辉

Mei Lanfang as Princess Tiejing and Ma Lianliang as Yang Yanhui in *Silang Visits His Mother*

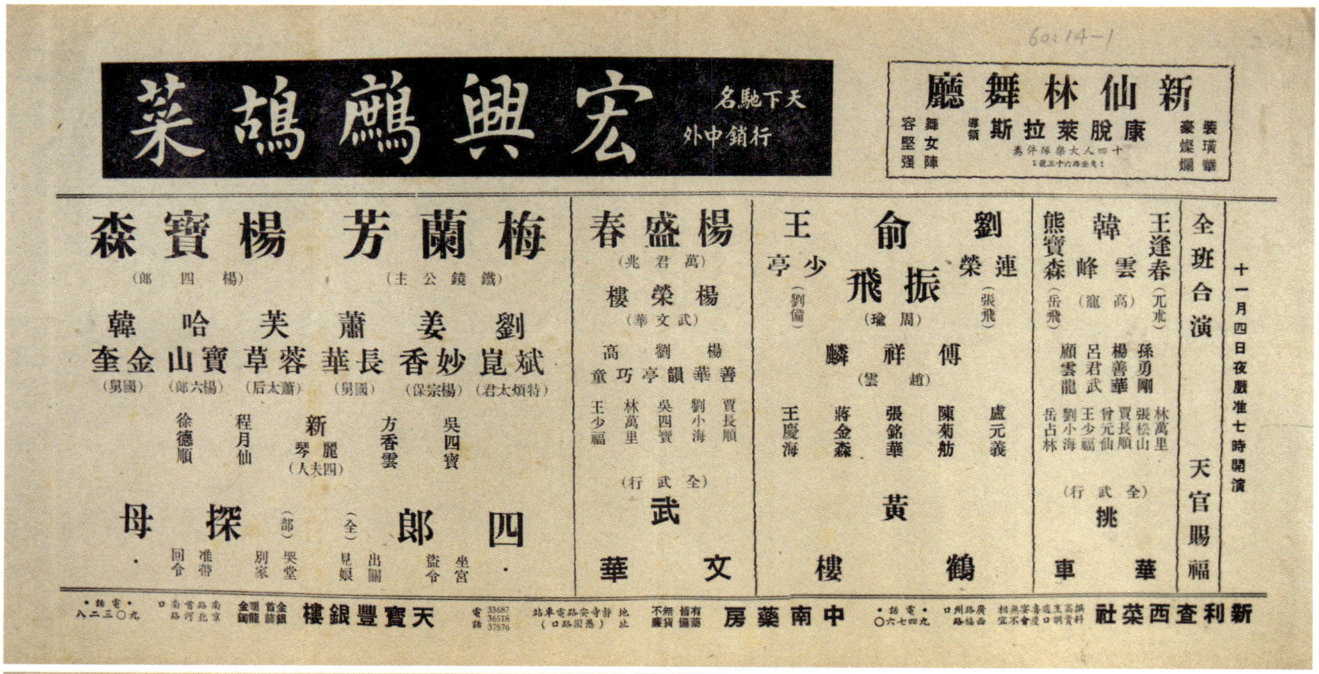

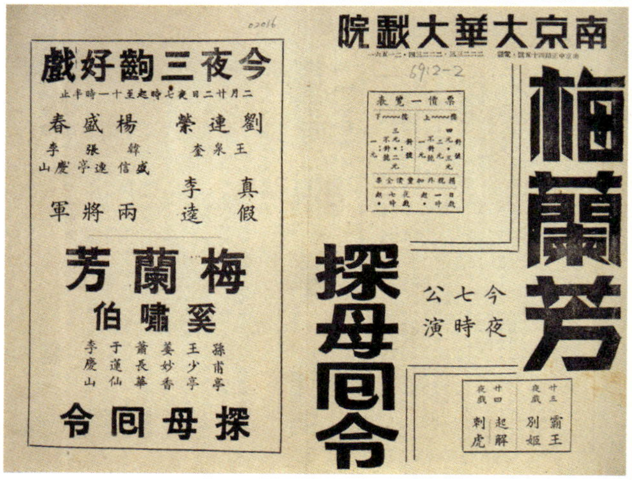

上图、下左 | 梅兰芳与杨宝森、奚啸伯合作演出《四郎探母》的戏单

The program of *Silang Visits His Mother*, performed by Mei Lanfang with Yang Baosen and Xi Xiaobo respectively

下右 | 梅兰芳饰铁镜公主

Mei Lanfang as Princess Tiejing in *Silang Visits His Mother*

《四郎探母》，梅兰芳饰铁镜公主，李少春饰杨延辉

Mei Lanfang as Princes Tiejing With Li Shaochun as Yang Yanhui respectively in *Silang Visits His Mother*

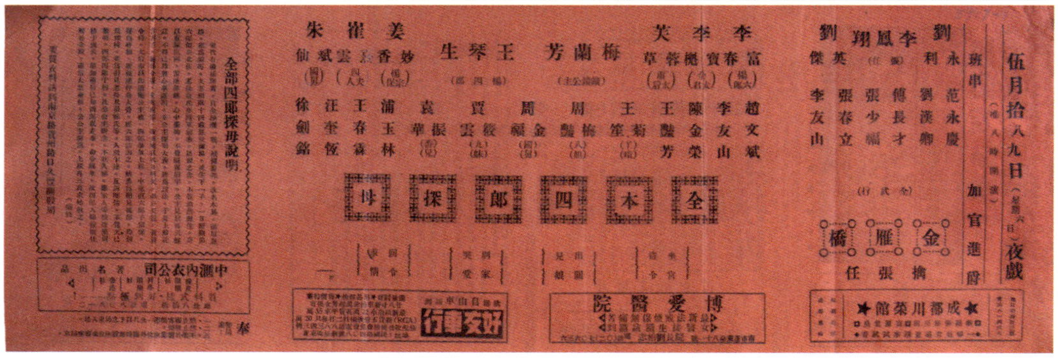

上、中图 | 《四郎探母》，梅兰芳饰铁镜公主，李少春饰杨延辉

Mei Lanfang as Princess Tiejing with Li Shaochun as Yang Yanhui respectively in *Silang Visits His Mother*

下图 | 梅兰芳与王琴生合作演出《四郎探母》的戏单

The program of *Silang Visits His Mother*, performed by Mei Lanfang with Wang Qinsheng respectively

《回荆州》，梅兰芳饰孙尚香，王少亭饰刘备（左一），杨盛春饰赵云（右一）
Mei Lanfang as Sun Shangxiang, Wang Shaoting as Liu Bei and Yang Shengchun as Zhao Yun in *Back to Jingzhou*

上图 | 《美人计》，梅兰芳饰孙尚香，谭富英饰刘备
Mei Lanfang as Sun Shangxiang and Tan Fuying as Liu Bei in *A Beauty's Ruse*
下图 | 《美人计》，梅兰芳饰孙尚香
Mei Lanfang as Sun Shangxiang in *A Beauty's Ruse* on stage

《樊江关》，梅兰芳饰薛金莲，魏莲芳（左）饰樊梨花
Mei Lanfang as Xue Jinlian and Wei Lianfang as Fan Lihua in *Fanjiang Pass*

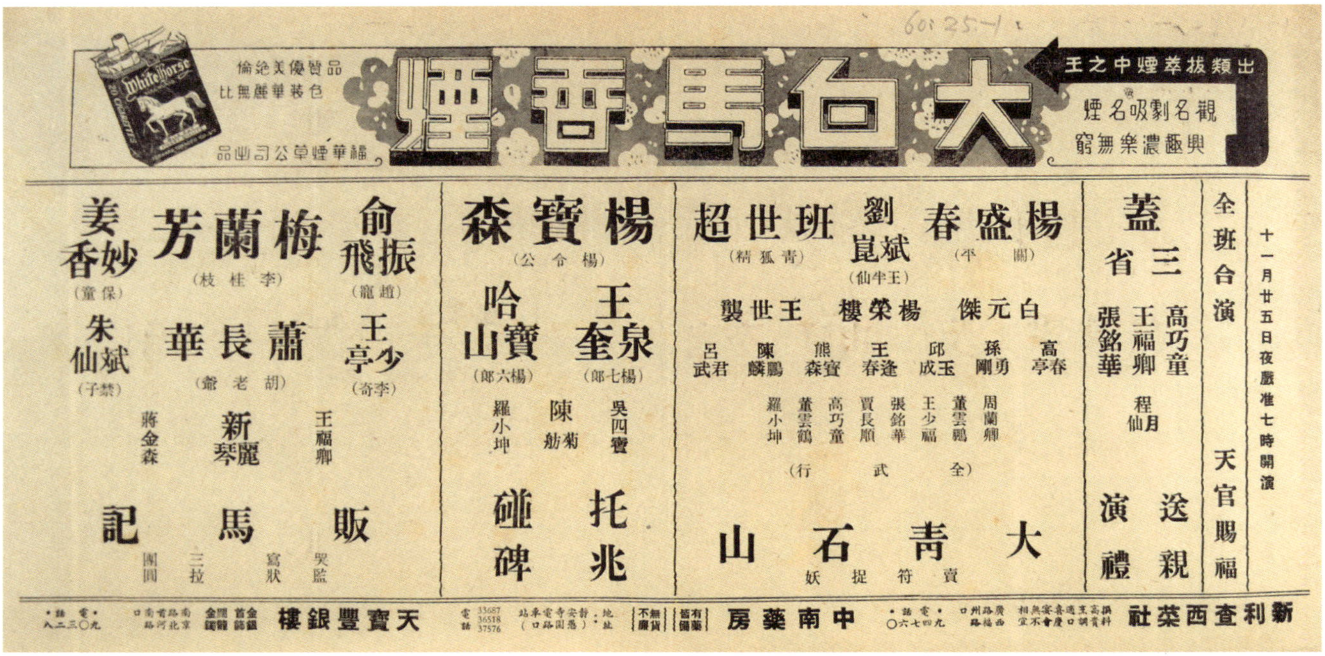

上图｜梅兰芳演《贩马记》的戏单

The program of *A Tale of Selling Horses*

下图｜《贩马记》，梅兰芳饰李桂枝

Mei Lanfang as Li Guizhi in *A Tale of Selling Horses*

《生死恨》，梅兰芳饰韩玉娘
Mei Lanfang as Han Yuniang in *A Wedding in the Dream*

上图、右页 | 拍摄《生死恨》电影剧照，梅兰芳饰韩玉娘，姜妙香饰程鹏举

Mei Lanfang as Han Yuniang and Jiang Miaoxiang as Cheng Pengju in the film *A Wedding in the Dream*

下图 | 1948 年，梅兰芳拍摄我国第一部彩色戏曲电影《生死恨》说明书封面

The cover of the synopsis of *A Wedding in the Dream*, the first Chinese technicolor film of Beijing Opera

梅兰芳在上海沪西俱乐部打高尔夫球（1947）
Mei Lanfang played golf at a club in Shanghai (1947)

左图｜梅兰芳在上海寓所与弟子李世芳（后排右一）、白玉薇等合影（1946）
With his disciples Li Shifang and Bai Yuwei in his house in Shanghai (1946)

右图｜梅兰芳在上海寓所与弟子李世芳（右二）等合影（1946）
With his disciple Li Shifang and other friends in his house in Shanghai (1946)

梅兰芳与张大千在上海（1948）合影
Mei Lanfang and Zhang Daqian in Shanghai (1948)

梅兰芳（右二）与丰子恺（右一）、郎静山（左二）等在上海合影（1947）
Mei Lanfang (right 2nd), Feng Zikai(right 1st) and Lang Jingshan(Left 2nd) in Shanghai(1947)

赈灾济贫

Raised Relief Funds to Aid the Victims of Natural Calamities and the Poor

梅兰芳对公益事业极为热心，经常义务演出。过去每至旧历年底，北京梨园界都会例行演出几场大型义务戏，俗称“窝窝头会”，所得票款全部救济贫苦同行，梅兰芳均鼎力支持（有时担任主持）并参加演出。梅兰芳迁居上海后，每到岁末仍组织此类义演，将票款汇到北京，分给贫苦同行。

新中国成立前，各地经常发生严重灾害，某些团体在举办济贫等公益活动时，一般均邀请梨园界人士义演募款。梅兰芳积极参加赈灾济贫的义演，多主演大轴戏，有时也反串角色以助声势，使募款大为增加。

Throughout his life,Mei was zealous for the commonweal to help the distressed and succor those in peril. He used to give benefit performances in Beijing, Shanghai and Hankou for aiding the victims of natural calamities and the impoverished colleague, Likewise, he raised funds for an oversea Chinese school in Kobe during his first tour to Japan in 1919, in 1923, he contributed a large sum to Japan for aiding the victims of the earthquake. In 1956, he gave several benefit performances in Tokyo.

举办义演的团体赠给梅兰芳“热心公益”的银盾

A silver shield-shaped prize medal presented to Mei Lanfang by an organization, which sponsored Mei's Benefit Performances, for his untiring zeal for the Public Welfare

上图 | 《虮蜡庙》，张伯驹饰黄天霸，钱宝森饰张桂兰，梅兰芳饰褚彪，李仲恩饰贺仁杰，徐兰沅饰关泰

Zhang Boju as Huang Tianba, Qian Baosen as Zhang Guilan, Mei Lanfang as Chubiao, Li Zhongen as He Renjie and Xu Lanyuan as Guantai in *Baza Temple*

下图 | 1928 年 1 月 13 日，北京第一舞台上演义务戏，图为《大登殿》剧照，梅兰芳饰王宝钏（左一），杨小楼饰薛平贵（左五），尚小云饰代战公主（左四），李多奎饰王夫人（左二）

A benefit performance at The First Stage of Beijing on January 13 th, 1928. *Come to the Throne*,Mei as Wang Baochuan(left 1st), Yang Xiaolou as Xue Pingui(left 5th), Shang Xiaoyun as Princess Dai zhan(left 4th), Li Duokui as Madame Wang(left 2nd)

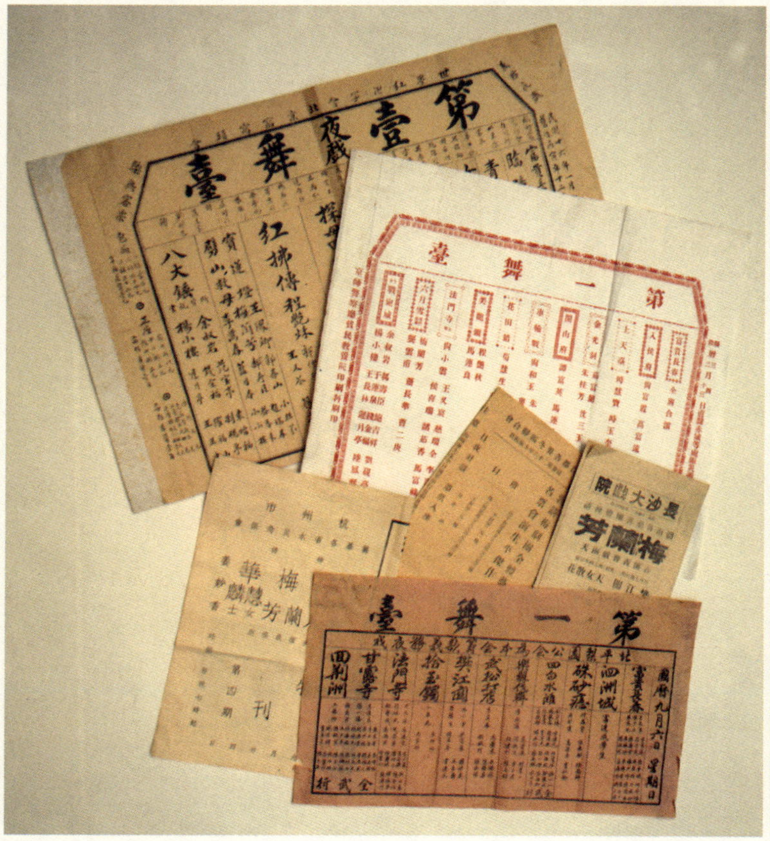

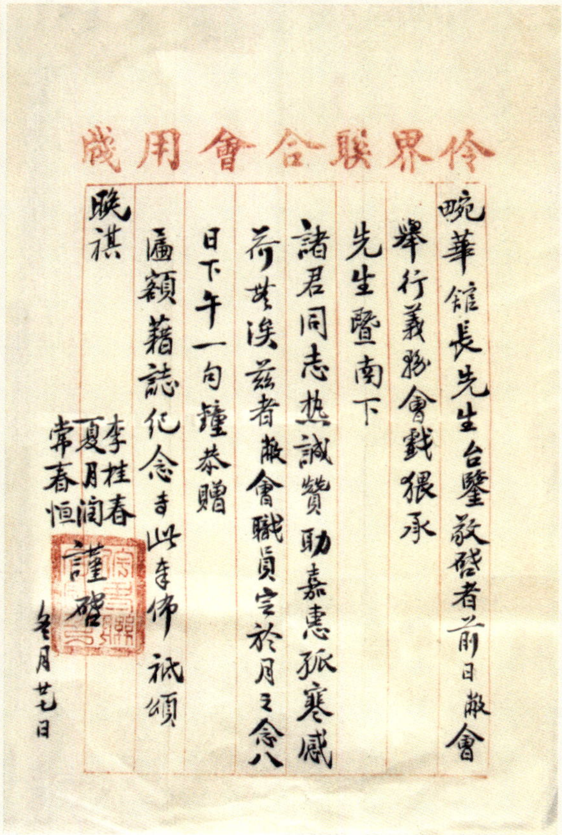
伶界聯合會用箋

畹華館長先生台鑒敬啓者前日敝會
舉行義務會戲猥承
先生暨南下
諸君同志熱誠贊助嘉惠孤寒感
荷莫溪茲者敝會職員定於月之念八
日下午一句鐘恭贈
匾額藉誌紀念并與李佛祇頌
暇祺
李桂春 夏月潤 常春恒 謹啓
冬月廿七日

左图｜梅兰芳参加义演的戏单

The program of the performances given by Mei Lanfang in several cities for aiding the victims of natural calamities

右图｜义演举办方写给梅兰芳的感谢信

Letter of gratitude for the benefit performance

右页｜梅兰芳佩戴义演举办方赠予的奖章

Wearing a medal awarded to him for his benefit performances to aid the victims of natural calamities and the poor

上图｜赈灾义演举办方赠送的奖杯、奖牌
Mei Lanfang and the souvenirs presented to him by the organizations which sponsored the benefit performances

下图｜20世纪30年代，梅兰芳在汉口参加义演后与金少山（右）、余洪元（中）合影
With Jin Shaoshan (right) and Yu Hongyuan (central) after a benefit performance in Hankou during the 1930s

在天津参加义演后，梅兰芳与杨小楼、尚小云、马连良、于连泉、李万春等合影
Mei Lanfang with Yang Xiaolou, Shang Xiaoyun, Ma Lianliang, Yu Lianquan and Li Wanchun after a benefit performance in Tianjin

在上海参加义演后，梅兰芳与金少山、谭小培、王少卿、李斐叔、姚玉芙及当地各界人士合影

Mei Lanfang with Jin Shaoshan, Tan Xiaopei, Wang Shaoqing, Li Feishu, Yao Yufu and some local deputies after giving a benefit performance in Shanghai

在汉口参加义演后，梅兰芳与萧长华、徐兰沅、南铁生及当地人士合影

Mei Lanfang with Xiao Changhua , Xu Lanyuan, Nan Tiesheng and others after giving a benefit performance in Hankou

伍

老骥伏枥

Vitality and Splendour

1949年，中华人民共和国成立后，梅兰芳在北京参加全国文代会、全国政协会议和全国人大会议，出任中国戏曲研究院、中国京剧院和中国戏曲学院院长。1959年加入中国共产党。他在全国各地巡回演出，受到各地群众的热烈欢迎。他率团访问日本、朝鲜、苏联、奥地利等国。1959年，他荣获国际舞蹈协会颁发的荣誉奖章。他拍摄彩色舞台艺术片，撰写回忆录，热心授徒传艺，晚年还编演了新戏《穆桂英挂帅》。1961年8月8日，他在北京因病逝世，终年67岁。

After the founding of the People's Republic of China in 1949, Mei went back to Beijing to attend the meetings of the People's Political Consultative Conference, the National People's Congress and the All-China Conference of Literary and Art Delegates. He was appointed President of the Research Institute of Traditional Chinese Drama and of the College of Chinese Drama, as well as Director of the National Beijing Opera Theatre. He joined the Communist Party of China in 1959. His tour of giving performances all around the country was warmly welcomed by the masses. In 1956, He led a national troupe of Beijing Opera to Japan. He also visited the Soviet Union, the Democratic People's Republic of Korea and Austria. In 1959, the International Association of Dance awarded him with a honourary medal. Many technicolour films of his masterpieces performed by himself were made during the fifties. His autobiography Forty Years On Stage was published, and he trained his students enthusiastically. In his late years, he produced and added to his repertoire a new opera Mu Guiying Takes Command. On August 8th, 1961, he died in Beijing at the age of 67.

《廉锦枫》

梅兰芳饰廉锦枫

Mei Lanfang as Lian Jinfeng in *Lian Jinfeng*

《木兰从军》

梅兰芳饰花木兰

Mei Lanfang as Hua Mulan in *Mulan, the Disguised Warrior Maiden*

《贵妃醉酒》

梅兰芳饰杨玉环

Mei Lanfang as Yang Yuhuan in *The Drunken Beauty*

《太真外传》

梅兰芳饰杨玉环

Mei Lanfang as Yang Yuhuan in *The Legend of Yang Yuhuan*

社会活动

Social Activities

梅兰芳在天安门城楼上参加开国典礼

Mei Lanfang attended the founding ceremony of the People's Republic of China at Tian'anmen rostrum (Oct. 1, 1949)

1949年10月1日，梅兰芳在天安门城楼上参加了开国典礼。从此他积极参加各种社会活动，先后当选为全国人民代表大会代表、中国人民政治协商会议全国委员会常务委员、中国文学艺术界联合会副主席和中国戏剧家协会副主席。1952年赴维也纳出席了世界人民和平大会，1953年参加中国人民赴朝慰问团，1957年赴苏联参加庆祝十月革命40周年的庆祝活动，1960年再赴苏联庆祝《中苏友好同盟互助条约》签订10周年，并访问阿塞拜疆共和国首都巴库。

On October 1st, 1949, Mei attended the founding ceremony of the People's Republic of China at Tian'anmen rostrum. He was then elected deputy to the National People's Congress and a member of the Standing Committee of the National Committee of the People's Political Consultative Conference. He was also elected a vice chairman of the China Federation of Literary and Art Circles and of the Chinese Dramatists' Union. In 1952, he went to Vienna to attend the People's Conference for World Peace. In 1957 and 1960, he went to Russia to attend respectively the celebrations for the 40th anniversary of the October Revolution and the 10th anniversary of the Sino-Soviet Treaty of Friendship, Alliance and Mutual Assistance.

上图｜梅兰芳与程砚秋（左一）、周信芳（右一）、袁雪芬（左二）出席政协会时合影

Mei Lanfang ,Cheng Yanqiu (left 1st), and Zhou Xinfang(right 1st) and Yuan Xuefen(left 2nd) at the First Plenary Session of the First People's Political Consultative Conference (1949)

下图｜梅兰芳与梁思成（右二）、老舍（右三）、华罗庚（左一）出席政协会时合影

With Liang Sicheng(right 2nd), Lao She(right 3rd) and Hua Luogeng (Left 1st) during the Session of the People's Political Consultative Conference

世界人民和平大會
維也納 一九五二·十二

代表證

姓名 MEI LAN FANG
Nom, prénom

國家 CHINE
Pays

組織委員會
Pour la Commission d'Organisation

上图｜梅兰芳出席在维也纳举行的世界人民和平大会时（第三排正中间）留影（1952）
At the People's Conference for World peace in Vienna, Austria (Mei at the center of 3rd row) in 1952

下图｜世界人民和平大会代表证
Delegate certificate of the People's Conferrence for World Peace

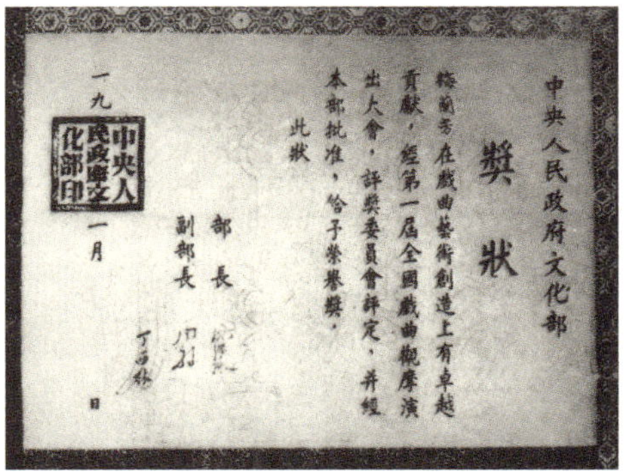
中央人民政府文化部

奬狀

梅蘭芳在戲曲藝術創造上有卓越貢獻，經第一屆全國戲曲觀摩演出大會，評奬委員會評定，并經本部批准，給予榮譽奬，

此狀

部長

副部長

一九　一月　日

中央人民政府文化部印

上图｜梅兰芳在第一届全国戏曲观摩演出大会上讲话（1952）

Mei Lanfang was giving a speech at the session of the 1st National Exhibition of Chinese Opera (1952)

中图｜文化部第一届全国戏曲观摩演出大会后领奖照（从右至左：王瑶卿、袁雪芬、梅兰芳、周信芳、程砚秋、常香玉、盖叫天）（1952）

Mei Lanfang at the first session of the repertoire fesetival organized bythe Ministry of Culture (1952)

下图｜文化部授予梅兰芳的荣誉奖状（1952）

The honourary certificate of merit awarded to Mei Lanfang by the Ministry of Culture (1952)

1957年4月18日，毛泽东陪同苏联最高苏维埃主席团主席伏罗希洛夫元帅观看梅兰芳演出后上台慰问演员

Accompanied by Chairman Mao Zedong, Marshal Voroshilov, Chairmen of the presidium of the Supreme Sovite of the U.S.S.R , came to the stage after watching Mei's performance

上图 | 1953 年，梅兰芳参加中国人民赴朝慰问团

Mei Lanfang as a member of the Chinese People's Delegation for Conveying Greetings and Appreciation went to the Democratic People's Republic of Korea in 1953

下左 | 梅兰芳在文代会上与盖叫天（左一）、周信芳（右一）合影

Mei Lanfang and Gai Jiaotian (left First), Zhou Xinfang (right 1st) at the Conference of Chinese Literary and Art Circles

下右 | 梅兰芳（前排右二）与宋庆龄（前排中）、郭沫若（前排左二）、常香玉（前排左一）出席苏联对外文化协会举行的招待会时与协会代表合影

Mei Lanfang (front right 2nd), Song Qingling (front right 3rd), Guo Moruo (front left 2nd) and Chang Xiangyu (front left 1st) with Soviet friends at the reception held by the VOKS in Moscow

上图｜梅兰芳在北京与阿塞拜疆外宾座谈时合影
With guests from Azerbaijan in Beijing
下图｜1954 年 10 月，印度总理尼赫鲁访华时会见梅兰芳
Indian Prime Minister Nehru met Mei Lanfang in Beijing
(October,1954)

上图｜梅兰芳（左三）出席全国人民代表大会时与田汉（左二）等合影（1954）
With Tian Han and others at the National People's Congress (1954)
下图｜梅兰芳在全国人民代表大会上投票
Mei Lanfang cast a vote at the National People's Congress

左图｜梅兰芳、周信芳在纪念大会上接受献花
Mei Lanfang and Zhou Xinfang receiving flowers at the commemoration meeting

右图｜梅兰芳在“梅兰芳周信芳舞台生活五十年纪念会”上讲话
Mei Lanfang gave a speech at the meeting in commemoration of the 50th anniversary of his stage life

1955 年 4 月，梅兰芳、周信芳与首都记者合影
Mei Lanfang，Zhou Xinfang with the journalists in Beijing(April, 1955)

1955 年 1 月 10 日，梅兰芳参加中国京剧院成立大会时与会者合影
At the ceremony of the founding of the National Beijing Opera Theatre (January. 10th, 1955)

大 會 一九五五年一月十日

上图｜梅兰芳演出《贵妃醉酒》后与罗马尼亚外宾合影（1955）
Mei Lanfang with Romanian guests after the performance of *The Drunken Beauty*(1955)
下图｜梅兰芳演出《洛神》后在舞台上与印度电影代表团团长普拉·卡普尔亲切握手（1955）
Mei Lanfang shook hands with the head of the Delegation of Indian Films after the performance of *The Goddess of the River Luo*(1955)

梅兰芳在北京向国际友人介绍京剧的服装和道具

Mei Lanfang introduced the costumes and properties of Beijing Opera to the foreigners

上左 | 梅兰芳登台拜见印度艺术家乌黛香卡（1957）
With Indian dancer Udaichenka (1957)

上右 | 梅兰芳在陕西演出后与印尼外宾及当地领导在舞台上合影（1957）
With Indonesian guests and Shanxi provincial officers in Shanxi after a performance(1957)

下左 | 梅兰芳在北京会见苏联舞蹈家乌兰诺娃（左一）时与田汉（右一）、小白玉霜（右二）等合影（1959）
With Soviet ballerina Galina Ulannowa (left 1st), Tian Han (right 1st) and Xiao Bai Yushuang (right 2nd) in Beijing (1959)

下右 | 梅兰芳接受国际舞蹈协会授予的奖章（1957）
Mei Lanfang accepted the medal awarded by the International Association of Dance (1957)

1960年7月23日，毛泽东（左一）接见梅兰芳（右二）、老舍（右一）、田汉（右三）
Mao Zedong received Mei Lanfang (right 2nd), Lao She(right 1st) and Tian Han(right 3rd)(July 23th 1960)

上图｜1957年7月，梅兰芳（左二）与韩世昌（左一）、白云生（左三）等庆祝北昆建院演出《游园惊梦》后，周恩来（右一）登上舞台接见演员

Zhou Enlai met Mei Lanfang , Han Shichang and BaiYunsheng after the performance of *The Peony Pavilion* in celebrating the founding of the North Kun qu Opera Theatre (1957)

下图｜程砚秋逝世一周年纪念时，周恩来（左四）和邓颖超（左一）在中南海接见梅兰芳（左五）及程砚秋夫人果素瑛（右二）等（1959）

Zhou Enlai and Deng Yingchao received Mei Lanfang and Guo Suying (Cheng Yanqiu's wife) and others in Zhong nan hai, Beijing, at the time of commemorating the 1st anniversary of the death of Cheng Yanqiu (1959)

1957年3月，庆祝“三八国际妇女节”演出后，陈毅（左六）与梅兰芳（左五）等合影

Mei Lanfang with Chen Yi after the performance for celebrating Women's Day in March 1957

1959 年 3 月，梅兰芳加入中国共产党
Mei Lanfang was taking an oath to join the Communist Party of China(March, 1959)

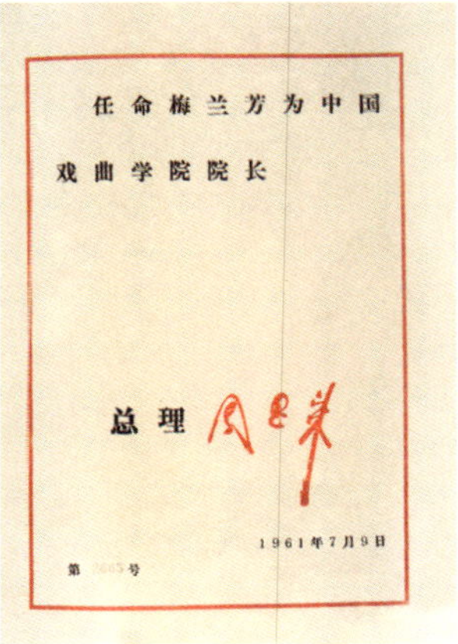

任命梅兰芳为中国戏曲学院院长

总理 周恩来

1961年7月9日

第[illegible]号

上图｜周恩来（前排右一）、陈毅（三排右一）、贺龙（四排右三）在中南海西花厅接见有关人员及梅兰芳、田汉、马少波等

China state leaders met the artist (including Mei Lanfang , Tian Han , Ma Shaobo etc)

下图｜周恩来任命梅兰芳为中国戏曲学院院长的任命书

The appointment of the presidest of the Academy of China Theatre given by Zhou Enlai

各地演出

Performances All Around the Country

新中国成立后，梅兰芳率领梅兰芳京剧团经常到全国各地巡回演出，常演的剧目有《贵妃醉酒》、《宇宙锋》、《断桥》、《霸王别姬》、《凤还巢》和《奇双会》等。每到一处，均受到当地各界群众的热烈欢迎。此外，梅兰芳还经常到各处举行慰问演出或义演。

After the founding of the People's Republic of China, Mei toured the country with his performing troupe and met warm welcome everywhere. In addition, he often gave benefit or salute performances here and there.

梅兰芳在全国各地演出的戏单

The programs of Mei's performance in various cities

《贵妃醉酒》，梅兰芳饰杨玉环
Yang Yuhuan in *The Drunken Beauty* performed by Mei Lanfang

《贵妃醉酒》，梅兰芳饰杨玉环的不同身段（左、右页）
Various gestures and postures of Yang Yuhuan in *The Drunken Beauty* performed by Mei Lanfang

《贵妃醉酒》，梅兰芳饰杨玉环，姜妙香饰裴力士，萧长华饰高力士（左、右页）

The Drunken Beauty on the stage , Mei Lanfang as Yang Yuhuan, Jiang Miaoxiang and Xiao Changhua as two royal attendants

《贵妃醉酒》剧照(左、右页)

The Drunken Beauty on the stage

《金山寺》，梅兰芳饰白素贞

Mei Lanfang as Lady White in *The Legend of White Snake Lady*

《金山寺》，梅兰芳饰白素贞，梅葆玖饰青儿

Mei Lanfang as Lady White and Mei Baojiu as Qing Er in *The Legend of White Snake Lady*

《金山寺》，梅兰芳饰白素贞，梅葆玖饰青儿

Mei Lanfang as Lady White and Mei Baojiu as Qing Er in *The Legend of White Snake Lady*

上图 |《金山寺》，梅兰芳饰白素贞，俞振飞饰许仙，梅葆玖饰青儿
Mei Lanfang as Lady White, Mei Baojiu as Qing Er and Yu Zhenfei as Xu Xian in *The Legend of White Snake Lady*

下图 |《金山寺》，梅兰芳饰白素贞，姜妙香饰许仙，梅葆玖饰青儿
Mei Lanfang as Lady White, Jiang Miaoxiang as Xu Xian and Mei Baojiu as Qing Er in *The Legend of White Snake Lady*

《穆柯寨》，梅兰芳饰穆桂英的不同身段（左、右页）

Various gestures and postures of Mu Guiying in *Mu's Village Fortress* performed by Mei Lanfang

《枪挑穆天王》，梅兰芳饰穆桂英

Mei Lanfang as Mu Guiying in *Triumph over Mu Tianwang*

《炝挑穆天王》，梅兰芳饰穆桂英，姜妙香饰杨宗保

Mei Lanfang as Mu Guiying and Jiang Miaoxiang as Yang Zongbao in *Triumph over Mu Tianwang*

《洛神》，梅兰芳饰洛神（左、右页）
Mei Lanfang as Goddess Luo in *The Goddess of River Luo*

上图 |《宇宙锋》，梅兰芳饰赵艳容
Mei Lanfang as Zhao Yanrong in *Beauty Defies Tyranny*

下图 |《宇宙锋》，梅兰芳饰赵艳容，刘连荣饰赵高，朱桂芳饰哑奴
Mei Lanfang as Zhao Yanrong, Liu Lianrong as Zhao Gao and Zhu Guifang as the maid in *Beauty Defies Tyranny*

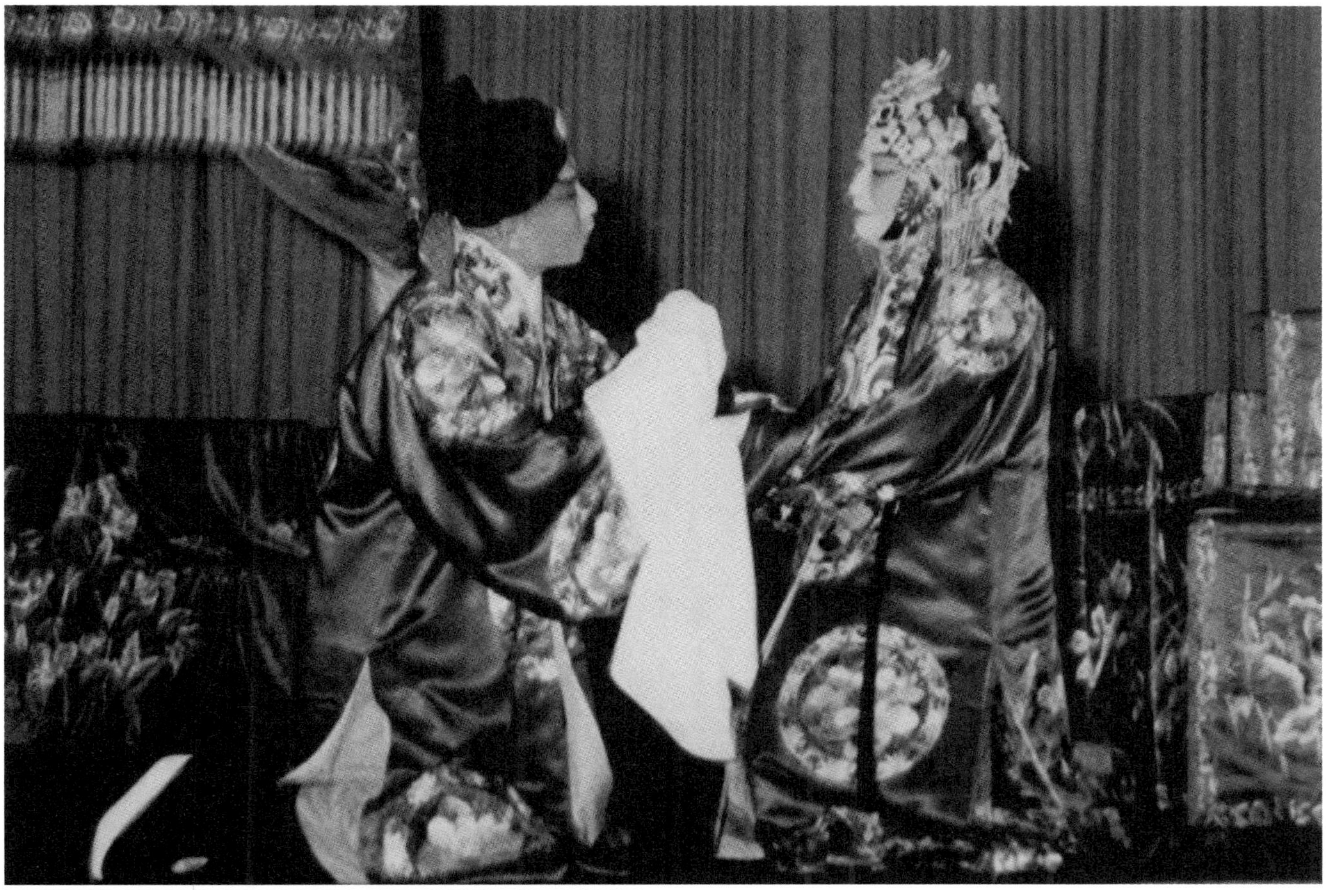

《凤还巢》，梅兰芳饰程雪娥，姜妙香饰穆居易

Mei Lanfang as Cheng Xue E and Jiang Miaoxiang as Mu Juyi in *The Phoenix Returns to Its Nest*

《凤还巢》全体演员谢幕，同台演出的有萧长华、姜妙香、王少亭、刘连荣、朱斌仙、李春林、耿世华

Mei Lanfang, Xiao Changhua, Jiang Miaoxiang, Wang Shaoting , Liu Lianrong, Zhu Binxian , Li Chunlin and Geng Shihui after the performance of *The Phoenix Returns to Its Nest*

《凤还巢》，梅兰芳饰程雪娥的不同身段（左、右页）

Various gestures and postures of Cheng Xue E in *The Phoenix Returns to Its Nest* performed by Mei Lanfang

《游园惊梦》，梅兰芳饰杜丽娘，姜妙香饰柳梦梅
Mei Lanfang as Du Liniang and Jiang Miaoxiang as Liu Mengmei in *The Peony Pavilion*

《游园惊梦》，梅兰芳饰杜丽娘，梅葆玖饰春香

Mei Lanfang as Du Liniang and Mei Baojiu as Chun Xiang in *The Peony Pavilion*

《西施》，梅兰芳饰西施

Mei Lanfang as Xi Shi in *Beauty Xi Shi*

《西施》，梅兰芳饰西施，同台演出的有王少亭、张蝶芬
Mei Lanfang as Xi Shi in *Beauty Xi Shi*.With Wang Shaoting and Zhang Diefen

左图 |《抗金兵》，梅兰芳饰梁红玉，王琴生饰韩世忠
Mei Lanfang as Liang Hongyu and Wang Qinsheng as Han Shizhong in *Fighting Against the Chins*

右图 |《抗金兵》，梅兰芳饰梁红玉
Mei Lanfang as Liang Hongyu in *Fighting Against the Chins*

《奇双会》，梅兰芳饰李桂枝，姜妙香饰赵宠（左、右页）
Mei Lanfang as Li Guizhi and Jiang Miaoxiang as Zhao Chong in *A tale of Double Reunion*

《奇双会》，梅兰芳饰李桂枝

Mei Lanfang as Li Guizhi in *A Tale of Double Reunion*

《奇双会》，梅兰芳饰李桂枝，同台演出的有俞振飞、王少亭等
Mei Lanfang as Li Guizhi in *A Tale of Double Reunion*, with Yu Zhenfei, Wang Shaoting and others

《霸王别姬》，梅兰芳饰虞姬（左、右页）
Mei Lanfang as Yuji in *The King's Parting with His Favorite*

梅兰芳在北京门头沟和煤矿工人在一起

Mei Lanfang with coal miners at Mentougou

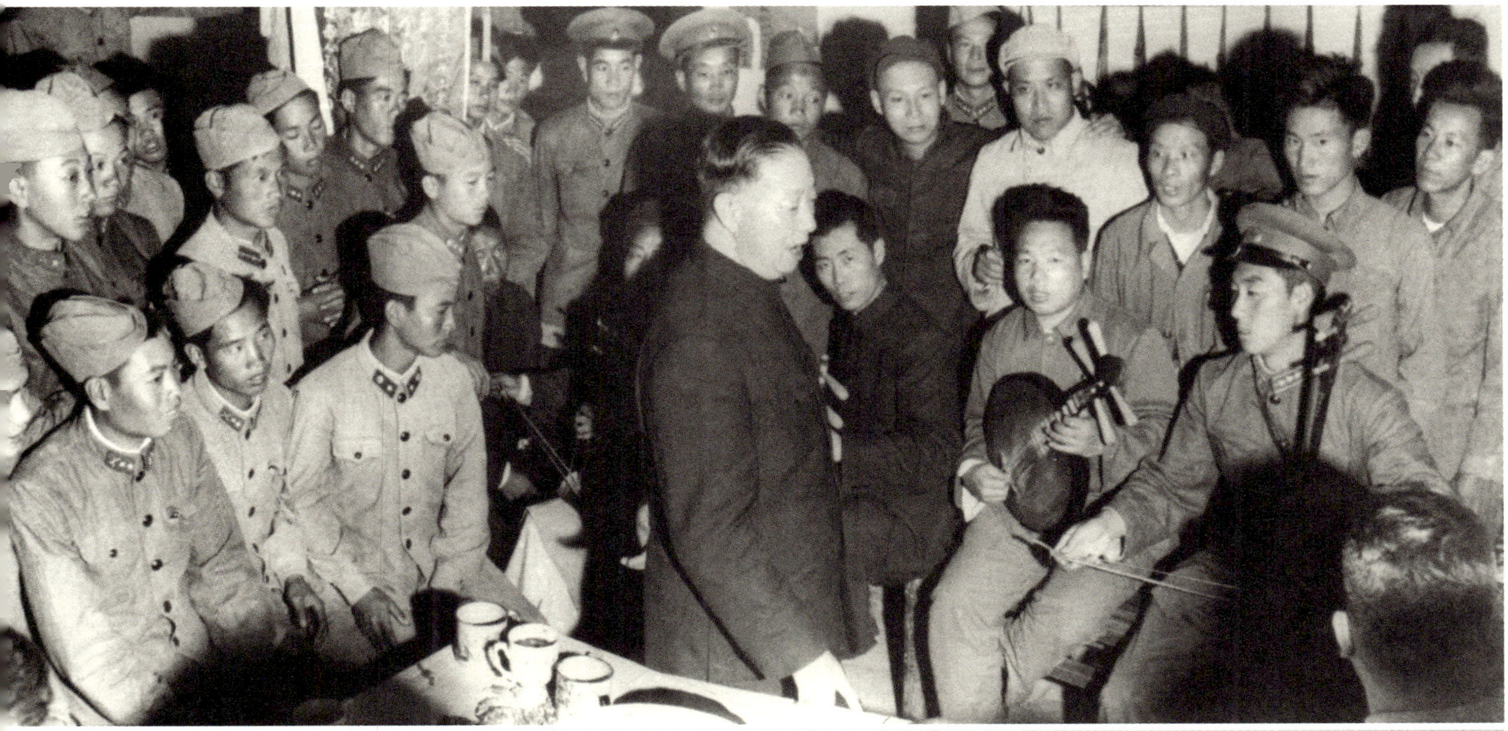

上图｜梅兰芳在福建与战士们联欢，战士操琴，梅兰芳清唱
With PLA soldiers in Fujian. Mei Lanfang sang to the accompaniment of the fiddle played by a soldier
下图｜梅兰芳在北京郊区与农民们在一起
With peasants at the suburb of Beijing

上左｜梅兰芳等在祖坟前肃立默哀

Meil Lanfang stood in silent tribute at his ancestral grave

上右、下右｜梅兰芳返乡演出盛况

Mei Lanfang returned to his hometown for a performance

下左｜梅兰芳在家乡与欢送者合影

Mei Lanfang with friends in his hometown

上图 | 梅兰芳在江苏扬州演出时与全体工作人员合影
Mei Lanfang in Yangzhou
下图 | 梅兰芳在江苏泰州演出时与亲友及领导合影
Mei Lanfang in Taizhou

上左｜梅兰芳在湖南长沙
Mei Lanfang in Hunan

上右｜1956年12月7日，梅兰芳参观毛泽东同志故居时在纪念册上签字留念
Mei Lanfang visited Mao Zedong's former Residence and wrote in an autograph album

下左｜梅兰芳等在毛泽东同志故居前合影留念
Mei Lanfang visited Mao Zedong's former Residence

下右｜梅兰芳等在毛泽东同志故居观看毛泽东少年时用的课本
Mei Lanfang watched Mao Zedong's textbook

梅兰芳离开湖南长沙，受到当地领导及民众的热情欢送
Mei Lanfang left Hunan

上图｜梅兰芳在陕西演出后谢幕
Mei Lanfang answered the curtain call in Xi'an
下图｜陕西省省长赵伯平与梅兰芳握手致谢
Mei Lanfang with the Governor of Shanxi

上图 | 梅兰芳夫妇与儿子葆玖观赏唐代宫中的银盘

Mei Lanfang viewed the galactic porcelain plate from the Tang Dy nasty

中图 | 梅兰芳等参观古代半坡村遗址

Mei Lanfang visited Banpo Village Ruins

下图 | 梅兰芳等在华清池合影

Mei Lanfang visited Huaqingchi Hot Spring

梅兰芳为西安戏曲界作报告
Mei Lanfang made a speech for the theatre circle of Xi'an

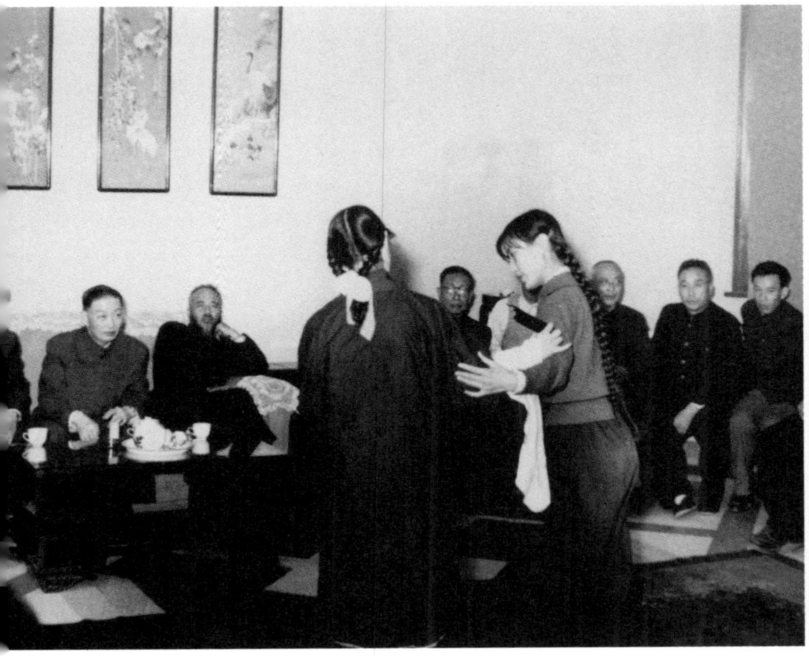

左图｜梅兰芳指导西安戏曲演员表演
Mei Lanfang guided the actresses to perform in Xi'an
右图｜车站送别
Farewell at the station

上图 | 梅兰芳在招待晚会上讲话
Mei Lanfang made a speech at the conference
下图 | 梅兰芳与天津市戏剧界人士座谈
Mei Lanfang talked to the theatre cirde in Tianjin

上图 | 梅兰芳在天津

Mei Lanfang in Tianjin

中图 | 梅兰芳演出后接受观众献花

Tianjin literary and art circles presented the flower to Mei Lanfang

中图 | 梅兰芳在天津演出后谢幕

Mei Lanfang arswered a curtain call in Tianjin

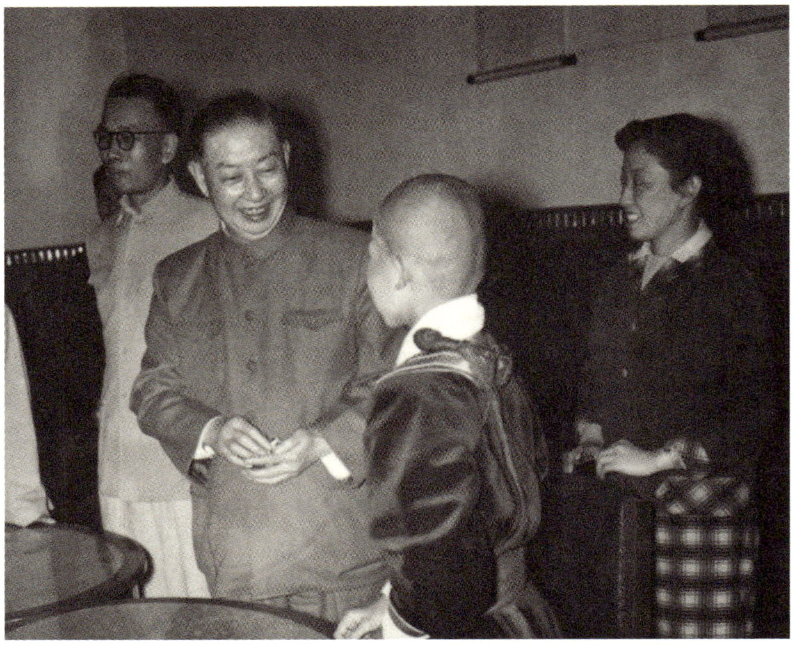

梅兰芳与天津戏校学生进行艺术交流

Talked with students from Tianjin Drama School

梅兰芳与参加晚会演出的天津小演员们合影

Mei Lanfang with young performers in Tianjin

左图｜梅兰芳在山西
In Shanxi
右上｜梅兰芳在太原演出后谢幕
Answered the curtain call in Taiyuan
右下｜梅兰芳在山西太原
In Taiyuan

左上｜梅兰芳在部队
In a PLA unit
左下｜梅兰芳在武昌
In Wuchang
右图｜梅兰芳在广州火车站
In Guangzhou Railway Station

全国各地群众热情欢迎梅兰芳剧团演出（左、右页）
Mei's performing troupe was welcomed by people all over the country

《穆桂英挂帅》，梅兰芳饰穆桂英

Mei Lanfang as Mu Guiying in *Mu Guiying Takes Command*

《穆桂英挂帅》，梅兰芳饰穆桂英（左二），李金泉饰佘太君（左三），李和曾饰杨宗保（右二）

Mu Guiying Takes Command on the stage. Mei Lanfang as Mu Guiying(left 2nd) , Li Jinquan as She Taijun(left 3rd) and Li Hezeng as Yang Zongbao(right 2nd)

左图｜梅兰芳演《穆桂英挂帅》"捧印"一场
Mei Lanfang as Mu Guiying in *Mu Guiying Takes Command*
右图｜梅兰芳演《穆桂英挂帅》"出征"一场
Mei Lanfang as Mu Guiying in *Mu Guiying Takes Command*

梅兰芳演《穆桂英挂帅》"出征"一场
Mu Guiying Takes Command on the stage

《穆桂英挂帅》，梅兰芳饰穆桂英（左、右页）

Mei Lanfang as Mu Guiying in *Mu Guiying Takes Command*

穆
令

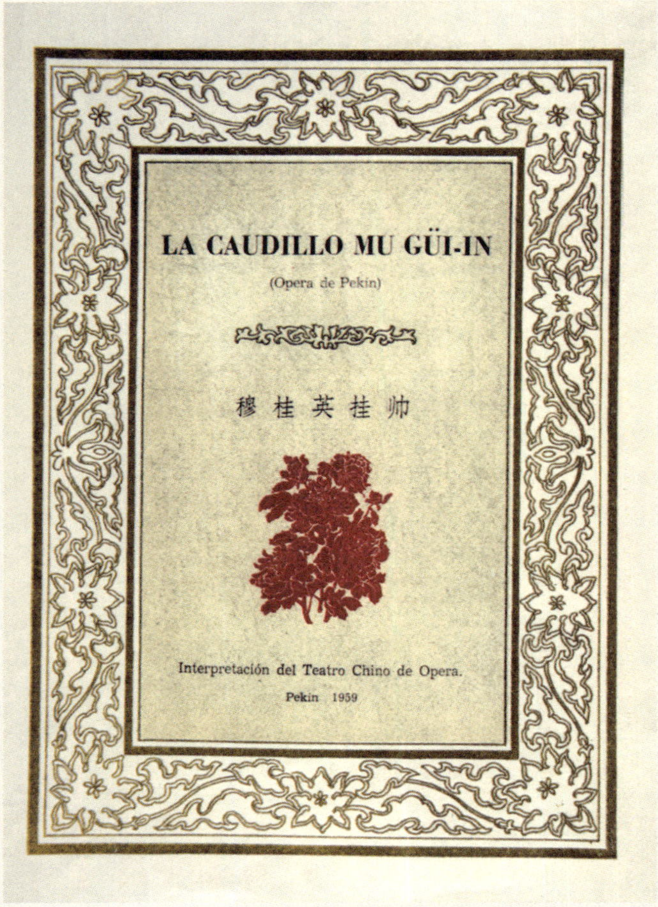

上左｜梅兰芳演出《穆桂英挂帅》说明书封面
The program of *Mu Guiying Takes Command* performed by Mei Lanfang

上右｜梅兰芳演出《穆桂英挂帅》世界语节目单封面
The program of *Mu Guiying Takes Command* in Esperanto

下图｜梅兰芳正在修改剧本
Mei Lanfang is amending a script.

上图 | 梅兰芳与徐兰沅研究剧目唱腔

Composing arias with Xu Lanyuan

下图 | 梅兰芳排练《穆桂英挂帅》，导演为郑亦秋（右二）

In rehearsing *Mu Guiying Takes Command* with the Director: Zheng Yiqiu(left 2nd)

率团访日

Visiting Japan with China Beijing Opera Delegation

梅兰芳率中国京剧代表团抵达东京羽田机场（1956）

The China Beijing Opera Delegation led by Mei Lanfang arrived at the Tokyo Airport in 1956

梅兰芳第三次访日是在新中国成立后的1956年。应日本《朝日新闻》等团体的邀请，在周总理的直接关心和帮助下，梅兰芳率领86人的中国京剧代表团赴日本各地演出。梅兰芳任团长，欧阳予倩等任副团长，团员有李少春、姜妙香、李和曾、侯玉兰、袁世海、梅葆玥、梅葆玖等著名演员。这是梅兰芳历次率团出国演出中阵容最齐整和规模最大的一次。这次演出了《贵妃醉酒》、《霸王别姬》、《奇双会》等名剧，不仅轰动了日本，还吸引了来自各国的观众。这次演出受到市川猿之助、松尾国三、千田是也等日本文艺界著名人士的大力支持，梅兰芳与他们建立了友谊，并与前两次访日认识的老朋友重逢话旧。日本国会破例招待了梅兰芳和主要演职人员，这是很少见的极高礼遇。1956年，中日两国尚未建交，梅兰芳率中国京剧代表团访问日本，进一步打开了两国文化交流的大门，增进了两国人民的了解，为两国关系正常化作出了贡献。

In 1956, Mei led the China Beijing Opera Delegation Company of 86 members including Li Shaochun, Jiang Miaoxiang, Yuan Shihai, Mei Baojiu and Mei Baoyue to visit Japan. They gave 23 performances in Tokyo, Kyoto, Osaka and other cities. The plays Mei performed were *The Drunken Beauty, The King's Parting with His Favourite, A Tale of Double Reunion* and other. Seventy thousands of people watched their performances. This tour made significant contributions to the mutual understanding and friendship between Chinese and Japanese peoples at the time when the diplomatic relation between the two countries has not yet been reestablished.

梅兰芳率中国京剧代表团抵达东京羽田机场时留影

The China Beijing Opera Delegation led by Mei Lanfang visited Japan and arrived at the Tokyo airport

-第五頁-

訪日京劇代表团日程单

六月八日 （星期五）

（上午10:00—正午12:00） 遊覧 福岡市内外、 中飯

（下午 1:30—下午 4:30） 遊覧 鋼網 地点：博多湾内

（松本治一郎先生之招待）

（下午 6:30— ） 歓迎会 地点：日活飯店 鶏尾酒式

（主持者 福岡県、市、商工会議所、朝日新聞社 日中友好協会）

六月九日 （星期六）

（下午 6:00—下午 9:30） 公 演 地点：大博劇場

六月十日 （星期日）

（正午12:00—下午 3:30） 公 演 （仝 上）

（下午 6:00—下午 9:50） 公 演 （仝 上） 幾回飯店

★（7） 14版 昭和31年5月27日 （日曜日）

中国京劇団が来日

梅蘭芳ら一行二十人

中国京劇の名優梅蘭芳、欧陽予倩氏ら訪日京劇代表団の一行二十名は二十六日午後三時四十五分羽田着のCPAL機で来日した。飛行場には中村翫右衛門、千田是也、岸輝子、猿之助氏夫人、秋田雨雀氏はじめ京浜地区の華僑や子供ら約二百人がにぎやかに出迎えた。

梅団長は六十二歳とは思えない若々しい元気さで「このような歓迎をうけて感謝いたします」とあいさつした。一行はホテル・ナイトに落ち着き三十日から歌舞伎座で公演する。

空港で花束を受ける京劇一行右から1人おいて梅蘭芳、欧陽予倩氏

團　　長：梅蘭芳　中國著名京劇演員。現任中國京劇院院長、中國戲曲研究院院長、中國戲劇家協會副主席。全國人民代表大會代表。

第一副團長兼總導演：歐陽予倩　中國著名戲劇家。現任中央戲劇學院院長、中國文學藝術界聯合會主席團委員、中國戲劇家協會副主席。全國人民代表大會代表。

副團長：馬少波　中國著名劇作家。現任中國京劇院副院長、中國戲曲研究院副院長、中國戲劇家協會常務理事。

副團長：劉　佳　中國著名導演。中國戲劇家協會理事。

副團長：孫平化　中國人民對外文化協會聯絡部副主任。

舞台監督：袁廣和　中國京劇院演出處處長。

演　　員：李少春　著名武生、老生、紅生。現任中國京劇院第三團團長、中國戲劇家協會理事。

演　　員：袁世海　著名花面。現任中國京劇院第三團副

—1—

左上｜中国京剧代表团访日行程表
The schedule of the China Beijing Opera Delegation Company

左下｜日本《读卖新闻》刊登中国京剧代表团访日消息
The news of Mei Lanfang visting Japan in Yoniuri Newpaper

右图｜中国京剧代表团名单首页
The staff list of China Beijing Opera Delegation Company

上图｜梅兰芳在机场受到日本文化交流协会会长片山哲（右）等人的欢迎

Mei Lanfang was welcomed by Mr. Trtu Katayama, the Chairman of the Association of the Cultural Exchange between Japan and China

下图｜中国京剧代表团在机场受到热烈欢迎

Mei Lanfang was welcomed by Japanese people at the airport

上图 | 梅兰芳等参加日本歌舞伎演员市川猿之助主办的欢迎会

A reception held by the distinguished Kabuki actor Ennosuke Ichikawa

下左 | 日本著名歌舞伎演员市川猿之助在寓所招待梅兰芳等并当场表演助兴

The Kabuki actor Ennosuke Ichikawa entertained Mei Lanfang and Chinese actors and actresses in his house and gave an ad lib performance

下右 | 梅兰芳在明治座舞台观摩《室町御所》后向市川猿之助献花（右二为梅葆玥）

Mei Lanfang presented the flowers to Ennosuke Ichikawa

上图｜梅兰芳在东京举行的欢迎会上讲话

Mei Lanfang gave a speech at the reception held in Tokyo

下左｜梅兰芳访问日本朝日新闻东京总社

Mei Lanfang visited Asahi News Agency in Tokyo

下右｜梅兰芳与日本《朝日新闻》东京总社的村山会长亲切交谈

Mei Lanfang visited the Asahi News Agency and talked with the director

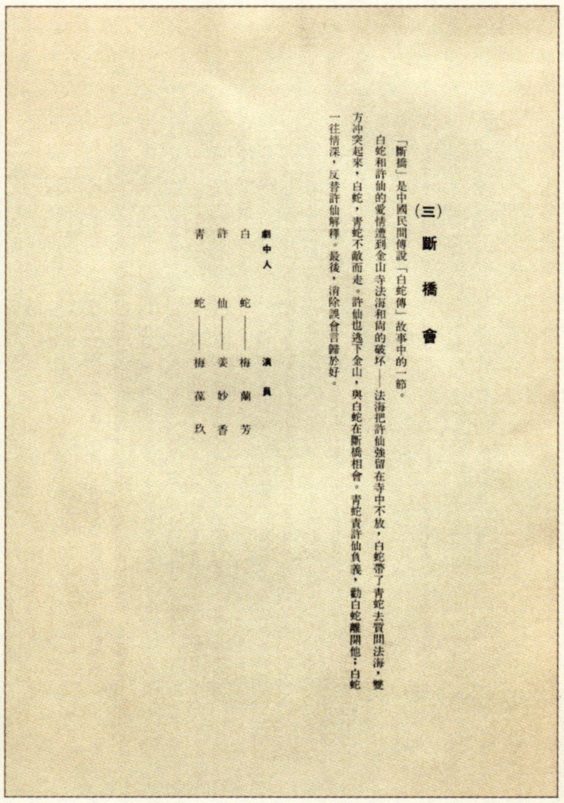

(三) 斷橋會

「斷橋」是中國民間傳說「白蛇傳」故事中的一節。

白蛇和許仙的愛情遭到金山寺法海和尚的破坏——法海把許仙強留在寺中不放，白蛇帶了青蛇去質問法海，雙方沖突起來，白蛇，青蛇不敵而走。許仙也逃下金山，與白蛇在斷橋相會。青蛇責許仙負義，勸白蛇離開他；白蛇一往情深，反替許仙解釋。最後，消除誤會言歸於好。

劇中人　演員

白　蛇——梅蘭芳

許　仙——姜妙香

青　蛇——梅葆玖

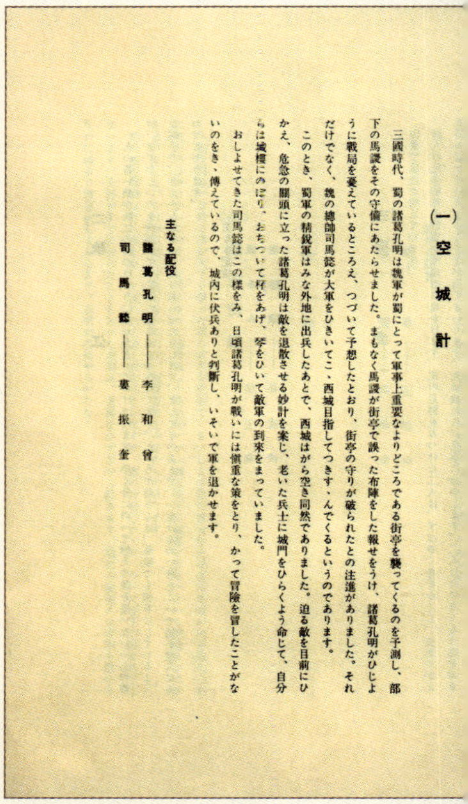

(一) 空城計

三國時代、蜀の諸葛孔明は魏軍が蜀にとって軍事上重要なよりどころである街亭を襲ってくるのを予測し、部下の馬謖をその守備にあたらせました。まもなく馬謖が街亭で誤った布陣をした報せをうけ、諸葛孔明がひじょうに戰局を憂えているところえ、つづいて予想したとおり、街亭の守りが破られたとの注進がありました。それだけでなく、魏の總帥司馬懿が大軍をひきいてこ、西城目指してつきす、んでくるというのであります。

このとき、蜀軍の精銳軍はみな外地に出兵したあとで、西城はがら空き同然でありました。迫る敵を目前にひかえ、危急の關頭に立った諸葛孔明は敵を退散させる妙計を案じ、老いた兵士に城門をひらくよう命じて、自分らは城樓にのぼり、おちついて杯をあげ、琴をひいて敵軍の到來をまっていました。

おしよせてきた司馬懿はこの樣をみ、日頃諸葛孔明が戰いには愼重な策をとり、かって冒險を冒したことがないのをき、傳えているので、城內に伏兵ありと判斷し、いそいで軍を退かせます。

主なる配役

諸葛孔明——李和曾

司馬懿——裘振奎

中国京剧代表团访日演出节目单

The program of Mei Lanfang's performance in Japan

"好々…梅蘭芳"のかけ声も飛ぶ
京劇の初公演

中国の古典芸術「京劇」を紹介するため来日した梅蘭芳氏ら中国京劇代表団の初公演は三十日午後六時から築地の歌舞伎座で行われた。日本では三十二年ぶりの公演である。開幕式ののち「将相和（しょうそうわ）」「拾玉鐲（しゅうぎょくたく）」「三岔口（さんさこう）」と続けて上演、最後に梅蘭芳が得意の「貴妃酔酒（きひすいしゅ）」を演じて満場のカッサイを浴びた。観客席には在日華僑も多く、さわりの場面では「ハオ、ハオ」という叫びがきかれた。なお「貴妃酔酒」公演の途中三階から「アジア青年反共連盟」の名で「反日家の梅蘭芳はなぜ日本に来たか？」という反共ビラがまかれたが、別に混乱はなく、同十時初の公演を終った。

京劇三十二年ぶりの公演「貴妃酔酒」で楊玉環を演ずる梅蘭芳（中央）＝歌舞伎座で

三笠宮夫婦與梅蘭芳

下圖：日本天皇三弟三笠宮夫婦，六月二日在東京觀看中國京劇團的演出後，特地到後台訪問京劇團團長梅蘭芳，與他談話，並向他表示祝賀。（本報東京特稿）

朝日新聞宴京劇團

作陪者有歐美國家使節及記者 各方面友人紛紛爲公演成功而乾杯

【新華社東京六日電】日本「朝日新聞」社五日晚間舉行宴會，招待中國訪日京劇代表團團長梅蘭芳、第一副團長歐陽予倩和全體團員。

日本方面出席作陪的有自由民主黨顧問會長石井光次郎、自由民主黨國會議員北村德太郎、日本學術會議會長茅誠司、日本演劇協會會長久保田萬太郎、日中友好協會副會長內山完造、日中文化交流協會理事長中島健藏、日本擁護和平委員會總書記平野義太郎，以及日本著名畫家、音樂家、作家、演員等各界代表約一百五十人。

出席作陪的還有印度、南斯拉夫、瑞士、智利、英國、法國、烏拉圭、奧地利、芬蘭、德意志聯邦共和國等國駐日本的外交使節等，以及美聯社、倫敦「泰晤士報」等外國駐日本的記者共三十多人。

宴會在歡樂友好的氣氛中進行。各方面的友人紛紛爲中國京劇代表團首次公演的成功而乾杯。

日本众議院副議長招待中国京剧团

据新华社东京4日电　日本国会众議院副議長杉山元治郎6月4日上午接待了中国訪日京剧代表团团長梅蘭芳、第一副团長兼总导演歐陽予倩等領导人員和著名京剧演員参观国会，并且举行招待茶会。这是日本国会第一次接待外国戏剧代表。

出席这个茶会的有各党派国会議員三十五人。

杉山元治郎在会上致詞，对中国京剧团到日本訪問演出，表示衷心的欢迎。他說，希望今后通过艺术和文化、科学以及各方面的交流，增进兩国人民的互相了解，并且把心和心連在一起，以达到兩国人民共同的和平願望。

自由民主党議員北村德太郎在会上致詞时說，中国京剧团前来日本訪問演出，在日本戏剧史上記下了偉大的一頁。他說，像这样的艺术交流是促进日中兩国友好亲善的最好方法。

社会党議員片山哲致詞說，从这一次中国京剧团訪日演出以后，要把日中兩国的文化、經济以及各方面的交流更加發展起来，并且希望日中兩国間的所有的一切問題，能够和平友好地解决。

在会上致詞的还有池田正之輔、須磨弥吉郎、山口喜久一郎等国会議員。

梅蘭芳代表中国京剧团对主人們的招待表示衷心的感謝。他說，去年以市川猿之助为首的日本歌舞伎团訪問了中国，受到中国人民热烈的欢迎，今年中国京剧团同样地受到日本人民热烈的欢迎。我們希望从今以后像这样的文化艺术交流更加發展，并且希望中日兩国的友好更加深厚。

欧陽予倩也在会上致詞。

最后，日本社会党国会議員穗积七郎代表主人方面說，日中兩国今天在文化上握手了，相信在不久的將来也能在政治上握手。

上左｜1956年5月31日，日本《每日新闻》刊登中国京剧代表团访日演出的消息

Asahi News reported the performance of Mei Lanfang in Japan

上右｜报载中国京剧团在日本的活动

The news of Mei Lanfang's activities in Japan

下图｜1956年6月6日，《光明日报》刊登中国京剧代表团的访日活动

Guangming Daily reported Mei Lanfang's activities in Japan

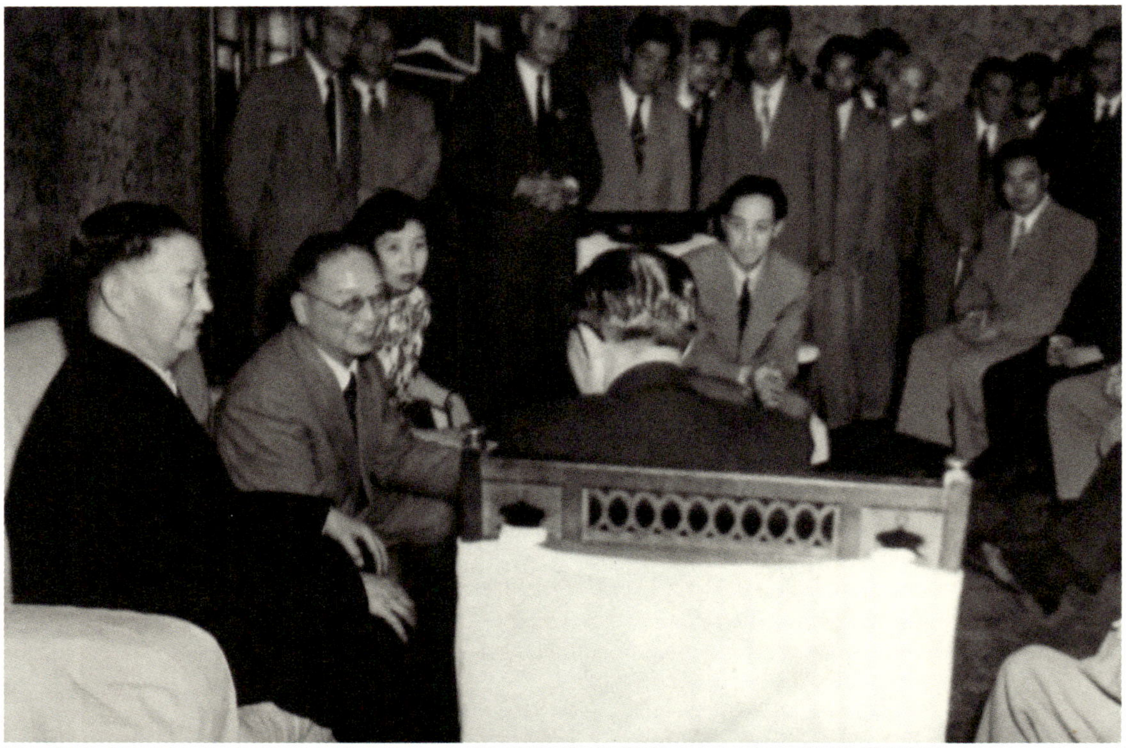

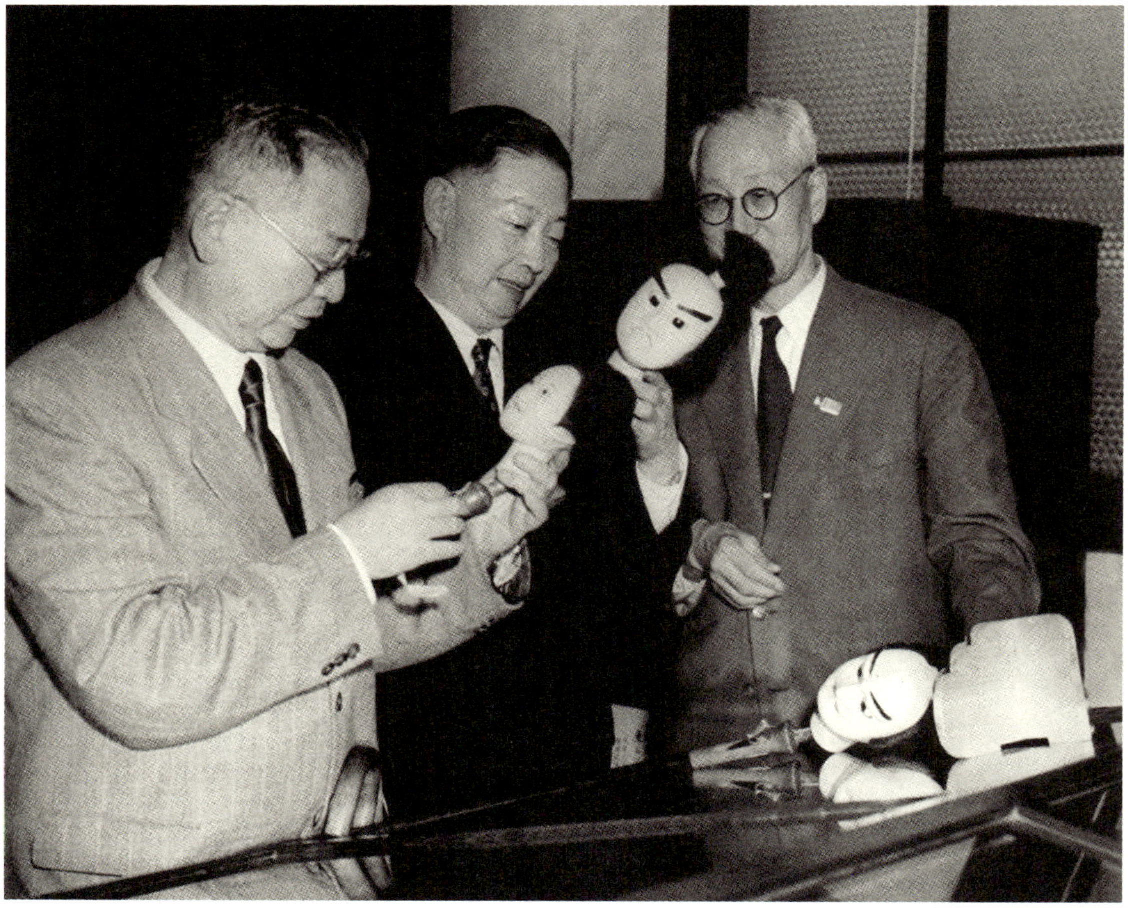

上图｜中国京剧代表团访问日本议事堂（国会）
Visited the Japanese Chamber
下图｜梅兰芳与欧阳予倩参观早稻田大学演出博物馆，馆长河竹繁俊热情接待
Visited the Theatre Museum in Waseda University

八幡行列一公里 等候入場看京劇

演員特為五千名觀衆加演了一齣

【新華社八幡十四日電】中國京劇代表團十三日晚上在八幡市的五千多名觀衆面前舉行了公演。京劇團是在當天下午從福岡到達這個九州的重工業城市的。

這一天，從上午九點開始觀衆就在門口等候入場，到下午三點排隊的人的行列長達一公里。公演開始時，密密層層的觀衆坐滿了八幡製鐵所體育館。觀衆中，八幡製鐵所的一千多工人是在工作剛剛完了就帶着飯盒前來看戲的。觀衆中還有許多從附近城市趕來的工人、青年、婦女、學生等。也有從福岡趕來再次觀看京劇的人。

中國京劇團演出了原定的「將相和」、「三岔口」、「拾玉鐲」和「貴妃醉酒」四個節目，又增演了「雁蕩山」。每一個節目都博得觀衆長時間的熱烈鼓掌。

演出結束時，八幡市市長守田道隆、小倉市市長林信雄、戶畑市市長白木正元、門司市市長柳田桃太郎、若松市市長吉田敬太郎等人的代表和八幡製鐵所工會代表以及和平友好團體的代表紛紛走上舞台，向梅蘭芳獻花，全場響起暴風雨般的掌聲，經久不息。

中國京劇團在九州的公演已經全部結束。十四日上午坐火車離開九州

左图｜1956年6月16日，香港《大公报》刊登中国京剧代表团在日本八幡市演出的盛况

Ta Kung Pao reported Mei's Performance in Japan

右上｜八幡体育场演出现场

Mei Lanfang's performance in the stadium in Japam

右下｜九洲华侨商会举办欢迎会并赠送锦旗

The overseas Chinese in Japan welcomed Mei Lanfang

京劇一行 大阪入り

批判を…… 梅・欧陽氏、車中で語る

上图｜梅兰芳在日本大阪欢迎会上讲话

Mei Lanfang gave a speech at the reception in Osaka

下左｜大阪饭店欢迎会

Mei Lanfang welcomed by the people in Osaka

下右｜1956年6月15日，日本《朝日新闻》刊登中国京剧代表团在大阪的活动

Asahi News reported Mei Lanfang's activities in Osaka

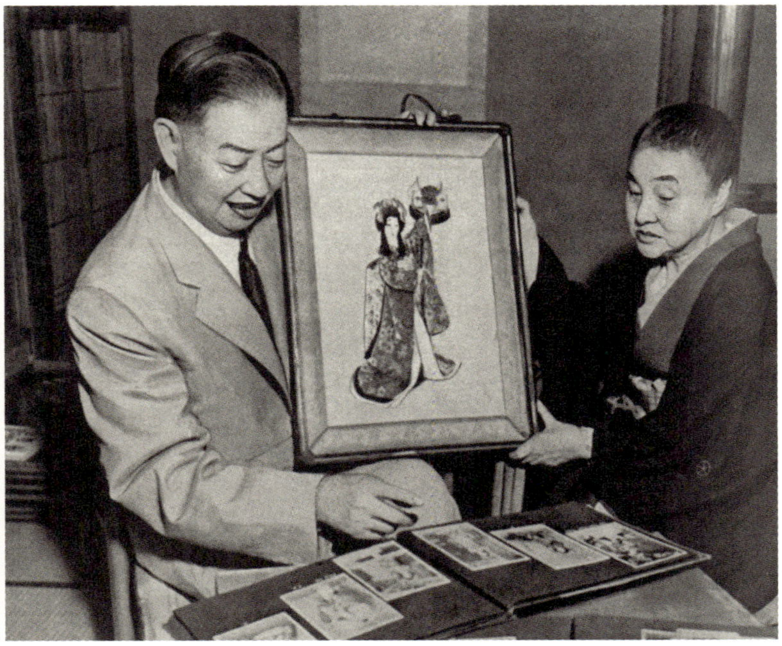

上左｜梅兰芳在中村雀右卫门夫人家中观看中村雀右卫门先生的剧照
Mei Lanfang watched the pictures of Nakamura Jakuemon's performance
上右｜中村雀右卫门夫人向梅兰芳赠送日本工艺品
Nakamara Jakuemon's wife presented a Japanese painting to Mei Lanfang
下图｜中村雀右卫门夫人赠送给梅兰芳的日本工艺品
The Japanese painting Nakamara Jakuemon's wife presentde to Mei Lanfang

中国京剧代表团游览奈良

China Beijing Opera Delegation Company Visited Nara

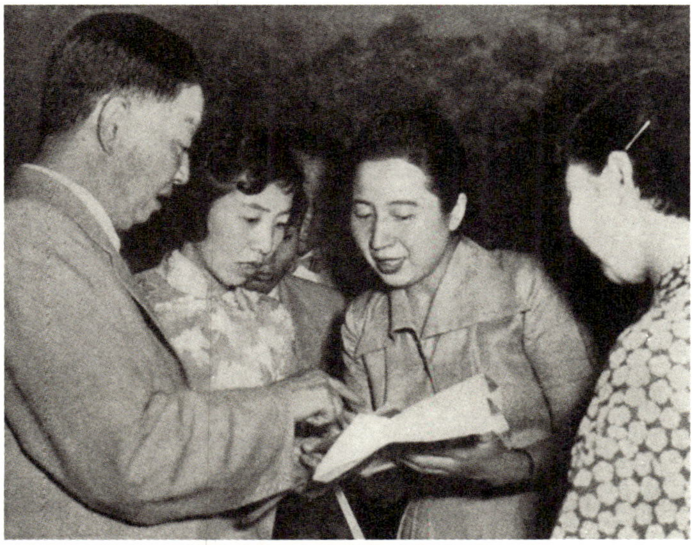

上图｜梅兰芳游览京都岚山时见到了老友今井泰藏的女儿京子

Mei Lanfang visited Arashiyama in Kyoto and met his old Japanese friend's daughter

下图｜梅兰芳在日本京都岚山游览

Sight-seeing at Arashiyama, Kyoto

上左 | 梅兰芳与欧阳予倩在爱知县参观美术史展览
Mei Lanfang and Ouyang Yuqian visited an Exhibition of Art History at Aichi-ken

上右 | 神户新闻会馆欢迎会
Mei Lanfang was welcomed by the people of Kobe in Japan

下图 | 梅兰芳等在名古屋市观看舞蹈演出
Watching dance performance at Nagoya

上左 | 梅兰芳、欧阳予倩在欢迎会上与日本戏剧界人士互赠礼品
Mei Lanfang, Ouyang Yuqian and Japanese dramatists exchanged gifts at a reception in Tokyo

上右 | 1956年6月30日，中村翫右卫门向梅兰芳赠送礼品
Japanese actor presented the gift to Mei Lanfang

下图 | 梅兰芳在福冈县欢迎会上致词
Mei Lanfang gave a speech at the reception held in Fukuoka

《贵妃醉酒》，梅兰芳饰杨玉环

Mei Lanfang as Yang Yuhuan in *The Drunken Beauty*

上左、上右 | 歌舞伎座闭幕式

The closing ceremony in Japan

下图 | 梅兰芳率团在为日本举行义演时的东京国际剧场外景

The exterior of the International Theatre in Tokyo where Mei Lanfang gave a benefit performance for aiding the orphans and the victims afflicted by the atomic bomb

我国京剧团在东京举行义演

野坂参三观剧后表示希望增进日中各方面的交流

据新华社东京13日电 中国訪日京剧代表团十二日在东京"国际剧場"为救济日本的战爭中的孤兒和原子彈受害者举行了兩場义演。这次义演是在和"朝日新聞社"共同主持下举行的。

剧場剛开門，成千上万的人源源不絕地涌进剧場来。他們都是东京和附近城乡的工人、机关职員、农民、青年学生和家庭妇女。兩場观众达到一万一千多人。

挤滿了剧場的观众，对每一个节目都报以雷鳴般的掌声和欢呼声。最后由"朝日新聞"社、經营电影和戏剧事業的松竹公司、日中友好协会等六个單位代表日本人民向代表团献花致謝。

日本共产党第一書記野坂参三看完戏以后說：中国京剧团前来日本訪問演出，向日本人民介紹优秀的中国古典艺术，尤其是今天特地給了广大群众看戏的机会，这个意义是非常大的。看过京剧的所有观众都被京剧的魅力迷住，受到深刻的感动。他还說：京剧代表团到日本演出和日本"歌舞伎"曾經在中国演出，同样地对促进中日兩国文化交流，恢复兩国邦交和兩国人民的友好关系有很大的作用。希望今后中日兩国各方面的交流，更向前發展。

在演出終了后，野坂参三还特意到后台向梅蘭芳致意問候，并且請梅蘭芳回国后向毛澤东主席、刘少奇委員長、周恩来总理轉达他和日本人民的謝意。

梅蘭芳代表全团对日本人民給予代表团的帮助表示感謝，并且对野坂参三这次当选国会参議員表示祝賀。

中国京剧团在义演这一天，还接到了日中友好协会事务总長伊藤武雄的感謝信。信上說：京剧团这次在日本各地公演，对日中友好运动將起重大的作用。他代表日本人民对中国人民的友好的誠意表示感謝。

梅蘭芳等在日最後演出

廿餘國使節看京劇

鳩山夫人也到場觀看

京劇團在東京等地演出觀衆共七萬

據新華社東京十一日電：中國京劇代表團七月十日晚上在東京「歌舞伎座」劇場舉行閉幕演出，結束了在日本各地五十多天的訪問。

在演出過程中，當每一個節目終了時，把劇場擠得滿滿的二千七百多個觀衆都報以熱烈的掌聲，再三要求演員們出來和他們見面。

京劇代表團在東京、大阪、京都、名古屋、福岡和八幡等地前後共演出了三十場，觀衆共達七萬人。

觀看閉幕演出的有日本首相鳩山一郎夫人鳩山薰，還有蘇聯駐東京代表團團長李契文斯基和英國、印度、巴西、印度尼西亞、墨西哥、奧地利、錫蘭、智利、南斯拉夫等二十幾個國家的駐日大使、公使和外交官員。

演出結束後舉行了閉幕儀式。東京的中國訪日京劇代表團歡迎委員會會長久保田萬太郎代表日本全國的觀衆致詞說：中國京劇團這次在日本的訪問演出，毫無疑問地對於增進中日兩國間的文化交流和兩國人民的友誼有了巨大的貢獻，並且給日本的演員、作家、導演家、詩人、畫家等文化界人士以很大的啓發。

久保田最後說：日本人民都盼望着你們能在不久的將來再一次來日本訪問。

京劇代表團第一副團長兼總導演歐陽予倩代表京劇代表團全體人員和中國戲劇界致答詞。他說，我們從每一個地方都感覺到日本人民對中國人民是友好的，這種深厚真誠的友誼正在迅速地發展。

接着，「朝日新聞」社、日中友好協會、日中文化交流協會、日本舞踊協會、日本演劇協會、「俳優座」劇團等日本各社會團體和東京華僑總會、橫濱華僑總會等華僑團體，向梅蘭芳和京劇代表團全體人員獻花或者贈送紀念品。市川猿之助夫婦和許多日本藝術家都上台和京劇代表團各位領導人員握手祝賀。

閉幕儀式在全體觀衆高呼中日友好萬歲的口號聲和如雷的掌聲中結束。

羅國再

先後裁

左图｜梅兰芳在日本与围棋名家吴清源合影
With the famous chess player Wu Qingyuan

右上｜《人民日报》刊登中国京剧代表团在东京举行义演的消息
People's Daily reported Mei Lanfang's performance in Japan

右下｜报载梅兰芳率领的中国京剧代表团在日本举行最后演出的消息
The news concerning the final performance of the China Beijing Opera Delegation in Japan on the newspaper

上左｜梅兰芳、欧阳予倩拜访松尾国三先生
Mei Lanfang and Ouyang Yuqian called on Mr. Matsuo Kunizo
上右｜梅兰芳与松尾国三先生的夫人交谈
Mei Lanfang called on Mr. and Mrs. Matsuo Kunizo
下图｜梅兰芳与代表团成员在松尾国三先生寓所合影
In the house of Mr. Matsuo Kunizo

上图｜在帝国饭店话别酒会上，野坂参三与梅兰芳等合影
With Sanzo Nosaka

下图｜梅兰芳、欧阳予倩、马少波等在东京羽田机场登机回国
Mei Lanfang, Ouyang Yuqian and others went back to China

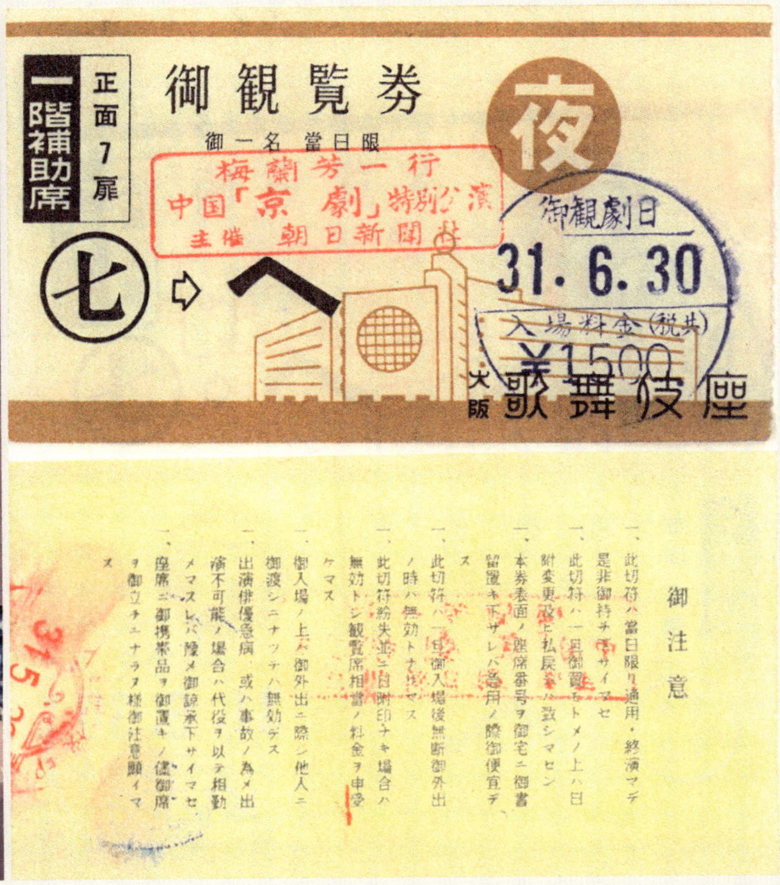

上左 | 日本朝日新闻社出版梅兰芳撰写的《东游记》（日译本）封面

The cover of the book *A Trip to Japan* written by Mei Lanfang (Japanese edition)

上右 | 梅兰芳在大阪歌舞伎座演出的门票

The ticket of Mei Lanfang's performance in Japan

下图 | 中国京剧代表团访日纪念章

The Commemorative Medal of China Beijing Opera Delegation Company

电影生涯

On Screen

梅兰芳拍摄电影舞台艺术片的海报

The postor of Mei's film

1955年，梅兰芳62岁时，由北京电影制片厂拍摄了《梅兰芳舞台艺术》彩色纪录片，记录了梅兰芳的舞台生活及《宇宙锋》、《断桥》、《贵妃醉酒》、《霸王别姬》、《洛神》等梅派精粹剧目，导演为吴祖光。1959年，他又拍摄了由崔嵬艺术指导，许珂导演的《游园惊梦》。

In 1955, when Mei was 62 years old, the Beijing Film Studio made *Mei Lanfang's Stage Art* directed by Wu Zuguang. In this film, several Mei's masterpieces, such as *Fighting Against the Chins*, *The King's Parting with His Favourite*, *Beauty Defies Tyranny*, *The Drunken Beauty*, *The Goddess of River Luo* and *The Broken Bridge* were included. In 1959, another film *The Peony Pavilion* was made with Xu Ke as director and Cui Wei as art supervisor.

梅兰芳拍摄电影《洛神》
Mei Lanfang in the film *The Goddess of the River Luo*

拍摄电影《洛神》，梅兰芳饰洛神，姜妙香饰曹子建

Mei Lanfang as Goddess Luo and Jiang Miaoxiang as Cao Zijian in the film *The Goddess of the River Luo*

梅兰芳拍摄电影《洛神》

Mei Lanfang in the film *The Goddess of the River Luo*

拍摄电影《宇宙锋》，梅兰芳饰赵艳容，刘连荣饰赵高

Mei Lanfang as Zhao Yanrong and Liu Lianrong as Zhao Gao in the film *Beauty Defies Tyranny*

拍摄电影《抗金兵》，梅兰芳饰梁红玉

Mei Lanfang as Liang Hongyu in *Fighting Against the Chins*

拍摄电影《霸王别姬》，梅兰芳饰虞姬，刘连荣饰项羽

Mei Lanfang as Yu Ji and Liu Lianrong as the King in the film *The King's Parting with His Favorite*

梅兰芳拍摄电影《霸王别姬》舞剑片段

Mei Lanfang as Yu Ji in the film *The King's Parting with His Favorite*

梅兰芳拍摄影片《游园惊梦》时与导演崔嵬（前排左二）、俞振飞（前排左四）、言慧珠（前排右二）、朱家溍（后排左二）、许姬传（后排左三）等合影（1959）

With director Cui Wei (front left 2nd),Yu Zhenfei (front left 4th),Yan Huizhu (front right 2nd), Zhu Jiajin (back left 2nd) and Xu Jichuan (back left 3rd) when the film *The Peony Pavilion* was being shot(1959)

拍摄电影《游园惊梦》，梅兰芳饰杜丽娘
Mei Lanfang in the film *The Peony Pavilion*

梅兰芳拍摄戏曲电影现场（左、右页）
The site of the film-making

陆

家庭交友

Mei Lanfang's Family and His Domestic Life

梅兰芳平日在家的生活很有规律，每天9点准时用完早餐，遂阅读书报，打太极拳，练功吊嗓。无论多么繁忙，他都坚持“拳不离手，曲不离口”，以永葆艺术青春。如无排练和晚上的演出，下午及其以后的时间，梅兰芳多半是作画，从不间断。每晚无论是否演出，他就寝均较晚。梅兰芳特别好客，几乎天天都抽时间接待或访问同行各界友人。稍有空暇，还不断亲自指导葆玥、葆玖练功学艺。梅兰芳的生活可以说是繁忙而有序，丰富而多彩。

Since 1951, Mei was busy with his performing and social activity. At his leisure, besides receiving friends, reading or painting, he usually trained his voice, did exercises or coached his son Baojiu and daughter Baoyue in their learning of theatrical arts. He led a happy life with his sons, daughters and grandchildren during the fifties.

《霸王别姬》

梅兰芳饰虞姬，杨小楼饰霸王

Mei Lanfang as Yu Ji and Yang Xiaolou as the King in *The King's Parting with His Favourite*

《宇宙锋》

梅兰芳饰赵艳容

Mei Lanfang as Zhao Yanrong in *Beauty Defies Tyranny*

《奇双会》

梅兰芳饰李桂枝，姜妙香饰赵宠

Mei Lanfang as Li Guizhi and Jiang Miaoxiang as Zhao Chong in *The Double Reunion*

《凤还巢》

梅兰芳饰程雪娥

Mei Lanfang as Cheng Xue E in *The Phoenix Returns Its Nest*

良师益友

Good Teachers and Helpful friends

梅兰芳与张謇

张謇，江苏南通人。梅兰芳于1914年在北京与张謇相识，是年，张62岁，梅21岁，从此建立了忘年厚谊。1926年，张謇辞世。

张謇是光绪二十年“恩科”状元，是近代爱国的实业家、教育家、政治家和思想家，是中国近代史上重要的代表人物。他一生抱定“实业救国、教育救国”的热忱，组织兴办工厂、公司、银行、学校、博物苑、图书馆和医院，积极推进戏曲改革，开发戏曲教育，在诸多领域作出了贡献。梅兰芳与张謇的友谊，就是建立在共同弘扬和改革中国传统戏曲艺术、造就新一代艺苑人才的基础上的。张謇不仅欣赏梅兰芳的艺术成就，而且赞赏他的创新精神，故时刻关心、激励这位高素质的艺术家。1919年、1920年和1922年，梅兰芳三次到南通。10余年中，两人除在京、沪和南通三地会面外，大部分时间保持通信来往和诗词唱和，体现出相互的深切情意。梅兰芳举世瞩目的艺术成就，也渗透着他们两位友谊的绚丽色彩。

Mei Lanfang and Zhang Jian

Zhang Jian is a modern patriotic industrialist, educator, politician and thinker. He is an important representative of modern Chinese history. He set up factories, companies, banks, schools, museums, libraries and hospitals, and actively promote the reform and development of the traditional drama education. He has contributed in many fields.

Zhang Jian and Mei Lanfang's friendship is built on the foundation of carrying forward the reform of Chinese traditional drama and art, creating a new generation of talent on the Chinese theatre. Zhang Jian not only enjoyed Mei Lanfang's artistic achievement, but also appreciated his innovative spirit, so he always concerned about and motivate this high qualified artist. In 1919, 1920 and 1922, Mei Lanfang went to Nantong three times. They met each other in Beijing, Shanghai and Nantong, and also maintain communication with the letters and poetry in more than ten years, and reflecting deep mutual affection. Mei Lanfang's remarkable artistic achievements also permeated their friendship with brilliant colors.

1922年，梅兰芳由上海去南通，与民族实业家张謇合影

Mei Lanfang With Chinese patriotic entrepreneur Zhang Jian in Nantong

上左 | 梅兰芳由上海赴南通所乘的“大升号”轮船

The liner Mei Lanfang taked from Shanghai to Nantong

上右 | 梅兰芳携夫人王明华等在南通码头

Mei Lanfang anf his wife Wang Minghua was welcomed by the people in Nantong

下图 | 梅兰芳（前排右六）与夫人王明华（前排右七）等人到达南通时合影（1919）

Mei Lanfang and his wife Wang Minghua were welcomed in Nantong (1919)

张謇（前排左五）在南通城南别业招待梅兰芳（前排左四）、欧阳予倩、姚玉芙（前排左三）、姜妙香（二排左二）、齐如山（二排左三）等人时合影

Zhang Jian received Mei Lanfang in Nantong

上图｜梅兰芳与张謇等在南通博物苑南馆门前合影（左起：薛秉初 、张孝若、欧阳予倩、张謇、齐如山、 梅兰芳、姜妙香、姚玉芙）

Mei Lanfang, Zhang Jian and others at Nantong Museum

下图｜1920 年 1 月 12 日，张謇在南通更俗剧场举行盛会欢迎梅兰芳

Zhang Jian welcomes Mei Lanfang at Gen su Theater on January 12th, 1920

上图 | 梅兰芳与张謇、王凤庆、姚玉芙、姜妙香在南通濠阳小筑别墅合影
Mei Lanfang with Zhang Jian and friends in Nantong
下左 | 中国银行总裁冯耿光是梅兰芳一生最重要的支持者，图为梅兰芳与冯耿光
Feng Gengguang,President of Bank of China, is the most important lifetime supporter of Mei Lanfang. The photo is Mei Lanfang and Feng Gengguang
下右 | 梅兰芳携夫人王明华等在南通码头受欢迎情况
Mei Lanfang was welcomed by the people in Nantong

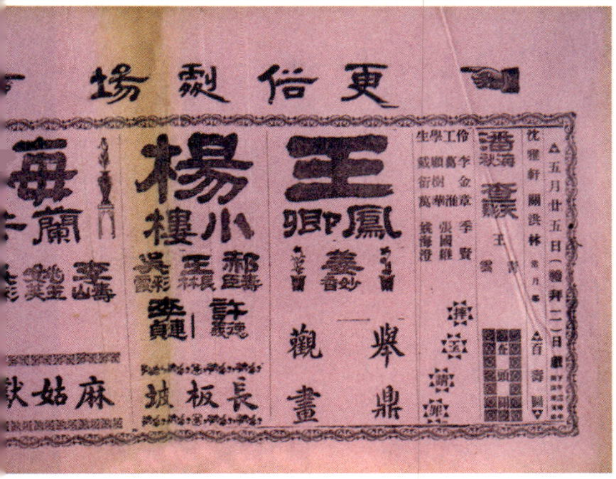

上左｜南通戏园（更俗剧场）外景（1919）
Nantong Gengsu Theater (1919)

上右｜南通戏园舞台（1919）
The stage of Nantong Gengsu Theater(1919)

下左｜梅兰芳在南通演《麻姑献寿》的戏单（1922）
The program of *Magu Wishing Godness Wang Mu a Long Life* performed bg Mei Lanfang at Nantong(1922)

下右｜南通戏园观众席（1919 ）
The auditorium of Nantong Gengsu Theatre (1919)

梅兰芳与齐白石 Qi Baishi and Mei Lanfang

齐白石与梅兰芳均为享誉20世纪中国的艺术大师，一个蜚声画坛，一个名满梨园，都活跃在民国以及新中国成立初期京城的文化界，在社会上享有极高的声誉。他们之间有着不同寻常的师友之谊，成为京华艺林的美谈佳话。齐白石初识梅兰芳是在19世纪20年代初，刚到北平的齐白石画名尚不显著，还处在广泛交游艺坛名流的时期。1920年秋天，齐白石经好友齐如山引荐到前门外北芦草园拜访梅兰芳，梅兰芳在他的书斋“缀玉轩”接待了齐白石等人。当时在场的还有画家汪霭士、诗人李释戡，也算是小型的名流雅集。梅兰芳理纸磨墨，请齐白石画草虫，在旁悉心观摩齐白石作画的动作，为自己的表演汲取素养。然后梅兰芳又即兴为众人唱了一段《贵妃醉酒》。次日，齐白石回赠诗曰：“飞尘十丈暗燕京，缀玉轩中气独清。难得善才看作画，殷勤磨就墨三升。”齐白石与梅兰芳结识后，每逢花期，齐白石必至梅处观赏，有诗记曰：“百本牵牛花碗大，三年无梦到梅家。”有一次，齐白石应邀到一个官宦之家参加聚会，因为穿着朴素，又没有熟人招呼，被冷落在一旁。这时梅兰芳到了，见到齐白石，就径直上前恭敬见礼。齐白石对此深为感激，后来特意画了一幅画送给梅兰芳，题曰《雪中送炭图》，并在画上题诗致谢：“记得前朝享太平，布衣尊贵动公卿。如今沦落长安市，幸有梅郎呼姓名。”新中国成立后，梅兰芳举家迁回北京，两位艺术家都在晚年欣逢新中国太平盛世，也都步入了事业上最后的辉煌时期。梅兰芳与齐白石同样担任国家文化机构的一些职务，见面交往的机会多了。1955年，梅兰芳在北京演出，特意邀请齐白石观剧，齐白石乘兴到剧场后台与梅兰芳交谈，这时照相师李维明突发奇想，拿起手中的照相机为两位艺术大师合影，把他们的艺苑盛事永远地定格在中国文化史上。

Qi Baishi and Mei Lanfang are renowned artists of the 20th century in China. Qi is famous in painting, and Mei is famous in Beijing Opera.They are active on the new Chinese cultural in the early Republic of China, enjoy a high reputation in the community. They have a deep friendship. Qi met Mei in the early 1920s. Mei Lanfang received Qi Baishi in his study in Autumn 1920. Mei Lanfang asked Qi Baishi to paint. Mei observed Qi's movements, nourishment for his performance. Then Mei sang The Drunken Beauty. Qi Baishi often went to Mei Lanfang's house to watch the morning glory flower. One time Qi was invited to an official family to attend a party, but Qi was not famous at this time, so nobody knew him. When Mei Lanfang came, Mei bowed and saluted him directly. Qi Baishi was deeply moved by Mei's respect.He has painted a picture for Mei Lanfang, and make a poem to Mei Lanfang:

"Remember the former and enjoy the peace.
Dressed in shabby clothes but distinguished and moved the lords.
Now I wandered in the street of Changan,
Thanks to Mei who recognized me."

上图 | 梅兰芳与齐白石
Mei Lanfang and Qi Baishi
下图 | 梅兰芳与齐白石（左二）、汪霭士（左一）、欧阳予倩（右一）
With Qi Baishi (left 2nd), Wang Aishi (left 1st) and Ouyang Yuqian (right 1st)

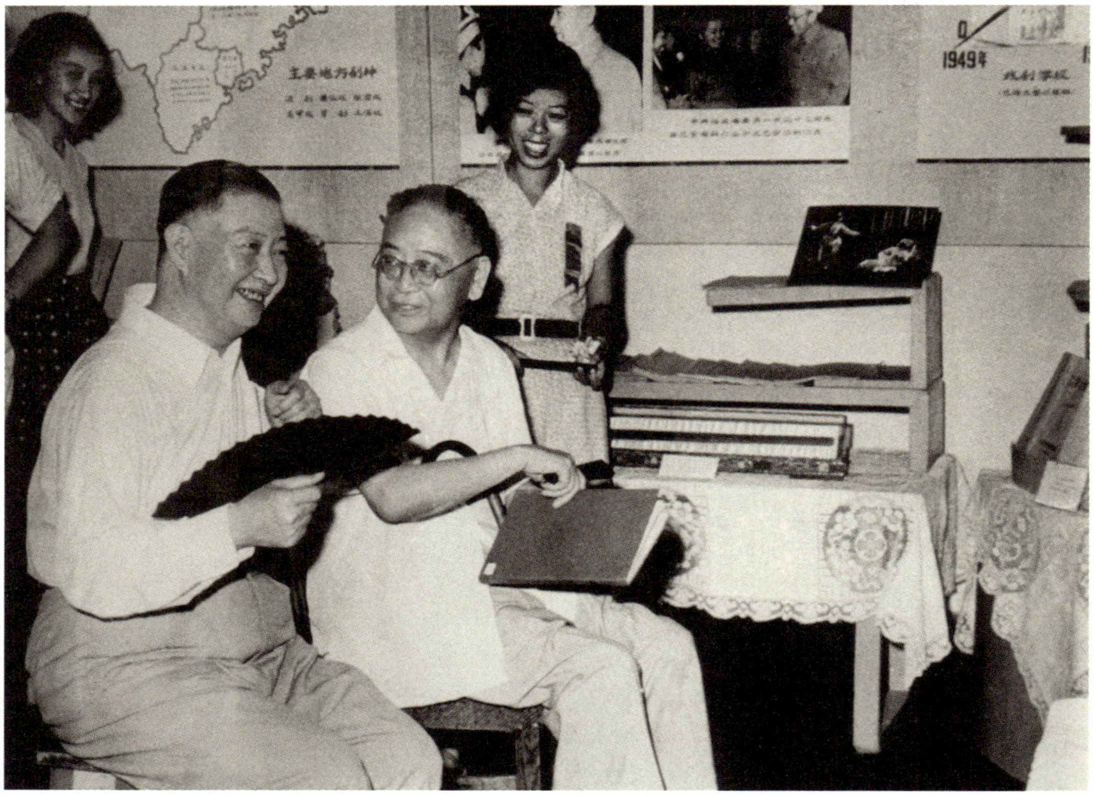

上图｜梅兰芳与粤剧演员红线女和马师曾
With Hong Xiannv and Ma Shizeng (famous actress and actor of Guangdong Opera)

下图｜梅兰芳与欧阳予倩参观展览会后会晤
With Ouyang Yuqian at an exhibition

梅兰芳与俞振飞
Mei Lanfang and Yu Zhenfei

上图｜梅兰芳与粤剧演员白驹荣、薛觉先
With Bai Jurong and Xue Juexian (famous actors of Guangdong Opera)
下图｜梅兰芳与周信芳
Mei Lanfang and Zhou Xinfang

梅兰芳与盖叫天

Mei Lanfang and Gai Jiaotian

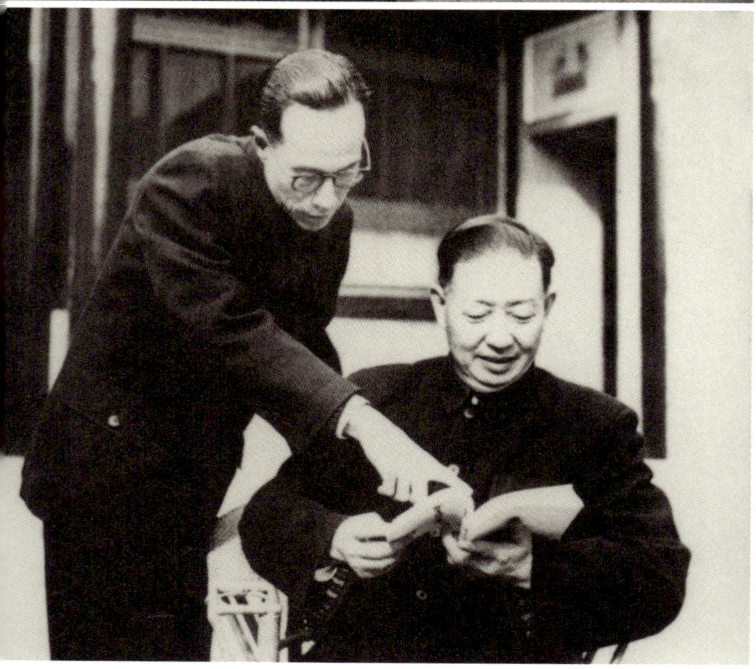

左上｜梅兰芳与姜妙香
Mei Lanfang and Jiang Miaoxiang

左下｜梅兰芳与秘书许姬传探讨戏剧问题
Mei Lanfang discussed with his secretary Xu Jichuan about the theatrical problems

右图｜梅兰芳（右）携孙儿卫平、卫东与徐兰沅合影
With Xu Lanyuan , and his grandsons Weiping and Weidong

左上｜梅兰芳在北京护国寺寓所院内练剑
Practising sword dance at his home in Beijing

左下｜梅兰芳在北京护国寺寓所院内与武术教师练功
Mei Lanfang was exercising martial skill with his teacher at his home in Beijing

右图｜梅兰芳与韩世昌
Mei Lanfang and Han Shichang

上图｜梅兰芳与沪剧演员俞杏元、陈宝荪
With Yu Xingyuan and Chen Baosun (famous actresses of Shanghai Opera)

下左｜梅兰芳与晋剧演员丁果仙
With Ding Guoxian (famous actress of Shanxi Opera)

下右｜梅兰芳与萧长华
Mei Lanfang and Xiao Changhua

梅氏夫人

Mei Lanfang's Wife

梅兰芳17岁时与王明华（名武生王毓楼之妹、名老生王少楼之姑母）结婚。王明华精明强干，持家有方，不但改善了并不宽裕的梅家境况，而且对梅兰芳演戏也有所帮助。她悉心照顾梅兰芳的起居饮食，并经常陪伴梅兰芳演出，在后台为梅兰芳梳头、化装和料理服装。1919年曾随梅兰芳赴日本演出。1928年，王明华因患肺结核病逝。育有一子一女，均不幸夭折。

福芝芳是梅兰芳的继室，自幼喜爱京剧，早年也从吴菱仙学唱青衣，在坤班"崇雅社"演出。她的扮相妍丽，嗓音圆润，基本功扎实，所饰《二进宫》中的李艳妃最受欢迎。1921年演出大轴戏《祭塔》后，即退出舞台，与梅兰芳结婚，专心照顾梅兰芳的生活和演出，成为梅兰芳的贤内助。每次梅兰芳演出，她必到后台协助，指点剧中人物的扮相及装束头饰等，使之增艳。她非常注重戏曲服装的设计和革新，往往亲自到绸缎店挑选适合角色的面料。《洛神》、《天女散花》等戏中的服装及风带就是她帮助调配的，为京剧界和广大观众所赞赏。排演《穆桂英挂帅》时，她又精心设计了中年穆桂英的装扮，使之光彩夺目。在扶掖梅派艺术的过程中，她倾心协力，立下了不可忽视的功劳。福芝芳育有9个子女，其中长成的只有4人，即葆琛（行四）、绍武（行五）、葆玥（行七）、葆玖（行九）。福芝芳因病于1980年逝世，享年75岁。她一生相夫教子，卓有成就，受到后人的尊敬与怀念。

Mei Lanfang married Wang Minghua at the age of seventeen. Wang Minghua was a clever, capable woman, not only improved Mei's family situation , but also help Mei Lanfang in his career. Wang Minghua was suffering from pulmonary tuberculosis and died in 1928. She had two children but all died so early.

Fu Zhifang is Mei Lanfang's second wife. She took care of Mei's life and performance, became Mei's better half. She played an important role in promoting Mei Lanfang's art. Fu has nine children, four of them grow up in adult. She died in 1980, and being remembered.

梅兰芳与夫人福芝芳在北京合影（1959）

Mei Lanfang and his wife Fu Zhifang in Beijing (1959)

左图 | 王明华
Wang Minghua
右图 | 福芝芳
Fu Zhifang

梅兰芳与夫人福芝芳
Mei Lanfang and his wife Fu Zhifang in Beijing

上图｜梅兰芳夫妇与许姬传（后排左一）及子女葆琛、绍武、葆玥和孙辈卫平、卫华在北京寓所接待族兄梅秀冬（中坐者）时合影

Mei Lanfang with his wife, sons, daughter, and grandchildren received a clan elder Mei Xiudong from Taizhou (sitting at the middle) at his home in Beijing with Xu Jichuan

下图｜1968年，梅兰芳的三个孙子、三个孙女及一个外孙子合影（前排左起：梅红红、范梅强、梅卫丽、梅卫文，后排左起：梅卫平、梅卫东、梅卫华）

Group photo of Mei Lanfang's grandsons and granddaughters in 1968(Front left: Mei Honghong, Fan Meiqiang, Mei Weili, Mei Weiwen Back left: Mei Weiping, Mei Weidong, Mei Weihua)

上图 | 梅兰芳在北京护国寺寓所院内看孙辈游戏
With his grandchildren in the courtyard of his Beijing house

下左 | 梅兰芳与孙子嬉玩
With his grandchild

下右 | 梅兰芳与女儿梅葆玥翻阅戏剧图书
Reading books with his daughter Baoyue

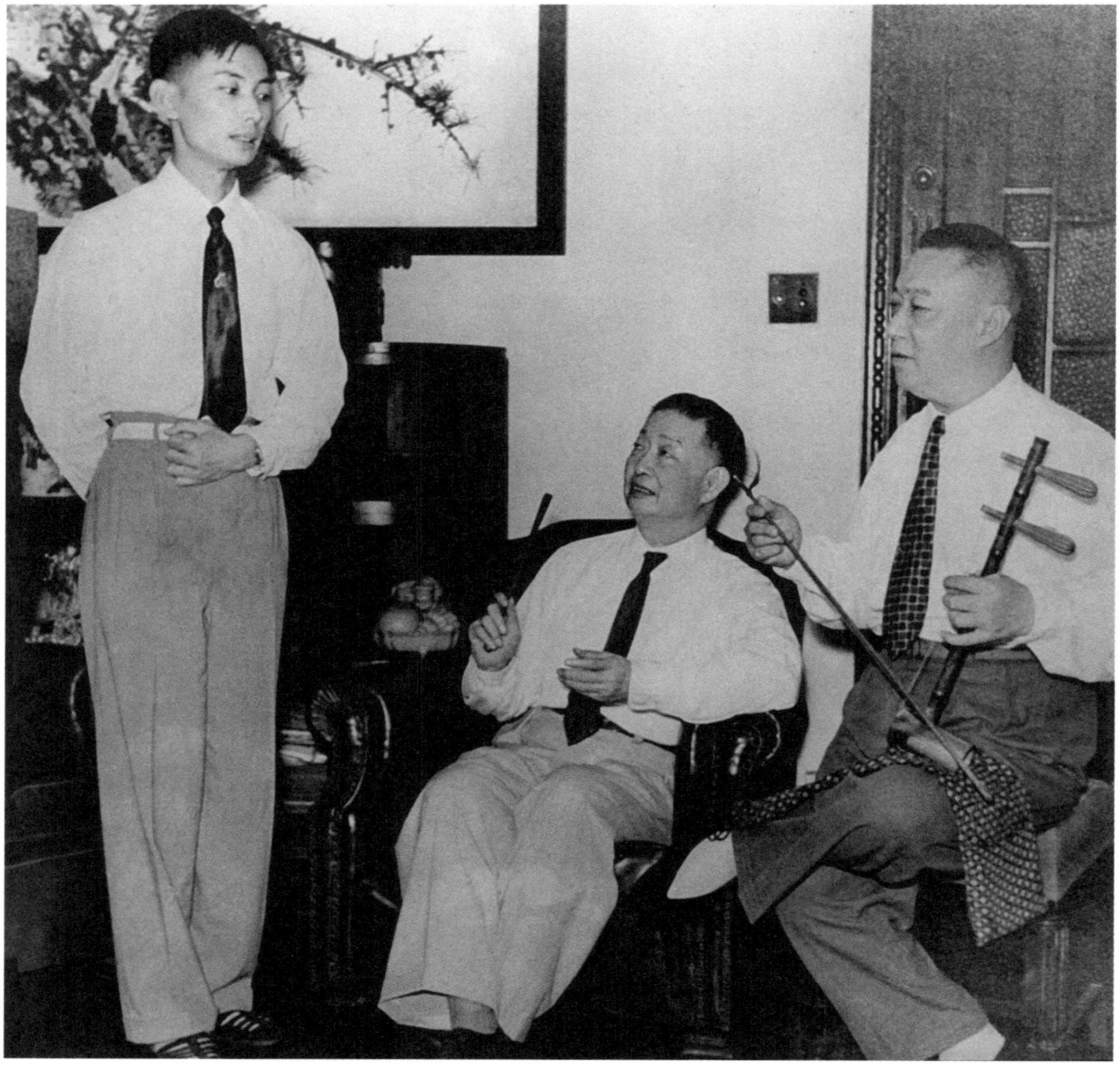

梅兰芳在上海沪寓所指点梅葆玖调嗓，操琴者为王少卿
Taught his son Baojiu the voice training with accompanist Wang Shaoqing

上图 | 梅兰芳在北京寓所客厅看报
Reading newspaper at home in Beijing
下图 | 梅兰芳在北京寓所客厅看书
Reading book at home in Beijing

梅氏子女及孙辈

Mei's Later Generations

梅氏第二代

梅兰芳长子 —— 梅葆琛

梅兰芳次子 —— 梅绍武

梅兰芳女儿 —— 梅葆玥

梅兰芳幼子 —— 梅葆玖

Mei's second generation

Mei Lanfang's eldest son:Mei Baochen

Mei Lanfang's second son:Mei Shaowu

Mei Lanfang's daughet:Mei Baoyue

Mei Lanfang's youngest son:Mei Baojiu

梅氏第三代

梅兰芳长孙，梅葆琛长子 —— 梅卫平

梅兰芳次孙，梅葆琛次子 —— 梅卫华

梅兰芳孙女，梅葆琛之女 —— 梅卫文

梅兰芳三孙，梅绍武之子 —— 梅卫东

梅兰芳孙女，梅绍武之女 —— 梅红红

梅兰芳孙女，梅绍武之女 —— 梅卫丽

梅兰芳外孙，梅葆玥之子 —— 范梅强

Mei Lanfang's grandchildren

Mei Baochen's first son: Mei Weiping

Mei Baochen's second son: Mei Weihua

Mei Baochen's daughter: Mei Weiwen

Mei Shaowu's son: Mei Weidong

Mei Shaowu's daughter: Mei Weili

Mei Shaowu's daughter: Mei Honghong

Mei Baoyue's son: Fan Meiqiang

梅氏第四代

梅兰芳长重孙 —— 梅玮

梅兰芳次重孙 —— 梅瑞琪

Mei Lanfang's great grandchildren

Mei Wei

Mei Ruiqi

梅兰芳与子女在北京寓所合影（前排左起：梅绍武、梅葆玖，后排左起：屠珍、梅葆玥、梅兰芳、林映霞、梅葆琛（1957）

Mei Lanfang and his family (Front from left) Mei Shaowu, Mei Baojiu, (Back from left) Tu Zhen, Mei Baoyue, Mei Lanfang, Lin Yingxia, Mei Baochen(1957)

梅兰芳夫妇与儿子葆琛、儿媳林映霞及孙辈卫平、卫文、卫华
Mei Lanfang with his wife, his eldest son Baochen, daughter in-law Lin Yingxia and grandchildren Weiping, Weiwen and Weihua

梅葆琛 Mei Baochen（1925—2008）

梅兰芳之长子。1925年生于北京。由于他生性稳重，乐于思考，梅兰芳便为他在理工科方面发展提供条件。后来，梅葆琛考上上海一所名牌大学理工学院的建筑系。毕业后，经过努力，成为北京建筑设计院的高级工程师。从小受到家庭的耳濡目染，梅葆琛拉得一手好胡琴，并得到王少卿的亲授。梅兰芳家里举行戏曲沙龙，梅葆琛经常承担琴师的工作。他酷爱梅派艺术，希望梅派艺术得到继承与发扬。他不仅关心弟弟梅葆玖的表演，而且精心培养下一代，将孙儿梅玮送到京剧名师身边学习梅派艺术，并在家中一句句辅导孙儿学唱京剧，亲自为孙子操琴吊嗓，为梅派艺术的传承倾注了自己的心血。

Mei Baochen is Mei Lanfang's first son, who was born in Beijing in 1925. He is a modest and intelligent man, and being an engineer in Beijing Architectural Design Institute. He is fond of the Mei School of art, cultivated his grandson carefully at home, and hope Mei School of arts can be inherited.

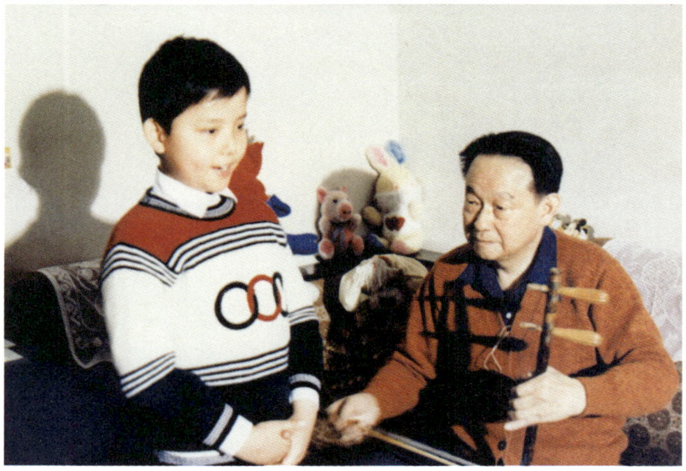

上图｜梅葆琛（右二）、林映霞（右三）夫妇与次子卫华（左一）、儿媳沈清（左二）、女儿卫文（右一）、孙子梅玮（前）合影

Meo Baochen(right 2nd), his wife Lin Yingxia(right 3rd), his 2nd son Weihua(left 1st), his daughter-in-law Shen Qing(left 2nd), his daughter Weiwen(right 1st) and grandson Mei Wei(front)

下左｜梅葆琛为孙子梅玮演唱操琴

Mai Baochen playing filddle for his grandson Mei Wei

下右｜梅葆琛、林映霞夫妇与长子卫平（右一）

Mei Baochen, his wife and their eldest son Weiping(right 1st)

上图｜梅兰芳教儿子葆琛操琴（1941）

Mei Lanfang taught his son Baochen to play fiddle(1941)

下图｜梅葆琛著《怀念父亲梅兰芳》封面（1994）

The cover of Mei Baochen's work in *Memory of My Father Mei Lanfang* (1994)

—— 梅绍武 Mei Shaowu（1928—2005）——

梅兰芳之次子 。1928年生于北京，原名梅葆珍。著名的英美文学翻译家、评论家、戏剧家、作家。毕业于燕京大学。第六、七、八、九届全国政协委员，梅兰芳纪念馆名誉馆长，中国梅兰芳文化艺术研究会会长，北京图书馆国际交换组干部，中国社会科学院美国研究所研究员。2004年被中国翻译协会授予“资深翻译家”荣誉称号。主要翻译作品有《一个匈牙利富豪》、《任性的凯琴姑娘 ——特罗洛普中短篇小说选》、《海尔曼老爷》、《灰烬的沉默》、《马克思和世界文学》、《微暗的火》、《瘦子》和尤金·奥尼尔、阿瑟·米勒的剧本等。此外，他也是第一个将俄裔美籍作家弗拉基米尔·纳博科夫介绍到中国的人。出版有《我的父亲梅兰芳》和《京剧与梅兰芳》等。

Mei Shaowu is Mei Lanfang's second son, who was born in Beijing in 1928. He is a famous translator, the honorary curator of Mei Lanfang Memorial Museum, the president of Mei Lanfang Research Association. researcher of the Institute of America in Chinese Academy of Social Sciences. Mei Shaowu is a famous American literary translator, critic, dramatist and writer, who is the author of *My Father Mei Lanfang, Beijing Opera and Mei Lanfang* etc.

梅兰芳与儿子绍武及儿媳屠珍合影（1957）

Mei Lanfang with his son Shaowu and daughter-in-law Tu Zhen(1957)

左图｜屠珍与婆婆福芝芳
Tu Zhen and Her Mother-in-law Fu Zhifang
右图｜梅绍武著《我的父亲梅兰芳》封面（1984）
The cover of Mei Shaowu's work *My Father Mei Lanfang* (1984)

上图 | 梅绍武与夫人屠珍（1994）
Mei Shaowu and his wife Tu Zhen(1994)

中图 | 梅绍武与夫人屠珍及子女梅红红、梅卫东、梅卫丽合影（1994）
Mei Shaowu, Tu Zhen and their son Weidong, daughters Honghong and Weili(1994)

下图 | 梅绍武与儿子卫东及孙子在梅兰芳墓前留影（1994）
Mei Shaowu, his son Weidong and grandson Ruiqi at Mei Lanfang's graveyard (1994)

梅兰芳与女儿葆玥
Mei Lanfang and Baoyue in the courtyard

梅葆玥 Mei Baoyue（1930—2000）

梅兰芳唯一的女儿。京剧老生。1930年生于北京。她自幼天资聪慧，父亲一有戏，总是闹着要一同去剧场。母亲福芝芳的师妹李桂芬是师从刘鸿声唱老生的第一代著名京剧女演员，她发现葆玥性格豪爽，嗓音高亢洪亮，韵味十足，于是毛遂自荐，从1943年起教葆玥学起了京剧老生。从此葆玥白天读书，晚上抽空学戏，吊嗓练功，春去冬来，从不间断。梅葆玥的演唱规范讲究，嗓音苍劲醇厚，中气充沛；扮相俊美儒雅，表演细腻严谨。其擅演的剧目有《红鬃烈马》、《四郎探母》、《捉放曹》、《文昭关》、《战太平》、《辕门斩子》等。

Mei Baoyue is Mei Lanfang's daughter. She is talented in Beijing Opera, and learned Beijing Opera in 1943. Her singing is standard and pure. Her appearance is pretty and elegant. She is a famous Laosheng actress of Beijing Opera.

左图｜梅兰芳为女儿葆玥做示范
Mei Lanfang was teaching his daughter Baoyue
右图｜梅葆玥与梅葆玖
Mei Baoyue and Mei Baojiu

上图｜梅葆玥演《大登殿》剧照
Mei Baojiu in *Come to the Throne*
下左｜梅葆玥演《战太平》剧照
Mei Baoyue in *Combat in Taiping*
下右｜梅葆玥演《四郎探母》剧照
Mei Baoyue in *Silang Visits His Mother*

上图｜梅葆玥、梅葆玖与梅玮合影
Mei Baojiu, Mei Baoyue and Mei Wei
下图｜梅葆玥（右一）、梅葆玖（左一）与张学良将军（左二）、陈立夫先生（右二）合影（1993）
Mei Baojiu and Mei Baoyue with General Zhang Xueliang and Mr. Chen Lifu (1993)

左上｜梅葆玥、梅葆玖合演《太真外传》剧照
Mei Baojiu and Mei Baoyue in *The Legend of Yang Yuhuan*
左下｜梅葆玥、梅葆玖合演《大登殿》剧照
Mei Baojiu and Mei Baoyue in *Come to the Throne*
右图｜梅葆玥、梅葆玖幼年时合演《四郎探母》剧照
Mei Baojiu and Mei Baoyue in *Silang Visits His Mother*

梅兰芳与夫人福芝芳及儿子梅葆玖
Mei Lanfang, his wife and their youngest son Baojiu

梅葆玖 Mei Baojiu (1934—)

梅兰芳之幼子。1934年生于上海。梅派领军人物，京剧表演艺术家，国家一级演员，北京京剧院梅兰芳京剧团团长，中国戏曲学院荣誉教授。10岁开始学艺，先后向王幼卿、陶玉芝、朱传茗、朱琴心等京剧名家学习，尤其得其父梅兰芳亲传。13岁正式登台演出，18岁开始与父亲同台演出。擅演《霸王别姬》、《贵妃醉酒》、《穆桂英挂帅》、《太真外传》、《洛神》、《西施》等梅派京昆剧目。梅葆玖嗓音甜美圆润，唱念字真韵美，其表演体现了端庄、典雅、细腻、自然的梅派神韵，充满诗情画意。为传承梅派艺术，梅葆玖先后培养了李胜素、魏海敏、董圆圆、张晶、胡文阁等38位弟子。1989年，梅葆玖荣获美国纽约林肯美华艺术中心授予的“亚洲杰出艺人奖”。2009年世界艺术家协会授予“艺术大师奖”和“终身成就奖”，2012年日本樱美林大学授予荣誉文学博士学位和联合国友好理事会等国际组织共同主办的世界和平祈祷大会“世界和平大使”奖章。

Mei Baojiu is Mei Lanfang's youngest son. He is the leader of Mei's school of art at present. He is a famous Beijing Opera artist and the president of Mei lanfang Troupe in Beijing Peking Opera Theater. He learned Beijing Opera at 10, and debut at 13. He got his father's capability and skills. His performance is dignified, exquisite and pure.

Mei Baojiu inherited Mei Lanfang's art,and trained 38 disciples as Li Shengsu, Dong Yuanyuan, Wei Haimin, Zhang Jing, Hu Wenge ect. In 1989, Mei Baojiu won the "Outstanding Asian Artist Award" issued by New York Lincoln Mei Hua Arts Center, and won the "Masters of the Art Award" and the "Lifetime Achievement Award" issued by the World Artists Association in 2009. He won the honorary degree of doctor of literature issued by Obirin University in Japan and "World Peace Ambassador" issued by the world peace prayer meeting award of UN in 2012.

上图｜梅葆玖与俞振飞演《玉堂春》剧照

Mei Baojiu and Yu Zhenfei in *Lady Magnolia*

下左｜梅葆玖幼年演《女起解》剧照

Mei Baojiu in *The Extradition of Su San*

下右｜梅葆玖 10 岁时第一次登台演《三娘教子》饰薛倚哥剧照

Mei Baojiu's debut on stage at the age of ten in *Mother Educated Her stepson*

左图｜梅葆玖演《太真外传》剧照

Mei Baojiu in *The Legend of Yang Yuhuan*

右图｜梅葆玖演《贵妃醉酒》剧照

Mei Baojiu in *The Drunken Beauty*

左图｜梅葆玖演《西施》剧照
Mei Baojiu in *Beauty Xi shi*
右图｜梅葆玖演《四郎探母》剧照
Mei Baojiu in *Silang Visits His Mother*

上左｜梅葆玖与谭元寿演《大登殿》剧照
Mei Baojiu and Tan Yuanshou in *Come to the Throne*
上右｜梅葆玖演《穆桂英挂帅》剧照
Mei Baojiu in *Mu Guiying Takes the Command*
下图｜梅葆玖演《宇宙锋》剧照
Mei Baojiu in *Beauty Defies Tyranny*

左图｜梅葆玖演《洛神》剧照
Mei Baojiu in *The Goddess of River Luo*
右图｜梅葆玖与袁世海演《霸王别姬》剧照
Mei Baojiu and Yuan Shihai in *The King's Parting with His Favorite*

柒

梅韵流芳

The Influences of Mei Everlasting

一代宗师梅兰芳在京剧艺术的发展上起到了承前启后的作用，把京剧艺术推向了高峰，并位列于世界戏剧之林。他创造的梅派艺术，其特点是唱腔圆润纯正，自然大方，婉转动听；表演简洁洗练，却包含着丰富的感情，蕴藏着深厚的功力；刻画人物细致入微，风格典雅大方。他一生在舞台上创造了为数众多、仪态万方的中国古代和近代妇女的优美形象，但他并非单纯地模仿女子的一姿一态，而是艺术地再创造妇女的本质和意象，刻意传达中国女性的温柔、秀丽、高雅、坚强等特征。他在艺术创作中善于辨别精、粗、美、丑，自始至终贯穿着独特风格，具有追求美、雅致和崇高的意向。梅派艺术之美，深得中华民族传统文化的精髓，欧阳予倩赞誉梅兰芳为“伟大的演员，美的创造者”。苏联著名芭蕾舞演员乌兰诺娃赞誉他为“美的化身”。他一生收徒百余人，倾心梅派艺术的人更是不计其数。梅派艺术享誉海内外，国内和海外经常举办纪念梅兰芳的活动。北京护国寺大街的故居被辟为梅兰芳纪念馆。梅兰芳及其梅派艺术将永远铭记在人们心中。正所谓：“梅质兰魂永芳香，音容笑貌五洲存。”

Having turned the Beijing Opera into a colorful comprehensive art of the highest stage effects and blazed a new path for his successors, Mei made a significant contribution to the development of the art of Beijing Opera, during his stage career over half a century. On stage he had created many lively unforgettable artistic images of both ancient and modern Chinese women. Though he played female parts, his acting was by no means imitation, but created essence and imagery-the gracefulness, elegance, fidelity, staunchness and other merits owned by the Chinese women. Through his performances abroad and relentless efforts, Beijing Opera won world recognition and Mei Langfang was accepted worldwide and applauded as a great artist and the embodiment of beauty.

During his lifetime Mei had more than a hundred disciples, while innumerable people love Mei Langfang's art in earnest. In recent years, commemorative activities in memory of Mei were often held both at home and abroad. In 1986. the Mei I.anfang Memorial Museum was founded at Mei's former residence in Beijing. which is now opened to the public.

The splendid image of Mei Lanfang and his brilliant performing art will forever live in the hearts of the people all over the world.

《抗金兵》

梅兰芳饰梁红玉

Mei Lanfang as Liang Hongyu *in Fighting against the Chins*

《生死恨》

梅兰芳饰韩玉娘

Mei Lanfang as Han Yuniang in *A Wedding in the Dream*

《穆桂英挂帅》

梅兰芳饰穆桂英

Mei Lanfang as Mu Guiyin in *Mu Guiying Takes Command*

穆
穆

大师辞世

The Death of the Great Master

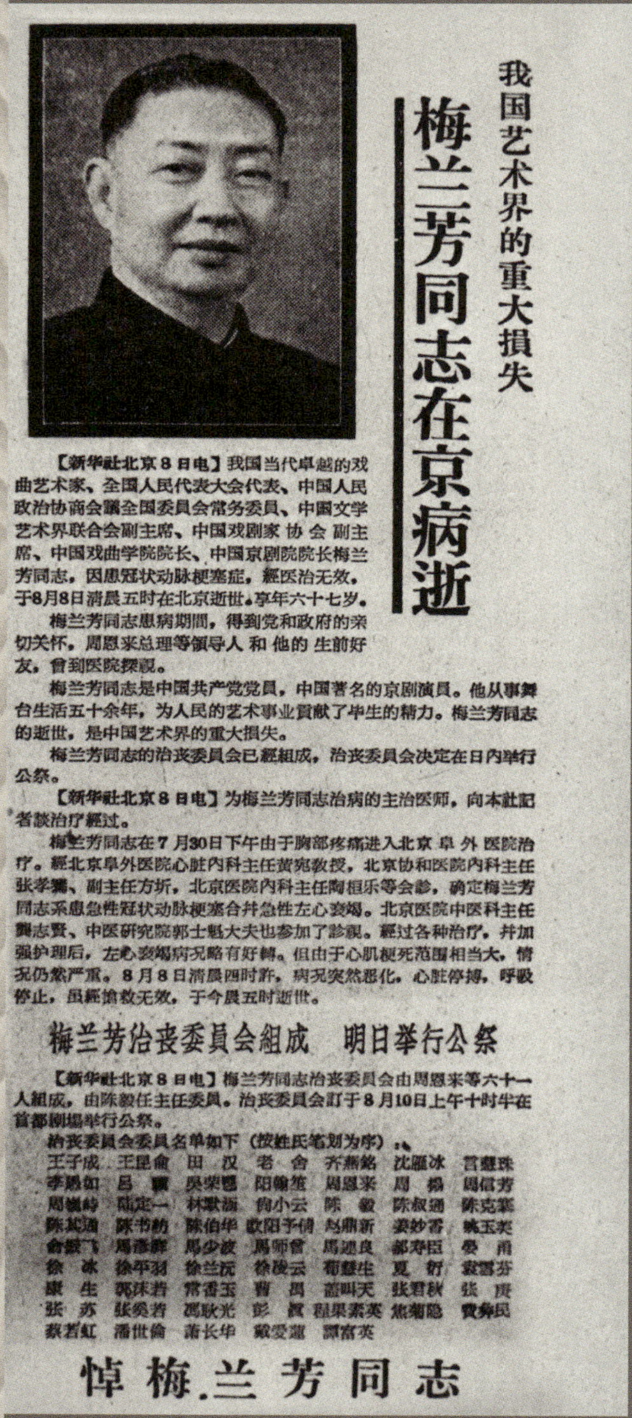

我国艺术界的重大损失

梅兰芳同志在京病逝

【新华社北京8日电】我国当代卓越的戏曲艺术家、全国人民代表大会代表、中国人民政治协商会議全国委員会常务委員、中国文学艺术界联合会副主席、中国戏剧家协会副主席、中国戏曲学院院长、中国京剧院院长梅兰芳同志，因患冠状动脉梗塞症，經医治无效，于8月8日清晨五时在北京逝世，享年六十七岁。

梅兰芳同志患病期間，得到党和政府的亲切关怀，周恩来总理等領导人和他的生前好友，曾到医院探視。

梅兰芳同志是中国共产党党員，中国著名的京剧演員。他从事舞台生活五十余年，为人民的艺术事业貢献了毕生的精力。梅兰芳同志的逝世，是中国艺术界的重大損失。

梅兰芳同志的治丧委員会已經組成，治丧委員会决定在日內举行公祭。

【新华社北京8日电】为梅兰芳同志治病的主治医师，向本社記者談治疗經过。

梅兰芳同志在7月30日下午由于胸部疼痛进入北京阜外医院治疗。經北京阜外医院心脏內科主任黄宛教授，北京协和医院內科主任张孝騫、副主任方圻，北京医院內科主任陶桓乐等会診，确定梅兰芳同志系患急性冠状动脉梗塞合并急性左心衰竭。北京医院中医科主任龚志贤、中医研究院郭士魁大夫也参加了診視。經过各种治疗，并加强护理后，左心衰竭病况略有好轉。但由于心肌梗死范圍相当大，情况仍然严重。8月8日清晨四时許，病况突然恶化，心脏停搏，呼吸停止，虽經搶救无效，于今晨五时逝世。

梅兰芳治丧委員会組成　明日举行公祭

【新华社北京8日电】梅兰芳同志治丧委員会由周恩来等六十一人組成，由陈毅任主任委員。治丧委員会訂于8月10日上午十时半在首都剧場举行公祭。

治丧委員会委員名单如下（按姓氏笔划为序）：

王子成	王昆侖	田　汉	老　舍	齐燕銘	沈雁冰	言慧珠
李颉如	吕　驥	吴荣恩	阳翰笙	周恩来	周　揚	周信芳
周巍峙	陆定一	林默涵	尚小云	陈　毅	陈叔通	陈克寒
陈其瑗	陈书舫	陈伯华	欧阳予倩	赵鼎新	姜妙香	姚玉英
俞振飞	馬彦祥	馬少波	馬师曾	馬連良	郝寿臣	娄　甬
徐　冰	徐平羽	徐兰沅	徐凌云	荀慧生	夏　衍	袁雪芬
康　生	郭沫若	常香玉	曹　禺	盖叫天	张君秋	张　庚
张　苏	张奚若	馮耿光	彭　真	[illegible]	焦菊隐	賀舜民
蔡若虹	潘世倫	萧长华	黎爱迪	譚富英		

悼梅兰芳同志

报纸刊登的梅兰芳病逝消息及梅兰芳治丧委员会名单

Announcement on the decease of Mei Lanfang on the People's Daily

梅兰芳先生因病于1961年8月8日5时在北京阜外医院逝世，享年67岁。《人民日报》等多家报纸均在第一版发表了讣告，并刊登了由周恩来总理等61人组成的治丧委员会名单（陈毅副总理任治丧委员会主任委员）。国外的许多报纸也报道了梅先生逝世的消息。

1961年8月10日上午，北京各界2000余人在首都剧场隆重举行梅兰芳先生追悼会。陈毅副总理主祭，并代表中共中央和国务院向梅兰芳的亲属表示深切慰问。文化部副部长齐燕铭致悼词。一些驻华使节及国际友人也参加了追悼会。8月29日，梅兰芳先生的灵柩移至北京香山碧云寺北麓万花山安葬。

On August 8th 1961, Mei died of heart disease at the age of 67. A mourning service was held in the Capital Theater in Beijing. Vice Premier Chen Yi gave the memorial speech. He was buried at the foot of the Flowers Hill at the suburb of Beijing.

1961年8月10日，在梅兰芳追悼会上，陈毅及各界人士向遗像默哀

Chen Yi and personalities of various circles mourned over Mei Lanfang at the memorial meeting on August 10th,1961

上图｜1961年8月10日，陈毅在梅兰芳追悼会上讲话
Chen Yi gave a memorial speech and the vice Minister of the Ministry of Culture Qi Yanming gave a funeral oration on August 10th 1961

下图｜日本人士在梅兰芳追悼会上献花圈
Japanese friends laid a wreath at the memorial service

梅兰芳追悼会会场（北京首都剧场）

The memorial meeting hall for mourning over Mei Lanfang at the Capital Theatre in Beijing

上图｜梅兰芳追悼会后，家属及各界人士走出会场

A funeral procession

下图｜梅兰芳灵车从北京首都剧场徐徐驶出

The hearse slowly went out of the Capital Theatre

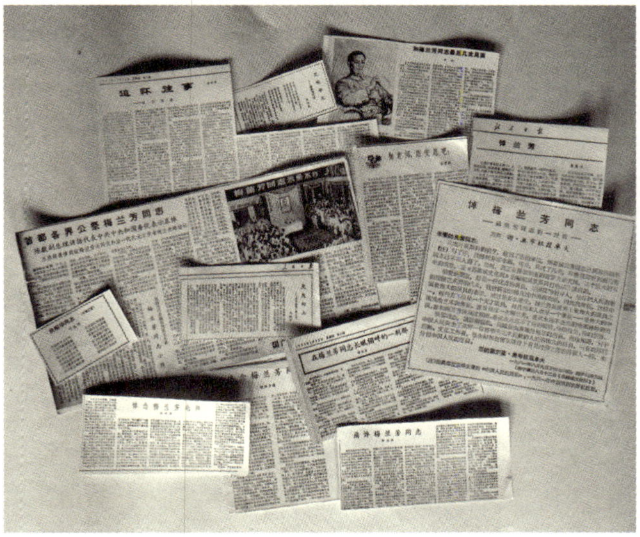

上图｜梅兰芳灵柩送至墓地后举行祭奠仪式
The funeral at the graveyard

下左｜梅兰芳生前好友发表的悼念文章
The articles mourning the death of Mei Lanfang written by Mei's friends

下右｜梅兰芳墓地坐落在北京西郊万花山
The graveyard located at the foot of Wanhua Hill of the west suburb of Beijing

梅门桃李

Mei's Disciples

梅兰芳20岁左右即已成名，1919年26岁时收程砚秋为开门弟子，一生共收弟子百余名，可谓桃李满天下。

梅兰芳先生弟子姓名一览表

（按姓氏笔画排序）

丁至云	马小曼	马金凤	于素秋	王凤燕
王志怡	王佩瑜	王素琴	王熙春	王慧萍
毛世来	毛剑秋	云燕铭	申丽媛	白玉薇
卢　燕	刘元彤	刘肖梅	刘淑华	阎立品
许守义	关肃霜	阳友鹤	毕谷云	吕慧君
红线女	任颖华	华慧麟	言慧珠	沈小梅
沈曼华	汪剑耘	李元芳	李世芳	李玉芝
李玉芙	李玉茹	李吟香	李　丽	李金鸿
李国粹	李香匀	李砚秀	李桂云	李湘君
李斐叔	李蔷华	李毓芳	李慧芳	李慧琴
李碧慧	李薇华	李燕香	杜近芳	杜丽云
杨玉娟	杨荣环	杨秋玲	杨维君	杨惠敏
杨畹农	张南云	张世孝	张君秋	张春秋
张志英	张曼玲	张淑娴	张蝶芬	张丽娟
陆素娟	陈书舫	陈永玲	陈正薇	陈伯华
吴若兰	邹慧兰	范玉媛	罗慧兰	周曼如
高玉倩	高　华	徐东来	徐再蓉	徐碧云
梁小鸾	唐富尧	赵文漪	赵慧娟	胡　蝶
胡芝风	胡漱芳	南铁生	陶默庵	郭建英
海碧霞	贾世珍	顾正秋	顾景梅	韩淑华
秦慧芬	章遏云	黄世恩	曹慧麟	崔秀茹
童芷苓	谢虹雯	谢黛琳	喻志清	舒昌玉
程砚秋	焦鸿英	新凤霞	新艳秋	醉丽君
冀韵兰	魏莲芳			

（根据梅兰芳纪念馆藏资料整理，共计117人）

Mei won national fame before he was twenty. When Mei was 26, Cher Yanqiu became the first of his disciples. Throughout his life, he had more tha a hundred disciples all around China and abroad.

A List of Mei's Disciples

Ding Zhiyun	Ma Xiaoman	Ma Jinfeng	Yu Suqiu	Wang Fengyan
Wang Zhiyi	Wang Peiyu	Wang Suqin	WangXichun	Wa Huiping
Mao Shilai	Mao Jianqiu	Yun Yanming	Shen Liyuan	Bai Yuwei
Lu Yan	Liu Yuantong	Liu Xiaomei	Liu Shuhua	Yan Lipin
Xu Shouyi	Guan Sushuang	Yang Youhe	Bi Guyun	Lv Huijun
Hong Xiannv	Ren Yinghua	Hua Huilin	Yan Huizhu	Shen Xiaomei
Shen Manhua	Wang Jianyun	Li Yuanfang	Li Shifang	Li Yuzhi
Li Yufu	Li Yuru	Li Yinxiang	Li Li	Li Jinhong
Li Guocui	Li Xiangyun	Li Yanxiu	Li Guiyun	Li Xiangjun
Li Feishu	Li Qianghua	Li Yufang	Li Huifang	Li Huiqin
Li Bihui	Li Weihua	Li Yanxiang	Du Jinfang	Du Liyun
Yang Yujuan	Yang Ronghuan	Yang Qiuling	Yang Weijun	Yang Huimin
Yang Wannong	Zhang Nanyun	Zhang Shixiao	Zhang Junqiu	Zhang Chunqiu
Zhang Zhiying	Zhang Manling	Zhang Shuxian	Zhang Diefen	Zhang Lijuan
Lu Sujuan	Chen Shufang	Chen Yongling	Chen Zhengwei	Chen Bohua
Wu Ruolan	Zou Huilan	Fan Yuyuan	Luo Huilan	Zhou Manru
Gao Yuqian	Gao Hua	Xu Donglai	Xu Zairong	Xu Biyun
Liang Xiaoluan	Tang Fuyao	Zhao Wenyi	Zhao Huijuan	Hu Die
Hu Zhifeng	Hu Sufang	Nan Tiesheng	Tao Moan	Guo Jianying
Hai Bixia	Jia Shizhen	Gu Zhengqiu	Gu Jingmei	Han Shuhua
Qin Huifen	Zhang Eyun	Huang Shien	Cao Huilin	Cui Xiuru
Tong Zhiling	Xie Hongwen	Xie Dailin	Yu Zhiqing	Shu Changyu
Cheng Yanqiu	Jiao Hongying	Xin Fengxia	Xin Yanqiu	Zui Lijun
Ji Yunlan	Wei Lianfang			

(Total 117, collected by Mei Lanfang Mcmorial Museum)

左图｜程砚秋赠送梅兰芳的个人照（1918）
Cheng's picture given to Mei Lanfang by Cheng Yanqiu(1918)
右图｜梅兰芳与程砚秋
Mei Lanfang and Cheng Yanqiu

左图｜梅兰芳弟子陶默庵演《四郎探母》剧照
Tao Moan in *Silang Visites His Mother*

右上｜张君秋与马连良演《赵氏孤儿》剧照
Zhang Junqiu and Ma Lianliang in *Orphan of the Zhaos*

右中｜李世芳与袁世海演《霸王别姬》剧照
Li Shifang and Yuan Shihai in *The King's Parting with His Favourite*

右下｜梅兰芳弟子毛世来演《十三妹》剧照
Mao Shilai in *The Thirteenth Sister*

上左 | 梅兰芳与弟子李斐叔（当时为梅兰芳的秘书）
Mei Lanfang and his disciple Li Feishu(his secratray)
上右 | 梅兰芳与弟子魏莲芳
Mei Lanfang and his disciple Wei Lianfang
下左 | 梅兰芳与弟子张君秋
Mei Lanfang and his disciple Zhang Junqiu
下右 | 梅兰芳与弟子李世芳、毛世来(1936)
Mei Lanfang and his disciple Li Shifang and Mao Shilai(1936)

左上 | 梅兰芳弟子童芷苓（右）与妹妹童葆苓演《樊江关》剧照
Mei's disciple Tong Zhiling and her sister Baoling in *Fanjiang Pass*

左下 | 梅兰芳弟子阎立品演《梵王宫》剧照
Mei's disciple Yan Lipin in *Brahma Palace*

右图 | 梅兰芳弟子杨荣环演《霸王别姬》剧照
Mei's disciple Yang Ronghuan as Yu Ji in *The King's Parting with His Favourite*

左图｜梅兰芳与夫人福芝芳及弟子李玉茹合影
Mei Lanfang, his wife Fu Zhifang and his disciple Li Yuru
右上｜梅兰芳与弟子顾正秋（1944）
Mei Lanfang and his disciple Gu Zhengqiu (1944)
右下｜梅兰芳与弟子张南云
Mei Lanfang and his disciple Zhang Nanyun

上图 |《大登殿》，梅兰芳弟子陈永玲饰代战公主（左），梅葆玖饰王宝钏（右）

Mei Baojiu(right) and Chen Yongling(left) in *Come to the Throne*

下图 | 梅兰芳弟子沈曼华演《虹霓关》剧照

Mei's disciple Shen Manhua in *The Rainbow Pass*

上左｜梅兰芳与弟子陈永玲
Mei Lanfang and his disciple Chen Yongling
上右｜梅兰芳与弟子顾景梅
Mei Lanfang and his disciple Gu Jingmei
下图｜梅兰芳与弟子丁至云
Mei Lanfang and his disciple Ding Zhiyun

左图｜梅兰芳弟子言慧珠演《凤还巢》剧照
Yan Huizhu in *The Phoenix Returns to Its Nest*
右图｜梅兰芳弟子白玉薇演《拾玉镯》剧照
Mei's disciple Bai Yuwei in *Picking Up a Jade Bracelet*

左图 | 梅兰芳与弟子白玉薇（右）及子女葆玥、葆玖合影
Mei Lanfang and his disciple Bai Yuwei(right),his children Baojiu and Baoyue

中图 | 梅兰芳与弟子言慧珠
Mei Lanfang and his disciple Yan Huizhu

右图 | 梅兰芳与弟子杜近芳（1949）
Mei Lanfang and his disciple Du Jinfang(1949)

左图｜梅兰芳弟子梁小鸾演《四郎探母》剧照

Liang Xiaoluan in *Silang Visits His Mother*

右图｜梅兰芳与夫人福芝芳及弟子梁小鸾（左）合影（1944）

Mei Lanfang, his wife Fu Zhifang and his disciple Liang Xiaoluan(left)(1944)

左图｜梅兰芳与弟子吕慧君
Mei Lanfang and his disciple Lv Huijun
中图｜梅兰芳与弟子周曼如(1937)
Mei Lanfang and his disciple Zhou Manru(1937)
右图｜梅兰芳与弟子汪剑耘(1951)
Mei Lanfang and his disciple Wang Jianyun(1951)

左图｜梅兰芳与弟子沈小梅（1953）
Mei Lanfang and his disciple Shen Xiaomei(1953)
中图｜梅兰芳与弟子杨维君（1954）
Mei Lanfang and his disciple Yang Weijun(1954)
右图｜梅兰芳与弟子喻志清（1957）
Mei Lanfang and his disciple Yu Zhiqing(1957)

左图｜梅兰芳与弟子李毓芳（1957）
Mei Lanfang and his disciple Li Yufang(1957)
中图｜梅兰芳与弟子王慧萍
Mei Lanfang and his disciple Wang Huiping
右图｜梅兰芳与弟子张曼玲
Mei Lanfang and his disciple Zhang Manling

左图 | 梅兰芳弟子王熙春演《十三妹》剧照
Mei's disciple Wang Xinchun in *The Thirteenth Sister*
右图 | 梅兰芳弟子陈书舫演《秋江》剧照
Mei's disciple Chen Shufang in *Autumn River*

上左｜梅兰芳弟子马金凤演《穆桂英挂帅》剧照
Mei's disciple Ma Jinfeng in *Mu Guiying Takes Command*

上右｜梅兰芳弟子高华演《凤还巢》剧照
Mei's disciple Gao Hua in *The Phoenix Returns To Its Nest*

下图｜梅兰芳弟子杨畹农演《法门寺》剧照
Mei's disciple Yang Wannong in *The Great Trial at the Famen Monastery*

左图｜梅兰芳与弟子李慧芳
Mei Lanfang and his disciple Li Huifang
右图｜李慧芳演《吕布与貂蝉》剧照
Mei's disciple Li Huifang in *Lv Bu and Diao Chan*

梅兰芳在上海“梅花诗屋”接受李碧慧（右二）拜师时合影，其中有夫人福芝芳（左三）、卢燕（左一）、梅葆玥（左二）、梅葆玖（右一）等（1946）

Mei Lanfang received Li Bihui(right 2nd) to be his disciple at his house, Mei's wife(left 3rd), Lu Yan(left 1st), Mei Baoyue(left 2nd) and Mei Baojiu(right 1st) were present(1946)

左图 | 梅兰芳弟子胡芝风演《凤还巢》剧照
Mei's disciple Hu Zhifeng in *The Phoenix Returns To Its Nest*

中图 | 梅兰芳弟子醉丽君演《思凡》剧照
Mei's disciple Zui Lijun in *Longing for Worldly Pleasures*

右图 | 梅兰芳弟子王志怡演《洛神》剧照
Mei's disciple Wang Zhiyi in *The Goddess of the River Luo*

梅兰芳在上海马斯南路寓所接受黄世恩（前排左五）拜师时合影，其中有夫人福芝芳、姜妙香、刘连荣、李世芳等（1946）

Mei Lanfang received Huang Shien(left 5th,front row) to be his disciple at his house, Mei's wife Fu Zhifang, Jiang Miaoxiang, Liu Lianrong and Li Shifang were present(1946)

梅兰芳与弟子谢黛林（小玲红）
Mei Lanfang and his disciple Xie Dailin (Xiao Linghong)

上左｜梅兰芳接受徐东来（二排中）拜师时合影，其中有夫人福芝芳、姜妙香（前排右二）、王少卿（前排右一）、梅葆玖、梅葆玥、许姬传、徐元珊、贾世珍、何海生等

Mei Lanfang received Xu Donglai to be his disciple at his house. Mei's wife Fu Zhifang, Jiang Miaoxiang, Wang Shaoqing, Mei Baojiu, Mei Baoyue, Xu Jichuan, Xu Yuanshan, Jia Shizhen, He Haisheng and others were present

下左｜梅兰芳弟子黄世恩演《凤还巢》剧照

Huang Shien in *The Phoenix Returns To Its Nest*

上右｜梅兰芳在上海“梅花诗屋”接受陈正薇（前排中）拜师时合影，其中有夫人福芝芳（前排右一）、言慧珠（后排左三）、王佩瑜、顾景梅、梅葆玥、梅葆玖等

Mei Lanfang received Chen Zhengwei to be his disciple at his house. Mei's wife Fu Zhifang, Yan Huizhu, Wang Peiyu, Gu ingmei, Mei Baojiu and Mei Baoyue were present

下右｜梅兰芳与弟子李金鸿

Mei Lanfang and his disciple Li Jinhong

上左 | 梅兰芳弟子陈正薇（左）、高玉倩（中）、李金鸿（右）合演《桃花扇》剧照

Chen Zhengwei(left), Gao Yuqian(central) and Li Jinhong (right) in *The Peach Fan*

上右 | 梅兰芳弟子关肃霜演《战洪州》剧照

Guan Sushuang in *The Combat in Hongzhou*

上左 | 梅兰芳弟子杨秋玲演《杨门女将》剧照

Mei's disciple Yang Qiuling in *The Women Generals of Yang Family*

上右 | 梅兰芳弟子新凤霞演《凤还巢》剧照

Mei's disciple Xin Fengxia in *The Phoenix Returns To Its Nest*

上图｜梅兰芳在北京接受范玉媛（二排右二）拜师时合影，其中有夫人福芝芳（前排右二）、姜妙香（前排左四）、萧长华（前排右四）等

Mei Lanfang received Fan Yuyuan to be his disciple. Mei's wife Fu Zhifang, Jiang Miaoxiang and Xiao Changhua were present

下图｜梅兰芳在北京接受关肃霜（二排左四）拜师时合影，其中有田汉、马彦祥、马连良、李多奎、张君秋等

Mei Lanfang received Guan Sushuang to be his disciple. Ma Yanxiang, Ma Lianliang, Li Duokui and Zhang Junqiu were present

上左｜梅兰芳弟子任颖华演《太真外传》剧照

Mei's disciple Ren Yinghua in *The Legend of Yang Yuhuan*

上右｜梅兰芳指导弟子陈伯华（汉剧演员）表演手势

Discussing acting techniques with Chen Bohua (a famous Hubei Opera actress)

下左｜梅兰芳与表演艺术研究班师生一起探讨表演艺术（前排左起：徐凌云、梅兰芳、红线女、袁雪芬、萧晴，后排左起：陈伯华、常香玉、俞振飞、马师曾）

Talking about performance with leading actors and actresses of various local operas (Back from left to right) Chen Bohua, Chang Xiangyu, Yu Zhenfei and Ma Shizeng. (Front from left to right)Xu Lingyun, Mei Lanfang, Hong Xiannv, Yuan Xuefen and Xiao Qing

下右｜梅兰芳与弟子毕谷云（1960）

Mei Lanfang and his disciple Bi Guyun(1960)

梅兰芳在北京接受李国粹（后排左八）拜师时合影，其中有夫人福芝芳、齐燕铭、夏衍、田汉、马彦祥、徐兰沅、姜妙香、姚玉芙、李慧芳、许姬传、梅葆玥、梅葆玖等（1960）

Mei Lanfang received Li Guocui(left 8th,back row) to be his disciple . Mei's wife Fu Zhifang, Qi Yanming, Xia Yan, Tian Han, Ma Yanxiang, Xu Lanyuan, Jiang Miaoxiang, Yao Yufu, Li Huifang, Xu Jichuan, Mei Baojiu and Mei Baoyue were present(1960)

纪念活动
Commemorative Activities

1962 年，梅兰芳逝世一周年，北京等地举行了隆重的纪念活动：邮电部发行了纪念邮票，文化部举办了梅兰芳艺术展览会，出版了《梅兰芳文集》，举办了“梅兰芳舞台艺术片电影周”；梅派弟子举行了纪念演出。

1984 年，文化部、中国文联和中国剧协联合举办了梅兰芳诞辰90 周年纪念活动。

1994 年，文化部，广播电影电视局，北京、上海、江苏三地人民政府、中国文联中国京剧艺术基金会在北京、上海、江苏等地联合举行隆重的纪念梅兰芳诞辰100周年的活动。

In 1962, Beijing and other cities held grand commemorative activities for the fist anniversary of the death of Mei Lanfang, issued the stamps, held the exhibition, published the collected works of Mei Lanfang, and held the memorial performance

In 1984, The commemorative activities were held by the Ministry of Culture and China Federation of Literary and Art for the 90th anniversary of the birth of Mei Lanfang.

In 1994, the Ministry of Culture, the goverment of Beijing, Shanghai and Jiangsu, China Federation of Literary and Art held grand memorial activities for the 100th anniversary of the birth of Mei Lanfang.

梅兰芳逝世一周年纪念会会场（1962 ）

The hall of the meeting in commemoration of the 1st anniversary of the death of Mei Lanfang (1962)

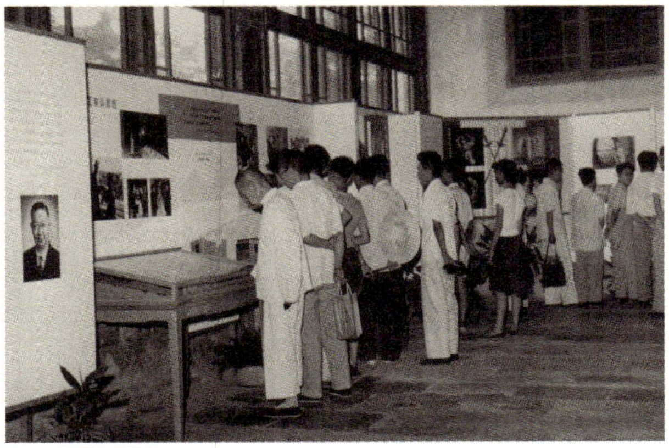

上图｜梅兰芳逝世一周年纪念会（主席台上就座者左起：姜妙香、阿英、齐燕铭、萧长华、田汉、老舍、徐兰沅、马彦祥（1962）

(From right to left)Ma Yanxiang, Xu Lanyuan, Lao She, Tian Han, Xiao Changhua, Qi Yanming, A Ying and Jiang Miaoxiang at the rostrum of a meeting in commemoration of the 1st anniversary of the death of Mei Lanfang (1962)

中左｜梅兰芳逝世一周年时，故宫武英殿举办了梅兰芳艺术展览会

An Exhibition of Mei Lanfang's art was held at the Wuying Hall of the Imperial Palace, in commemoration of the 1st anniversary of the death of Mei Lanfang

中右、下图｜梅兰芳逝世一周年时发行的纪念邮票

The commemorative stamps issued in 1962

弘扬民族艺术　振奋民族精神

江泽民与京剧、戏曲艺术家专家座谈并发表重要讲话　李瑞环主持

梅兰芳周信芳诞辰一百周年纪念活动拉开帷幕

江泽民乔石李瑞环朱镕基出席开幕式

据新华社讯　卓越的戏曲艺术大师、杰出的京剧表演艺术家梅兰芳、周信芳先生诞辰100周年纪念活动，昨天在首都正式拉开帷幕。

党和国家领导人江泽民、乔石、李瑞环、朱镕基出席了昨晚的梅兰芳、周信芳诞辰100周年纪念演出开幕式。

李铁映、王光英、吴阶平、万国权等也参加了开幕式。

开幕式由文化部常务副部长、梅兰芳周信芳诞辰一百周年纪念委员会组委会主任高占祥主持。中宣部副部长、文化部部长刘忠德致开幕辞。

梅兰芳、周信芳诞辰100周年纪念活动由文化部、广播电影电视部、北京市人民政府、上海市人民政府、江苏省人民政府、中国文联、文化部振兴京剧指导委员会、中国剧协、中国京剧艺术基金会联合主办。

纪念活动从昨天起到明年1月10日，在北京、上海、江苏以及全国许多地方隆重举行。

在昨晚演出结束后，江泽民、乔石、李瑞环、朱镕基等领导同志走上台去，祝贺演出成功，并同演员们一起合影留念。

文艺界隆重纪念梅兰芳诞生九十周年

习仲勋到会讲话　梅兰芳研究学会成立

新华社北京10月26日电　（记者秦杰、冯瑛冰）近千名文艺工作者今天在政协礼堂集会，隆重纪念京剧表演艺术家梅兰芳诞生九十周年。习仲勋、宋任穷、邓力群、叶圣陶、贺敬之等出席了纪念大会。

京剧艺术的一代宗师梅兰芳1894年生于梨园世家。他八岁学戏，十岁登台，在半个世纪的舞台生涯中，承前启后，精心钻研，勇于创新，塑造了赵艳容、白娘子、林黛玉、晴雯、梁红玉等众多优美动人的艺术形象。他熔青衣、花旦、刀马旦于一炉，表演自然和谐，富于节奏感，质朴中见俏丽，妩媚中显大方，形成一个独具特色、蜚声海内外的艺术流派，世称“梅派”。他是把中国京剧传播到国外并获得国际盛誉的第一个艺术家。他还是一位忠诚的爱国者。抗战期间，他不向侵略者低头，息影舞台，蓄须明志，表现出崇高的民族气节。解放后，他的艺术才华得到充分发挥。建国十周年时，他以六十七岁高龄排演新戏《穆桂英挂帅》。这一年，他加入中国共产党。1961年他因病去世。

中共中央政治局委员习仲勋在讲话中称赞梅兰芳对京剧艺术无限热爱、精益求精、勇于探索，有高度的爱国热情和政治觉悟，为人忠厚、公道正派、与人为善、和衷共济、乐于助人，对年轻一代关怀备至、精心培养。习仲勋说，这些值得我们学习，希望大家以此共勉，并身体力行。这也就是我们对梅兰芳同志最好的纪念。

文化部部长朱穆之在会上说，我们今天纪念梅兰芳同志，就要学习和继承他那永不停步的革新精神，让戏曲艺术同我们的伟大新时代相结合，同广大的人民群众相结合，开创出一个民族的戏剧艺术事业的新局面。

中国作家协会副主席冯牧代表中国文联主席周扬讲话，向梅兰芳表示敬意和缅怀之情。

梅兰芳的夫人福芝芳1965年将梅兰芳生前珍藏的艺术文物和戏剧资料三万余件捐赠国家。今天，文化部副部长周巍峙代表文化部向梅兰芳的家属梅葆琛、屠珍、梅葆玥和梅葆玖颁发了奖状。

纪念大会上宣布成立梅兰芳研究学会，周扬任会长。会后将举行梅兰芳艺术学术讨论会和六场纪念演出。梅兰芳纪念馆也将在梅兰芳故居——北京护国寺一号建立。

这次纪念活动由文化部、中国文联、中国戏剧家协会、中国艺术研究院、中国京剧院和北京京剧院联合主办。

上图｜1994 年12 月20日，梅兰芳、周信芳诞辰100周年纪念委员会全体会议与会者合影

The members of the committee in commemoration of the centenary of the birth of Mei Lanfang gathered at the People's Hall on December. 20, 1994

下左、下中｜梅兰芳、周信芳诞辰100 周年纪念活动剪报（1994）

The news about the commemoration of the centenary of birth of Mei Lanfang on the newspaper (1994)

下右｜梅兰芳诞辰90 周年纪念活动剪报（1984）

The news about the commemoration of the 90th anniversary of the birth of Mei Lanfang on the newspapers (1984)

上图｜在大型电视剧《梅兰芳》开拍招待会上，梅葆琛（左八）、林映霞（右八）、梅绍武（左七）、屠珍（左五）、梅葆玥（右一）等合影（1994）

Mei Baochen, Lin Yingxia, Mei Shaowu , Tu Zhen and Mei Baoyue at the reception for announcing the starting of making the TV serial Mei Lanfang (1994)

下图｜泰州举办纪念梅兰芳诞辰100 周年活动时，梅葆琛（左四）与夫人林映霞（左三）及梅绍武（左六）与夫人屠珍（左二）等合影

Mei Baochen, Lin Yingxia, Mei Shaowu, Tu Zhen and others during the commemoration of the centenary of birth of Mei Lanfang in Taizhou

梅馆故居

Mei Lanfang Memorial Museum

邓小平同志为梅兰芳纪念馆题写的匾额

The horizontal tablet with the inscription—Mei Lanfang Memorial Museum—written by Deng Xiaoping, hangs at the top of the gate of the museum

为纪念梅兰芳大师，北京和泰州先后建立了梅兰芳纪念馆。1986 年10 月，由邓小平同志题写馆名的北京梅兰芳纪念馆对外开放，习仲勋副总理参加了开馆仪式。1987年，由国家主席李先念题写馆名的泰州梅兰芳纪念馆对外开放。1990年，李瑞环和习仲勋亲自为梅兰芳汉白玉半身塑像揭幕。1994年，为纪念梅兰芳诞辰100周年，江泽民等国家领导人出席纪念大会，江泽民发表了重要讲话。

梅兰芳纪念馆成立以来，对梅兰芳的研究与宣传工作起到了积极的推动作用。在新时代，梅兰芳纪念馆将进一步努力为中国京剧传统文化的推广、传播与发展作出更大的贡献。

As a landmark figure in the art of Beijing Opera, Mei Lanfang dedicated his life to promote and develop Chinese culture and Chinese traditional drama. He left tremendous cultural wealth for future generations.

His skills and talent are deeply treasured and loved by world, and he has become an irreplaceable symbol for Chinese art. Mei Lanfang's impressive personal works are not only dedicated to the arts, but also dedicated to human beauty in "truth, goodness and beauty" the spirit of perseverance. Even till now, Mei Lanfang is still greatly respected and loved by the people.

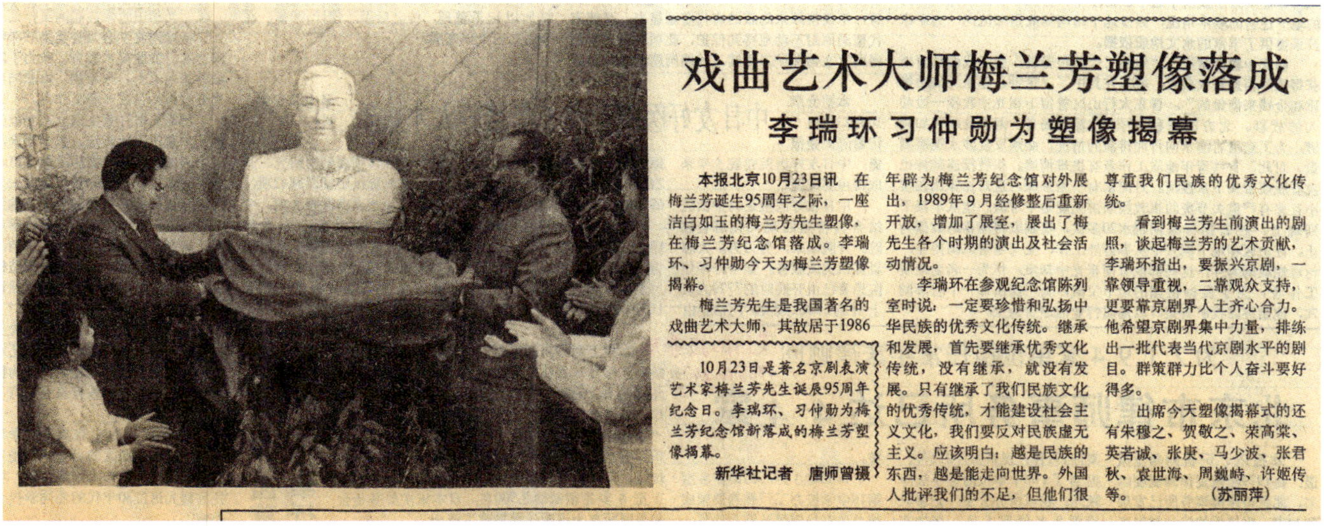

戏曲艺术大师梅兰芳塑像落成

李瑞环习仲勋为塑像揭幕

10月23日是著名京剧表演艺术家梅兰芳先生诞辰95周年纪念日。李瑞环、习仲勋为梅兰芳纪念馆新落成的梅兰芳塑像揭幕。

新华社记者　唐师曾摄

本报北京10月23日讯　在梅兰芳诞生95周年之际，一座洁白如玉的梅兰芳先生塑像，在梅兰芳纪念馆落成。李瑞环、习仲勋今天为梅兰芳塑像揭幕。

梅兰芳先生是我国著名的戏曲艺术大师，其故居于1986年辟为梅兰芳纪念馆对外展出，1989年9月经修整后重新开放，增加了展室，展出了梅先生各个时期的演出及社会活动情况。

李瑞环在参观纪念馆陈列室时说：一定要珍惜和弘扬中华民族的优秀文化传统。继承和发展，首先要继承优秀文化传统，没有继承，就没有发展。只有继承了我们民族文化的优秀传统，才能建设社会主义文化，我们要反对民族虚无主义。应该明白：越是民族的东西，越是能走向世界。外国人批评我们的不足，但他们很尊重我们的民族的优秀文化传统。

看到梅兰芳生前演出的剧照，谈起梅兰芳的艺术贡献，李瑞环指出，要振兴京剧，一靠领导重视，二靠观众支持，更要靠京剧界人士齐心合力。他希望京剧界集中力量，排练出一批代表当代京剧水平的剧目。群策群力比个人奋斗要好得多。

出席今天塑像揭幕式的还有朱穆之、贺敬之、荣高棠、英若诚、张庚、马少波、张君秋、袁世海、周巍峙、许姬传等。　（苏丽萍）

上图｜《光明日报》1989年10月24日有关李瑞怀（左）、习仲勋（右）为梅兰芳塑像揭幕的报道。

A report by Guamgming Daily on 24 October 1989. Mei's statue was inaugurated by Li Ruihuan(left) and Xi Zhongxun(right)

下左｜1984年，梅兰芳故居成为北京文物保护单位

The fromer residence of Mei Lanfang is designated as one of the place for the preservation of cultural relics in Beijing

下右｜梅兰芳塑像

The marble statue of Mei Lanfang at the Museum

上图｜梅兰芳纪念馆正门
The gate of the Mei Lanfang Memorial Museum
中左、中右｜梅兰芳纪念馆院落一角
A corner in the courtyard
下图｜梅兰芳纪念馆内影壁前的石质小水池
A small marble-carving fish pool in front of the screen wall

上左 | 书房一角
A corner of the study

上右 | 客厅
The drawing room

下左 | 梅兰芳书画展览
The painting exhibition

下右 | 戏装展览
The costumes exhibition

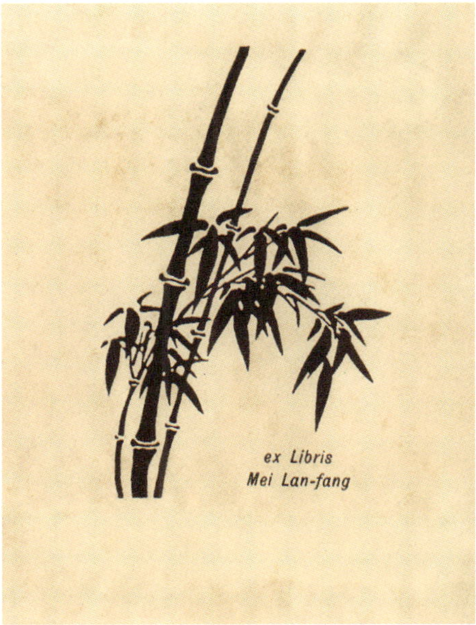

梅兰芳藏书签
Mei Lanfang's Exlibris

泰州市梅兰芳纪念馆

Taizhou Mei Lanfang Memorial Museum

泰州市梅兰芳纪念馆位于泰州市海陵区迎春东路90号，是一座以明清建筑为主体的园林式纪念馆。梅兰芳纪念馆始建于20世纪80年代初，1988年建成并正式对外开放。馆区占地22000平方米，建筑面积3500平方米，地理位置三面环水，一面临街，地势高敞，环境优美。

泰州市梅兰芳纪念馆汇集了当代众多名家名人的智慧，包括刘开渠、赵朴初、萧娴、陈从周、戴广文等；拥有大量的图文资料，以及江泽民、李先念、李铁映等领导人的亲笔题字等近千件藏品。开馆20多年来，已接待上百万的游客和来宾，为弘扬先进文化，扩大泰州知名度发挥了重要作用。纪念馆展厅建筑面积3500平方米，以丰富的实物资料和先进的科技手段向人们立体地展示梅兰芳先生的辉煌人生。

泰州市梅兰芳纪念馆是一个集观光、休闲、娱乐、审美和传播知识于一体的泰州特色文化旅游景点，是生态园林与京剧（戏曲）文化相结合的人文景观，也是全国小型园林式名人纪念馆中的精品。我们会以全新的姿态和更好的服务迎接四方宾客的到来。

Taizhou Mei Lanfang Memorial Museum is located in No.90,Yingchun Donglu , Hailing District, Taizhou. The Museum covers an area of 22000 square meters, and opening in 1988. It is surrounded by water on three sides, one facing the street,The environment is very beautiful.

Taizhou Mei Lanfang Memorial Museum is a tourist attraction combining the function of leisure, entertainment, spreading knowledge in Taizhou. It is a site with a nice landscape and an ecological garden for Beijing Opera cultural heritage.

The Memorial Museum's building area is 3500 square meters, in which Mei Lanfang's brilliant life is showed to the people with rich collections and advanced technological ways.

上图｜泰州梅兰芳纪念馆大门
The Main Gate of the Museum
下图｜梅像广场
The Square of Mei Lanfang Statue

上图 | 泰州梅兰芳纪念展厅
The Museum Exhibition Hall
下图 | 雪中梅亭
The Snow Covered Pavilion

左图 |《太真外传》梅兰芳扮相雕塑
The Statue of Mei Lanfang as Yang Yuhuan in *Concubine Yang's Unofficial Story*

右上 | 滨河水榭
Waterside Pavilion

右下 | 仿古戏台
The Antique-like Stage

附录

Appendix

梅兰芳在表演中的各种规范姿势

手部示范

练习眼神

梅兰芳年谱

Various standard postures and gestures performed by Mei Lanfang

Standard gestures

Exercise of glances

A chronicle of Mei's life

梅兰芳在表演中的各种规范姿势
various stawdard postures and gestures performed by Mei Lanfang

上左 | 坐式
Posture of sitting

上中 | 立式
Posture of standing

上右 | 卧式
Posture of dozing

下左 | 望式
Posture of watching

下中 | 指式
Posture of pointing

下右 | 羞式
Posture of shyness

上左 | 托物式
Posture of holding thing with the plam

上中 | 思式
Posture of considering

上右 | 提物式
Posture of carrying things

下左 | 搬物式
Posture of moving things

下中 | 抱物式
Posture of holding things

下右 | 捧物式
Posture of holding things by both hands

手部示范
stawdard gestures

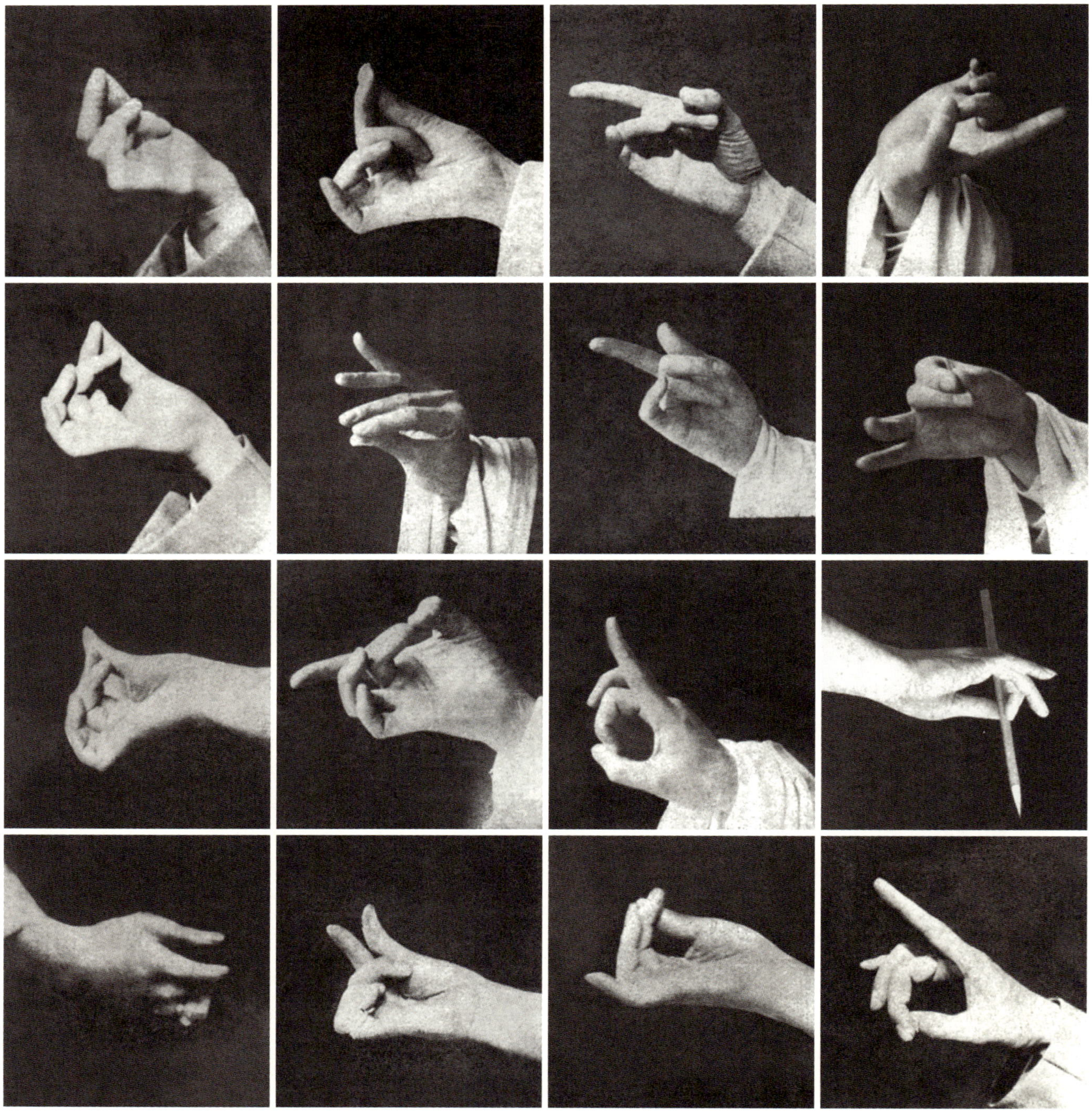

含苞
Handling a letter
初纂
Handling the needle and thread
避风
Praising
握蒂
Holding with finger

含香
Another style of expressing praise
陨霜
Holding a fan in reverse form
映日
Pointing somewhere far
吐蕊
Handling something small

护蕊
Pointing out
伸萼
Holding the whip
迎风
Pointing the void
醉红
Holding a basket

露滋
Self pointing
蝶陨（一）
Holding a writing brush
蝶陨（二）
Holding a writing brush
雨润
Pointing with rage

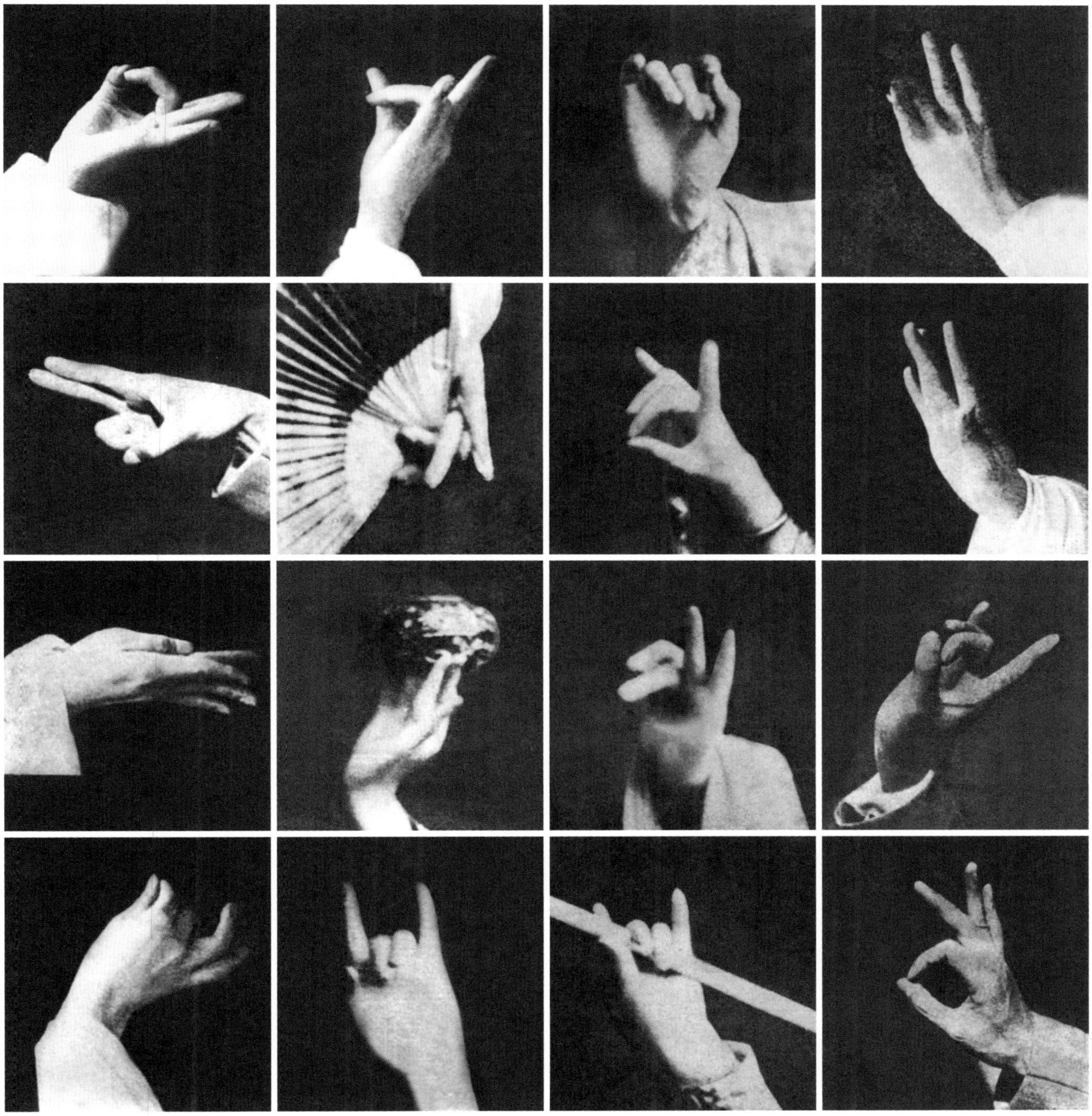

泛波
Brushing off tears
怒发
A gesture of sword dance
蝶恣
Self pointing
映水
Holding flowers

弄姿
Holding a tray
茁芽
Handling a fan in reverse form
掬云
Holding a bok
双翘
Expressing surprise lightly

翻莲
Expression of shock
拂云
Holding something while pointing
媚箧
Unfolding a fan
握蒂
Holding a of spear

滴露
Holding a fan
耐寒
Pointing the void
笑日
Self pointing one's head
指风
Denoting three

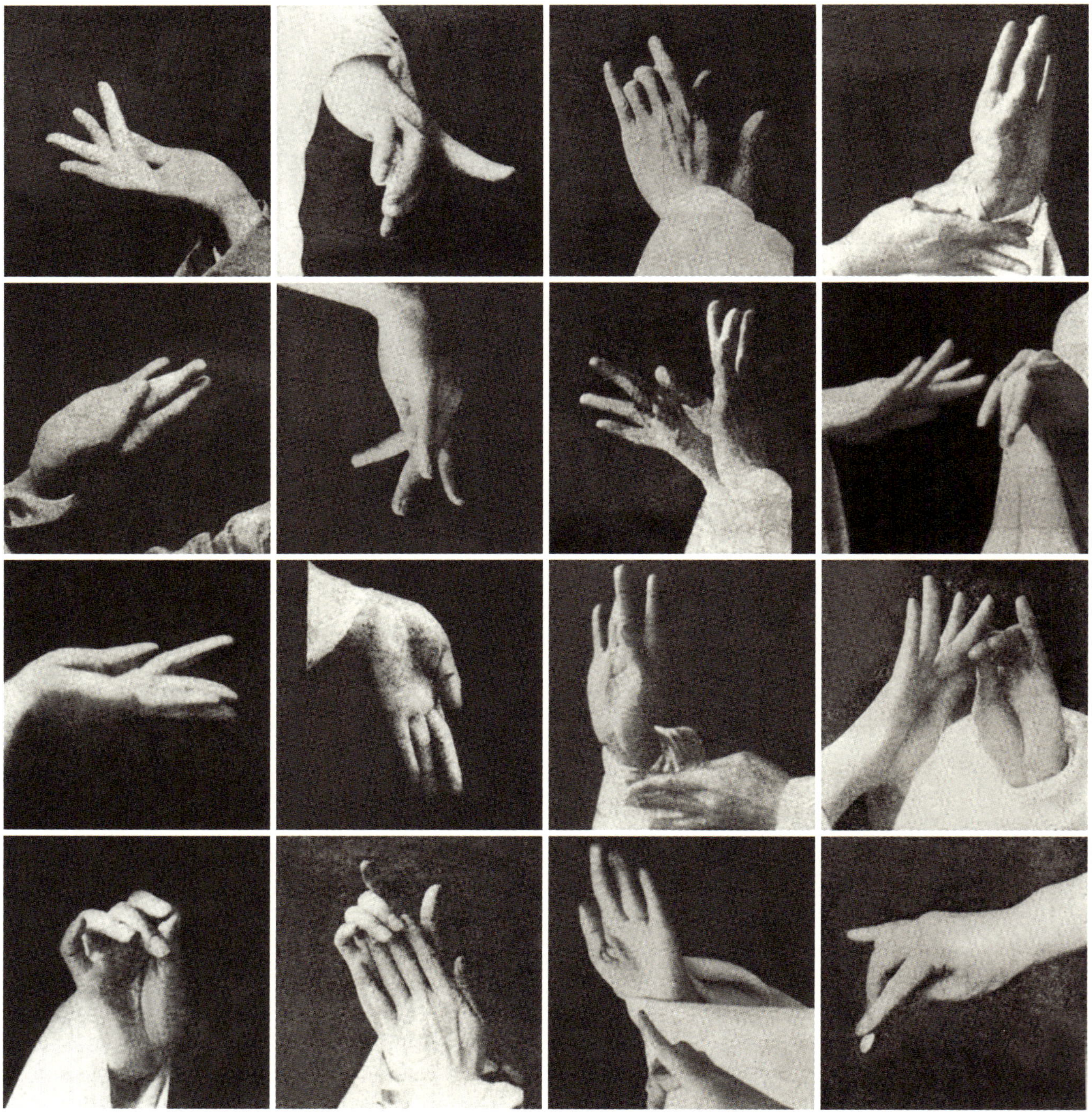

舒瓣
Fingers spreading out
浮香
Expression of fear
承露
Holding a tray
垂露
Holding a small thing

倒影
Pointing downwards
垂丝
With arms akimbo
垂颖
Courtesy of inviting
花态
Courtesy with hands clasped

含笑
Expression of helplessness
并蒂
Clapping
招蝶
Adjusting sleeves
散馥
Handling a thin paper

蒨蒨
Adjusting sleeves
逗花
Expression of respect
斗芳
Expression of salutation
避日
Holding a fan

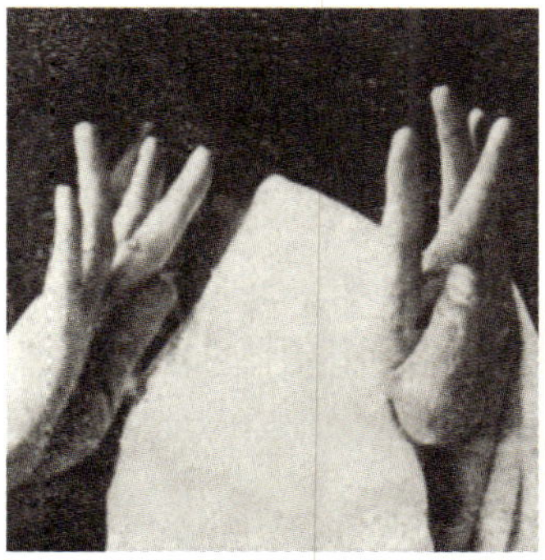

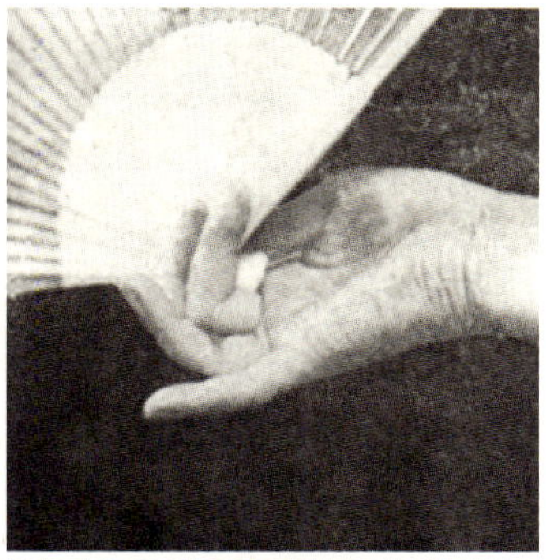

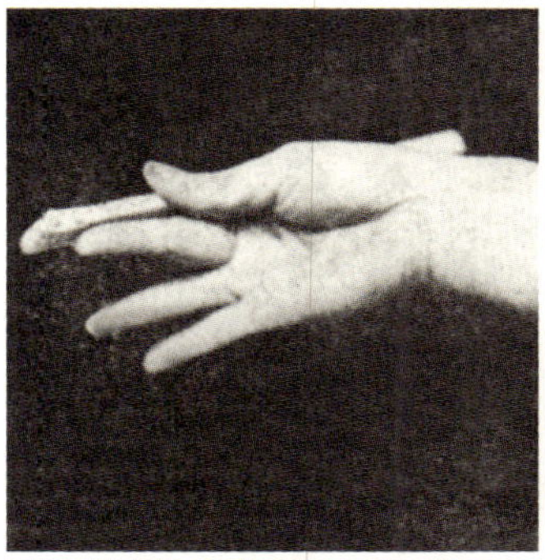

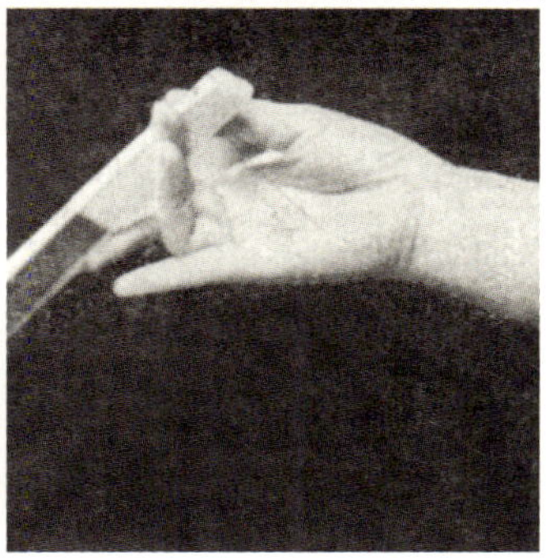

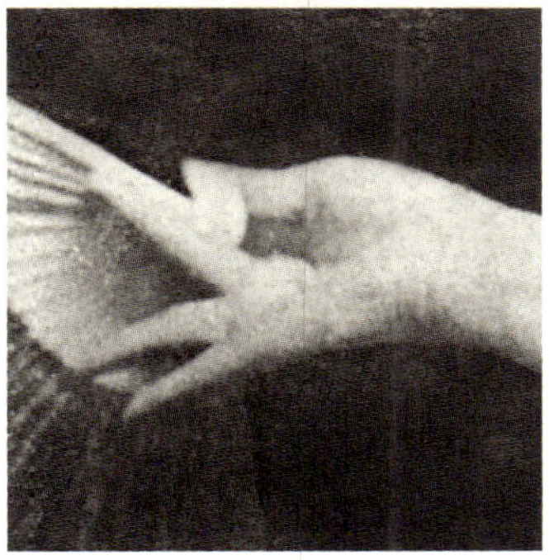

双双
Waving hands
聚头
Holding a fan
弄簪
Holding a fan

挹翠
Holding a fan
挥芬
Holding a fan

练习眼神
Exercise of glances

梅兰芳年谱

- 1894年10月22日生于北京前门外李铁拐斜街一座梨园世家的旧居。
- 1899年，梅兰芳在北京百顺胡同附近一家私塾读书。
- 1902年正式拜吴菱仙为师，学习青衣戏，学的第一出戏是《战蒲关》，后又学习了《二进宫》、《三娘教子》等共约30余出戏。
- 1904年8月17日（农历七月初），在北京广和楼戏馆第一次登台，在《长生殿·鹊桥密誓》中饰织女。
- 1907年，梅兰芳家从百顺胡同移居卢草园。正式搭班"喜连成"演出。
- 1908年8月14日，母亲杨长玉病逝。后全家移居鞭子巷头条。
- 1910年，梅兰芳与王明华结婚。本年起开始养鸽子。
- 1912年，第一次与谭鑫培同台演出，演出的剧目《桑园寄子》。
- 1913年10月31日，接受上海许少卿邀请首次赴上海演出（梅兰芳第一次离开北京）。11月16日，第一次贴演扎靠戏《穆柯寨》，也是他第一次唱大轴戏。本年，开始研究新腔并学习昆曲。全家移居北京鞭子巷三条。
- 1914年1月，在庆丰堂与王蕙芳同拜陈德霖为师。同年，先后从师乔蕙兰、李寿山、陈嘉梁学习昆曲。又从师路三宝、王瑶卿学戏。7月至10月，在"翊文社"最初尝试创编时装新戏《孽海波澜》。本年，梅兰芳对化装、头饰进行改革。
- 1915年4月10日，在北京吉祥园上演创编时装新戏《宦海潮》。4月16日，在北京吉祥园上演创编时装新戏《邓霞姑》。10月31日，在北京吉祥园首演创编古装新戏《嫦娥奔月》。第一次在京剧舞台上使用追光，把灯光的作用向前推进了一步。本年，梅兰芳开始学习绘画，绘画老师为画家王梦白。此后，又结识了画家陈师曾、金拱北、姚茫父、陈半丁、齐白石等。同时与收藏家朱翼庵订交，广泛观赏书画和古器物。
- 1916年1月14日，在北京吉祥园上演创编的新戏《黛玉葬花》。4月19日—21日，在北京吉祥园上演创编时装新戏《一缕麻》。
- 1917年，梅兰芳创编神话歌舞剧《天女散花》。
- 1918年，梅兰芳演出《游园惊梦》。同年，还创编演出了《麻姑献寿》、《红线盗盒》。
- 1919年4月21日—5月27日，应日本帝国剧场邀请，携"喜群社"赴日本东京、大阪、神户等地演出。12月，应近代实业家张謇邀请，第一次到江苏南通演出。

· 1920年，第一次拍摄无声电影《春香闹学》。

· 1921年年初，与杨小楼合作组织“崇林社”剧团。年末，与福芝芳结婚。

· 1922年2月15日，在北京第一舞台首演创编新戏《霸王别姬》。夏季，梅兰芳独自组建“承华社”剧团。10月15日—11月22日，应香港太平戏院邀请，率“承华社”剧团140余人赴港演出。

· 1923年，首创在京剧伴奏乐器中增加了二胡，使京剧音乐更加丰富。11月，在北京开明戏院上演创编新戏《洛神》，在北京真光剧场上演创编新戏《廉锦枫》。

· 1924年5月，在北京寓所接待印度著名学者、诗人、作家泰戈尔。10月9日—11月22日，应日本帝国剧场社长邀请，第二次访问日本，先后在东京、大阪、京都等地演出。

· 1925年，创编新戏头本、二本《太真外传》。

· 1926年，创编新戏三本、四本《太真外传》。在北京东城无量大人胡同梅宅接待来访的瑞典王储夫妇。

· 1927年，被评为京剧“四大名旦”之首。创编新戏《俊袭人》。

· 1928年4月6日，在北京中和戏院首演创编新戏《凤还巢》。夏季，在北京编演了新戏全本《宇宙锋》。第二次赴香港演出。

· 1930年1月18日—7月，率“承华社”剧团部分演员经日本横滨、加拿大维多利亚赴美国演出，先后在西雅图、芝加哥、华盛顿、纽约、旧金山、洛杉矶、圣地亚哥、檀香山等地演出72天。美国波摩拿学院、南加利福尼亚大学分别授予梅兰芳文学荣誉博士学位。

· 1931年5月，与余叔岩、齐如山、张伯驹等人创办“国剧学会”。第三次率团赴香港演出。

· 1932年，梅兰芳从北京迁居上海。

· 1933年，在上海天蟾舞台上演创编新戏《抗金兵》。

· 1935年2月21日—4月21日，率剧团赴苏联访问演出，先后与戏剧大师斯坦尼斯拉夫斯基、布莱希特会面。4月—8月，赴波兰、德国、法国、比利时、意大利、英国等国进行戏剧考察。后经埃及、印度回国。

· 1936年2月26日，在上海天蟾舞台上演创编新戏《生死恨》。

· 1938年年初，携家眷和剧团演职人员再次赴香港演出，全家留居香港。

· 1941年，蓄须明志，息影舞台。

· 1942年夏，由香港返回上海。从此，杜门谢客。

· 1945年10月，重新登台，在上海美琪大戏院与俞振飞合作演出昆曲《断桥》、《游园惊梦》等剧目。

· 1948年6月—11月，在上海联华三厂拍摄彩色戏曲片《生死恨》。

· 1949年7月，出席中华全国第一次文学艺术工作者代表大会。9月30日，当选全国政协常务委员。10月1日，参加中华人民共和国和中央人民政府成立典礼活动。

· 1951年4月，梅兰芳被任命为中国戏曲研究院院长。7月，全家从上海迁回北京，定居护国寺街1号（今梅兰芳纪念馆）。

· 1952年12月，出席在奥地利首都维也纳举行的世界人民和平大会。与苏联著名舞蹈大师乌兰诺娃在北京会面。

· 1953年10月，梅兰芳当选中国戏剧家协会副主席。

· 1954年9月，梅兰芳当选中华人民共和国第一届全国人民代表。

· 1955年1月，梅兰芳任命被为中国京剧院院长。4月，文化部、中国文联、中国戏剧家协会联合为梅兰芳、周信芳举办了舞台生涯50年纪念活动。2月—8月，拍摄戏曲片《梅兰芳舞台艺术》，12月制作完成。

· 1956年5月26日—7月16日，应日本朝日新闻社等团体邀请，在周恩来总理的直接关心和帮助下，组建了阵容最强大的访日京剧代表团，梅兰芳任团长。这是梅兰芳第三次访问日本，先后在东京、九州、大阪、京都、名古屋等地演出。

· 1957年6月7日，国际舞蹈协会主席海尔格来到北京授予梅兰芳荣誉奖章。

· 1959年5月25日，在北京人民剧场上演创编新戏《穆桂英挂帅》。

· 1960年1月21日，《游园惊梦》彩色电影片拍摄完成。4月15日，北京市人民委员会任命梅兰芳为梅剧团团长。

· 1961年5月31日，为中国科学院的科学家们演出《穆桂英挂帅》，这是梅兰芳舞台生涯中的最后一次演出。7月9日，梅兰芳被任命为中国戏曲学院院长。8月8日凌晨5时，梅兰芳在北京病逝。

A chronicle of Mei Lanfang

- October 22nd,1894, born in an old residence of Pear Garden family Li TieguaiXiejie outside Qianmen, Beijing.
- In 1899, Mei Lanfang studied at a old-style private school near Baishun Alley, Beijing.
- In 1902, he became a formal apprentice of Wu Lingxian specializing in plays of Qingyi role. The first play he learned was Fighting in Pu Pass, then he learned Entered the Palace a Second Time, Sanniang Teaches His Son and other 30 plays.
- On August 17th, 1904 (early July of lunar calendar), he staged first at Guanghelou Theatre House and performed as Weaver Girl in the act Secret Oath of Queqiao from Palace of Eternal Youth.
- In 1907, Mei Lanfang's family moved to Lucao Yuan from Baishun Alley. He formally joined in Xiliancheng Company.
- On August 14th,1908, his mother Yang Changyu died of sickness and his family moved to Toutiao of Bianzi Alley.
- In 1910, Mei Lanfang and Minghua married. From the beginning of this year, he started feeding pigeons.
- In 1912, he performed Entrusting the Son at Mulberry Field with Tan Xinpei at the same stage.
- On October 31st,1913, he went to Shanghai for performing under the invitation of XuShaoqing (It was the first time he left Beijing). On November 16th, he first performed military play Muke Fortress as the chief actor in the final scene. This year, he began to study new tunes and learned Kunqu Opera. His family moved to Santiao of Bianzi Alley.
- In January 1914, he and Wang Huifang acknowledged Chen Delin as their master together in Qingfengtang. In the same year, he studied Kunqu Opera with QiaoHuilan, Li Shoushan and Chen Jialiang. He also learned Peking Opera from Lu Sanbao and Wang Yaoqing. From July to November, he created a new-fashion play Waves in the Sinful Ocean in Yiwen Society. In the same year, he innovated makeup and headwear.
- On April 10,1915, he performed The Vicissitudes of Official Life, a newly-written

fashion play in Jixiang Theatre. On April 16, he performed a new play with contemporary costumes in Jixiang Theatre too. On October 31,he made a debut Chang'e Flies to the Moon in Jixiang Theate where he used the spotlight on the Beijing Opera stage and pushed the role of lighting forward. This year, Mei Lanfang began studying painting. His drawing teacher is the painter Wang Mengbai. Since then, he became acquainted with the painter Chen Shizeng, Jin Gongbei, Yao Mangfu, Chen Banding, Qi Baishi and so on. Meanwhile, he and Zhu Yi'an, a collector became friends. He learned to appreciate paintings and artifacts.

- On January 14th, 1916, he staged a new play Daiyu Buried Flowers. From 19th -21th April, he performed a new play with contemporary costumes A Thread of Hemp.
- In 1917, Mei Lanfang created a mythological song and dance drama The Heavenly Maid Scattered Flowers.
- In 1918, Mei Lanfang performed Peony Pavilion. In the same year, he created and performed Magu Celebrates Birthday and Hongxian Steals Box.
- At the invitation of Imperial Theatre in Japan, Mei led Xiqun Troupe to perform in Tokyo, Osaka and Kobe from 21st April to 27th May, 1919. In October, he was invited by Zhang Jian, a modern industrialist, to perform for the first time in Nantong, Jiangsu Province.
- In 1920, a silent file Chunxiang Upsets Study was made for the first time.
- In 1921, he organized Chonglinshe Troupe with Yang Xiaolou. By the end of the year, he married Fu Zhifang.
- On February 15, 1922, Farewell My Concubine, a new play made a debut at Beijing First Stage. From 15th October to 22nd November, he was invited by Taiping Theatre, Hong Kong to lead Chenghua Company with more than 140 performers and staffs to perform.
- In 1923, he added erhu in the accompaniment instruments of Beijing Opera and made Beijing Opera richer. In November, he created and performed Goddess Luo in Kaiming Theatre and performed a new play LianJinfeng in Zhenguang Theatre in Beijing.
- In May 1924, he received Rabindranath Tagore, the famous scholar, poet, and writer in his residence in Beijing. From October 9th to 22nd November, he was invited by the director of Imperial Theatre, Japan to pay the second visit and performed in Tokyo, Osaka , Kyoto and other places.
- In 1925, he created Part 1 and Part 2 of The Legendary Story of Concubine Yang Yuhuan.

- In 1926, he continued to create Part 3 and 4 of The Legendary Story of Concubine Yang Yuhuan. He received the Crown Prince and Princess of Sweden in Mei's residence in Wuliang Daren Alley.
- In 1927, he was elected No.1 of Four Great Dan Roles and composed a new play Beautiful Xiren.
- On April 6th,1928, he made a debut of a new paly Phoenix Returns Home in Zhonghe Theatre, Beijing. In summer, he composed and performed full-length Yuzhoufeng Sword and performed in Hong Kong for the second time.
- From January 18th to July, he led some of actors from Chenghuase Troupe to perform via through Yokohama, Japan and Victoria, Canada in the United States. He had performed in Seattle, Chicago, Washington, New York, San Francisco, Los Angeles, San Diego, Honolulu and other places for 72 days. He was awarded honorary doctorate in literature by Pomona College and University of Southern California.
- In May 1931, Mai Lanfang, Yu Shuyan, Qi Rushan and Zhang Boju founded National Opera Society. He led his troupe to perform in Hong Kong for the 3rd time.
- In 1932, Mei Lanfang moved from Beijing to Shanghai to settle down.
- In 1933, he performed a new paly Resistance to Jin Army.
- From February 21st to April 21st , 1935, he led a delegation to pay a visit in Soviet Union and met master dramatists Stanislavsky, Bercht. From April to August, he went to Poland, Germany, France, Belgium, Italy, Britain and other countries for theater visits. After that, he returned to China via Egypt and India.
- On February 26th, 1936, he performed a new play Hatred of Life and Death in Tianchan Stage, Shanghai.
- In early 1938, he led his family and members of his troupe to perform in Hong Kong again. The whole family stayed in Hong Kong.
- In 1941, he grew a moustache and kept himself away from the stage.
- In the summer of 1942, he returned to Shanghai from Hong Kong. Since then, he did not receive guests.
- In October 1945, he was back on stage and cooperated with Yu Zhenfei to perform Kunqu Opera Broken Bridge, Peony Pavilion and so on in Majestic Theatre, Shanghai.
- From June to November, 1948, Hatred of Life and Death, a color operatic film was shot by Studio 3 of Shanghai Lianhua.
- In July 1949, he attended the First China National Literary and Art Workers

Assembly. On September 30, he was elected CPPCC Standing Committee. On October 1, he attended the Inaugural Activities of the People's Republic of China and the Central People's Government.

- In April 1951, Mei Lanfang was appointed President of the Chinese Opera Research Institute. In July, the family moved back to Beijing from Shanghai and settled No.1, Huguosi Street (now Mei Lanfang Memorial Museum).
- In December 1952, he attended the World Peace Conference of the People in Vienna, Austria. He met Ulanova, famous dance master of the Soviet Union in Beijing.
- In October1953, Mei Lanfang was elected Vice Chairman of China Dramatists Association.
- In September 1954, Mei Lanfang was elected the deuty to the First National People's Congress People's Republic of China.
- In January 1955, Mei Lanfang was appointed as China Beking Opera Institute. In April, the Ministry of Culture, China Federation of Literary and Art Cirlces of China and China Dramatists Association united to hold a 50-year stage career celebration for Mei Langfang and Zhou Xinfang. From February to August, the opera film "Stage Art of Mei Lanfang," was shot, which was finished in December.
- From May 26th to July 16th, at the invitation of Japan's Asahi Shimbun and other organizations and with the direct care and help of Premier Zhou Enlai, the most powerful delegations of Beijing Opera was organized to visit Japan Mei Lanfang was the head. This is the third visit of Mei Langfangto Japan. He had performed in Tokyo, Kyushu, Osaka, Kyoto, Nagoya and other places.
- On June 7,1957, Halger, Chairman of International Dance Association came to award him Medal of Honor in Beijing.
- On May 25,1959, he performed a new play Mu Guiying Takes Command in Renmin Theatre, Beijing.
- On January 21st, 1960, the color film Peony Pavilion was finished. On April 15th, he was appointed Head of Mei Lanfang Troupe by Beijing Municipal People's Committee.
- On May 31,1961, Mei Lanfang performed Mu Guiying Takes Command for scientists from the Chinese Academy of Sciences. It was his last performance in Mei Lanfang's stage career. On July 9th, Mei Lanfang was appointed President of National Academy of Chinese Theatre Arts. At 5:00 on August 8, Mei Lanfang died in Beijing.